English Language Teaching

Recent Approaches

Edited by
Mohit K. Ray

ATLANTIC
PUBLISHERS & DISTRIBUTORS (P) LTD

ATLANTIC
PUBLISHERS & DISTRIBUTORS (P) LTD
7/22, Ansari Road, Darya Ganj, New Delhi
Tel.: +91-11-4077 5252, 2327 3880
E-mail: orders@atlanticbooks.com
Web: www.atlanticbooks.com

Reprint 2021, 2026

Published by Atlantic Publishers & Distributors (P) Ltd.

Printed & bound in India by Atlantic Print Services

Preface

One of the linguistic consequences of colonialism is that English is now one of the official languages of India, and both the English literature and the English language are studied all over India. After Independence and historical decolonization of the country, English naturally lost its glory as the ruler's language, but, paradoxically, it is studied by more people now than it was prior to 1947. The number of learners of English in India would easily exceed the total population of many countries of Europe. But the emphasis has significantly shifted from literature to language. The importance of English as a link language or as a world language has been steadily growing. It is increasingly felt that the need of the hour is communicative competence and the focus of English language teaching in India is therefore on learning English as a means of effective communication in all the spheres of life. Twenty-two essays included in this volume explore in depth various aspects of English language teaching.

Dr Meenakshi Raman calls attention to the need of effective communication in becoming a better businessman, a better leader or a more likeable personality. With many supporting illustrations she makes her point quite convincingly.

In his well-researched paper based on a careful survey made by him, Brigadier Mahendra Singh Dhaka brings under sharp focus the need for communicative competence for success in every sphere of life and the hopelessly poor communicative skill of students of various levels. He carefully analyses the dismal situation for which the teachers are as much to blame as the thoughtless expansion of higher education. He identifies the problem very convincingly and suggests some practical steps for the solution of the problem.

Dr Karan Singh Yadav lays bare the deficiencies in the studies of English in Indian colleges where thousands of students learning English cannot properly articulate their feeling in speaking or writing. The only solution, Dr Yadav feels, is the teaching of communicative English which can effectively counter the adverse effects of teaching through literature.

Dr K. Balachandran makes a fine anatomy of the malaise that plagues most educational institutions and makes a detailed, careful recommendation which he believes will change the face of classroom situation.

Dr Krushna Chandra Mishra in his perceptive study of the English language situation in India examines the views of many distinguished educationists and seems to agree with Jayasudha T. that in teaching of English as a second language the communicative aspect of English is often ignored, and believes that sympathetic awareness of the cultural level and educational background of the learners, and the use of the educational technology can help develop the communicative competence of the learners.

Dr Pratibha Gupta calls attention to the linguistic realities prevailing in Jharkhand where for the tribal students English is the fourth or fifth language. She makes out a strong case, with solid supporting documentation, for a proper language planning that would take into consideration the actual language situation of the learner, for effective teaching of English.

In another well-researched paper, Dr Pratibha Gupta points out that in the flood prone areas of Bihar, flood has a retarding effect on the development of the linguistic skill of a learner. This is so, because the displaced and rehabilitated pattern of the learner's situation on account of the flood, affects the curriculum development of the learner. She pleads that in view of this situation an appropriate teaching methodology should be introduced to counter the pedagogic problem.

In another interesting paper Dr Krushna Chandra Mishra and N.P. Mahapatra reiterate the need for using the latest educational technology to revolutionize English language education in India.

Dr Mallikarjun Patil has mapped out the political circumstances leading to the establishment of English as a global language. He also calls attention to the flexibility of the English language to adapt to new situations and developments. He further makes a strong case for the learning of many languages, because it widens the cultural outlook.

K. Ponni provides an elaborate "skill focal model" of remediation at the tertiary level for the socially disadvantaged students. She identifies the various reasons for the fact that the objectives of the primary and secondary English syllabus are not realized, and advocates a multiple line approach to make the learners realize the flaws and develop real skill. She contends that, if properly introduced, the model she recommends "would make the Utopia L2 competence a reality for the socially disadvantaged".

Dr Pushp Lata explores the viability of multimedia and Internet language teaching, students' adaptability in learning English with the aid of multimedia computers and the pedagogical implications of using multimedia and the Internet. She contends that the success of using these media largely depends on the careful preparation of materials and computer friendly attitude on the part of both the teachers and the students.

Dr Hitesh D. Raviya highlights the needs of the introduction of ESP (English for Special Purposes) courses in India where students across disciplines are not very good at communication and lack enough proficiency in English to meet the demands of the job market. In order to develop his paper he makes a short but succinct historical survey of the development of ESP in the West and makes a detailed analysis of the various aspects of ESP with conviction.

In his well-researched paper Dr Prashant Mishra makes a critical survey—both synchronic and diachronic—of the concepts of modality, mood and modal auxiliaries. Mood, we learn, is considered as grammatical category, formal category, syntactic category, inflectional category, etc. by different grammarians while TG grammarians are silent about mood. Dr Mishra argues that modality is a semantic notion and that modal auxiliaries are the chief means of expressing modality.

Dr K. Balachandran calls attention to the socio-cultural aspects of language learning. Starting with the assumption that educational excellence calls for a well-developed society he examines in detail the proficiency in English among students of various classes and holds that the students from the middle class are best equipped in the second language learning. He examines the role of the parents, teachers and friends, among others, in the development of the language skill of a student.

In their tribute to Rajul Bhargava, Dr Bernice J.M. West and Dr Michael H. Lyon analyse four alternative literary forms—diary excerpts, social exchange, participatory dialogue and a poem—to justify Bhargava's claim that "language makes meaning by transforming meaning".

Dr J. Samuel Kirubahar and Ms. Anita Evelyn introduce Ebonics, which generally refers to the evolved form of a kind of Pidgin English spoken in the United States, and discuss various aspects of Ebonics including the differences of opinion about whether it is a slang or a dialect, and argue that it is not slang as it has a distinct structure of its own.

Dr Prashant Mishra discusses the relevance of Stylistics in teaching literature at the college level. He tries to acquaint the readers with the pedagogical, potential and practical viability of Stylistics with many illustrative references to various texts.

Dr Harish Narang makes out strong case for globalizing English studies in India. Since English is spoken and written by more people outside the British isles than within it, the syllabus should be revised accordingly to accommodate new literatures in English.

Dr C. Kannan deplores the fact that the education system in India still carries the burden of colonialism. The course contents have no touch with the reality or the experience of the learners, resulting in a culture shock and communication breakdown. It is time, Dr Kannan argues, that in view of the contemporary Indian scenario and the needs of the nation the curriculum was reformulated. The new decolonized pedagogics should inculcate human values and challenges to live in peaceful co-existence and strike a balance between traditional culture and global exposure.

Mallikarjun Patil makes broad historical survey of the various influences that have gone into the making of the English language.

Dr R. Chanana makes a fine analytical and evaluative study of the nature and function of gestures in fine arts and poetry.

Dr K. Sudha Rao examines in detail the role of regulatory bodies in monitoring the quality of technical education in India. He thinks that in view of the various constraints under which a regulatory body is forced to function, its role is virtually reduced to that of a facilitator.

I thank all the contributors for their excellent papers. I also thank my former colleague Professor Rama Kundu for her valuable assistance in readying the volume.

I am grateful to Dr K.R. Gupta, Honorary Advisor, Atlantic Publishers and Distributors (P) Ltd., New Delhi, for the confidence evinced in me and for seeing the book through the press.

Mohit K. Ray

Contents

1

Using Effective English to Meet the Various Communicative Functions of Business Conversations

Meenakshi Raman

Introduction

You are awake 16 hours a day—5840 hours a year. You spend more time contacting other people than in any other single activity. How well you converse with these people is the magic key to whether your days will be pay-off days filled with personal and social popularity.

—James A. Morris

I wish I had said....

Why didn't he promote me into the new job?

Why wasn't I invited to the party?

I could have made a better impression if....

These silent thoughts cross everyone's mind now and then. That's but natural. We all wish to do better and we all feel we'll do better if only we have a few hints to help us master the art of conversing in such an engaging manner that people feel drawn toward us.

The ability to create relationships of trust and sharing, so valued in family life, has taken on new importance in the workplace (Sreevalsan, 2001). As our economy is based more on knowledge, the single most important asset in many organizations is the knowledge worker who has the ability to learn from others, create new knowledge, and transfer what is known to co-workers (Adler and Elmhorst, 2002). Learning, creating and transferring—all these three endeavors are possible through one single, significant form of business communication, namely, conversation.

Developing conversational ability is vital for achieving success in one's professional career (Robbins and Coulter, 1996). Teachers instructing students in the areas of business communication have a major role to play in developing conversational skills in their students so as to enable them not only to carry out their managerial responsibilities successfully in future but also to earn reputation in the society in which they live. By breaking down conversation into various communication functions and enabling their students use appropriate expressions in English, teachers of business communication/business English may develop the requisite skills in them. Beginning with a brief discussion on the various types of conversation, this paper elaborates on the seven categories of verbal behavior exhibited in successful business conversations and the practical expressions to be used in carrying out the communication tasks involved therein.

Types of Conversation

The six types of conversation are:

Chat: The least formal of all conversations, whether it's a father talking to his son about girls or two women talking about their wayward husbands.

Tête-à-tête: French for head to head, meaning a confidential conversation.

Dialogue: A two-way conversation that may involve opposing points of view.

Parley: It is a formal discussion between enemies regarding the terms of a truce.

Colloquy: The most formal of all conversations (a colloquy on nuclear disarmament); it can also be used to jocularly describe a guarded exchange (a brief colloquy with the arresting officer).

Communion: A form of conversation, well—one that may take place on such a profound level that no words are necessary (communion with nature). (*Oxford Thesaurus*, p. 132)

Each type of conversation is important, interesting and indispensable in its own way. But whatever the type of conversation you may be involved in, it's in your hands to make it interesting, inspiring and influential.

Strategies for Effecive Conversations

Given below are some strategies and tools that facilitate a profound shift in the course of a conversation and a relationship, when you practise them consciously:

- Involve Everyone
- Arouse and Sustain Interest
- Shift from Blame to Contribution
- Engage in Empathic Listening
- Develop the Ideas Adequately
- Move from Certainty to Curiosity
- Separate Impact from Intent
- Make Effective Requests
- Use Verbal Cues Appropriately

Using Verbal Cues

This is the most difficult aspect of a conversation. We use language in conversations to convey our ideas and feelings, paraphrase the presented thoughts, appreciate others, reflect upon implications and underlying feelings, and to invite further contributions (Ludlow and Panton, 1999).

How to do this? Given below are some practical hints to accomplish these purposes:

- Acknowledge Emotions
- Encourage
- Acknowledge Ideas
- Question
- Inform

- Direct
- Criticize

Acknowledge Emotions

Acknowledging Emotion is a key for reducing defensiveness and for building trust. Acknowledge Emotion when:

- Emotions dominate.
- Emotions are important to problem-solving.
- Emotions are in the way.

How to Acknowledge

First, pay attention to the feelings expressed by the other person, either verbally (words like mad, sad, glad and scared) or non-verbally (volume, intensity, hesitancy, tight jaw, clenched fist, tears). Then, repeat the feelings as you understand them, to demonstrate empathy.

Examples:

Counterpart: 'I'm really upset with how the project is going; I thought we'd be finished by now.'

You: 'You're disappointed.'

Counterpart: Slaps table.

You: 'Frustrating, huh?'

(Often, when an emotion is directed at you, your first tendency may be to respond defensively. When you Acknowledge Emotion first, you remind yourself that you are to focus on your counterpart, not yourself. Thus, you may avoid being "hooked" by this tendency.)

Counterpart: 'I can't believe you just did that!'

You: 'You're annoyed with me. I guess I hadn't told you that...'.

[Second sentence changes category.]

Encourage

Encouragement is a key-factor for successful communication (Madhukar R.K., 2001). It gives the other person permission to go on with what he or she is saying, promotes the other person's further exploration of an idea can start the other person taking.

Typically, encourage when:

- you want more information about ideas, facts, or feelings.
- the other person appears hesitant.

How to Encourage

- Say things like, 'Go on', 'Tell me more', and 'uh-huh'.
- Use non-verbal cues, like head nodding and hand gestures.
- Maintain good eye-contact, use appropriate body language, and remain quiet.

Examples:

Counterpart: 'I've been having a problem motivating my team.'

You: 'Tell me more.'

Counterpart: 'They just don't seem to work together well enough.'

You: 'Could you tell me a bit more about that?'

Counterpart: 'They just don't seem to work together well enough.'

You: 'Go on. What happened then?'

Counterpart: 'I think additional security guards will reduce theft.'

You: 'That's an excellent idea.'

A few more examples:

'Had it happened to me I'd have been rather upset.'

'That must have been rather satisfying.'

'I guess that must make you rather anxious.'

Acknowledge Ideas

You focus on the other person's content—the ideas—rather than the emotion. In acknowledging ideas, you let the other person know that you are paying attention to the content (Lesikar, et. al., 2002). It:

- demonstrates that you have listened actively.
- summarizes your understanding of the information presented to you.
- provides a basis for clarifying what you may have misunderstood.
- establishes rapport.

Typically, acknowledge ideas when:

- you think ideas should dominate.
- you want more information about what has been said.
- you are confused or unclear.
- you have been given a lot of information.
- you want to make sure that you heard and understood correctly.

First, listen to understand—not to judge—the ideas expressed by the other person. Then, repeat almost verbatim, or paraphrase using the other person's words as much as you can. Your restatement can interrupt, clarify, or summarize the other person's presentation. When you acknowledge ideas, refrain from adding some of your own comments and avoid evaluating what you are hearing.

Examples:

Counterpart: 'This policy manual is outdated. It cites procedures no longer in effect. We need annual revisions.'

You: 'You think we should start revising the policy manual annually.'

Counterpart: 'We must abandon all projects other than those which have a direct bearing on production.'

You: 'Earlier, I understood that you wanted annual revision of the policy manual. Now, I think you're saying that we should engage only in projects having direct bearing on production.'

Counterpart: 'Flex-time could really solve a lot of problems around here. There are too few typewriters and wordprocessors to go around. I'd love to drive in at 7:30; it would make commuting a snap for me. The only problem might be for the company carpool. I guess they'd have to co-ordinate time schedules.'

You: 'Let me see if I understood this correctly. You believe that if we institute flex-time, we can increase the use of office equipment, and alleviate some traffic problems, but there will be some implications for carpooling.'

Question

Questioning is the single most used category in conversations. Questions can clarify meaning and avoid problems. Insufficient or incorrect information can lead to an improper response or action (Anderson, 2003). The intent of questioning is to:

- seek information.
- gather additional information.
- clarify information.
- help lead the other person to an insight not yet his or hers.

There are two types of questions, open and closed. An open question allows the respondent wide latitude and opens up the conversation. It is phrased so that it requires a descriptive response. A closed question allows less latitude because it requires a 'yes' or 'no' response or a specific fact. It causes the respondent to focus narrowly his or her thoughts.

Typically, question when:

- you know what information you need.
- you are unclear about something.
- you want to guide the conversation.

How to Ask an Open Question: Phrase your question so your counterpart can choose from a variety of responses and can be descriptive.

How to Ask a Closed Question: Phrase your question so that it limits the range of your counterpart's response.

Examples:

Open: 'What factors could interfere with your meeting the deadline for the report?'

Closed: 'Will we get the report on time?'

Open: 'We need to address the dependent care needs of our employees. What are some of the things we can do?'

Closed: 'What companies have programs for employees' dependents?'

Open: 'How have these insurance claims been handled in the past?'

Closed: 'Have past insurance claims been answered using this approach?'

Open: 'How could that help with the problem of absenteeism?'

Inform

Informing conveys a message to your counterpart. The ability to share information is critical in the business world (Guffey, 2000). Most discussions revolve around giving information and centre on an exchange of messages. The sender states facts, thoughts, feelings, and concerns about the subject. The receiver processes the message and gives back his/her own information.

Informing may:

- make your counterpart aware of something.
- answer your counterpart's question.
- move the discussion in a particular direction.
- change the subject under discussion.
- build on another's idea(s).

- contribute to problem solving or decision making.
- stimulate discussion, as in a brainstorming session.

Typically, inform when:

- more information is needed by your counterpart to go further in the interaction.
- explaining.
- your counterpart is ready to listen.
- time is critical.

How to Inform

- Know your audience.
- State your message clearly, in appropriate language.
- Keep to the point.
- Offer only the quantity of information you believe your counterpart can assimilate at a time.
- Identify your opinion as such.
- Question to check for understanding before informing further.

Examples:

You: 'You have an opportunity to participate in a training programme, Conversations that Work, that will help you to achieve your communication goals. The program will help you effectively use skills you already know but, perhaps, haven't thought to organize in this particular way.'

You: 'I think there are two key audiences our newsletter must address: our clients and our board of directors.'

Some more examples of sentences that inform:

'I was very pleased when I read your report.'

'Fantastic! How do you keep coming with such good ideas?'

'What a memory! Wish mine were as good....'

'You learn fast! I wish I too....'

Praise, implied in the last few examples, often has some of the elements of the encouragement. Because praise often reflects the judgement of the speaker and its intent is to share opinion, it is frequently classified as information.

Direct

Directing involves one person giving instructions to another. In the most common business use, directing is the act of delegating. Directing helps you to:

- guide someone.
- clarify expectations.

Typically, direct when:

- you expect compliance from the other person.
- you are delegating responsibility.
- you are teaching.
- you do not have time to do anything else.
- you believe that the other person has the knowledge and skill to carry out the direction.

How to Direct

- State the directions clearly.
- State the directions in sequence.
- Use imperative sentences.
- Be constructive.
- Question to check understanding.

Examples:

You: 'Please review the year-end totals for last year and compare those with the year-end totals from the previous year.'

You: 'I'd like you to retype the proposal, substituting the new regional manager's name for John's name.'

You: 'I need your help in the beginning phase of this project. Please complete the following by March 1: identity five experts, interview them, summarize the information in a report, send the summary to me and mail copies to each interviewee. Do you have any questions?'

In giving directions, one of the most important things is to be clear. Therefore be concise, and check for understanding.

Criticize

Criticizing intends to redirect negative behavior to positive. It is necessary in business interactions because everyone can make mistakes. Since criticism increases defensiveness in the receiver, criticizing should be done carefully and with tact (Adair, 2002). Criticizing:

- allows you to give feedback and change the direction of another's behavior.
- allows you to point out someone's weakness and redirect him or her to a more positive action.
- can repair and improve conditions.
- can promote mutual satisfaction.

How to Criticize

- Describe the unacceptable behavior and specify the acceptable behavior and possible consequences.
- Avoid blame.
- Acknowledge the counterpart's emotions or ideas if necessary and/or if time permits.
- Be certain that the counterpart understands the corrective action and the consequences.

Examples:

You: 'John, the situational analysis you did was excellent. The bottom-line approach was very helpful. There is some change I'd like. I think the section on marketing strategies lacks explanatory charts and graphs. It would make things clearer to the non-technical audience. Would you add those to the final copy?'

You: 'Margaret, your report doesn't follow the guidelines set by our client. Would you please review Section III of those guidelines and revise it by 3 pm?'

You: 'John, you've missed two deadlines on this project. Let's work this out so that the project gets back on schedule. I'd like you to prepare a status report showing where each step actually stands. Set priorities for each point. If conditions warrant, I'll get you extra help.'

Useful Phrases

Given below are phrases and expressions helpful in putting forth preferences and opinions, offering explanations and disagreeing with other's views:

Opinions, Preferences: I think..., In my opinion..., I'd like to..., I'd rather..., I'd prefer..., The way I see it..., As far as I'm concerned..., If it were up to me..., I suppose..., I suspect that..., I'm pretty sure that..., It is fairly certain that..., I'm convinced that..., I honestly feel that..., I strongly believe that..., Without a doubt....

Disagreeing: I don't think that..., Don't you think it would be better..., I don't agree, I'd prefer..., Shouldn't we consider..., But what about..., I'm afraid I don't agree..., Frankly, I doubt if..., Let's face it, The truth of the matter is..., The problem with your point of view is that....

Giving Reasons and Offering Explanations: To start with, The reason why..., That's why..., For this reason..., That's the reason why..., Many people think...., Considering..., Allowing for the fact that..., When you consider that....

Conclusions

To sum up, conversing involves use of appropriate verbal cues besides other factors such as active listening, involvement of every member, understanding of implications, use of non verbal cues, and so on. Words do matter in a business conversations and hence it is imperative that the conversationalists use appropriate language expressions during their conversation so as to make them more effective. By understanding the various communication functions involved in business conversations and also the appropriate verbal cues to be used in carrying out these functions, we can bring in success to our conversations. As we all know, practice makes perfect, and the more conversations we are engaged in, the better conversationalists we become. We always need to remember that acquiring conversational skill is the magic key to our professional success and our social popularity.

REFERENCES

Adair, John, *The Effective Communicator*. Jaico Publishing House, Mumbai, 2002, p. 108.

Adler, Ronald B. and Jeanne Marquardt Elmhorst, *Communicating at Work*, 7th Edition. McGraw Hill Higher Education, NY, 2002, p. 118.

Anderson, Paul V., *Technical Communication*, Fifth Edition. Thomson Asia Pte Ltd., Singapore, 2003, p. 407.

Guffey, Mary Allen, *Business Communication: Process and Product*. Thomson Asia Pte Ltd., Singapore, 2000, p. 108.

Lesikar, Raymond V. et.al., *Lesikar's Basic Business Communication*, Eighth Edition. Tata McGraw-Hill Publishing Company Limited, New Delhi, 2002, p. 442.

Ludlow, Ron and Fergus Panton, *The Essence of Effective Communication*. Prentice-Hall of India, New Delhi, 1999, pp. 2-3.

Madhukar, R.K., *Business Communication and Customer Relations*. Vikas Publishing House Pvt. Ltd., New Delhi, 2001, p. 125.

Robbins, Stephen P. and Mary Coulter, *Management*, Fifth Edition. Prentice Hall of India Private Limited, Delhi, 1996, p. 625.

Sreevalsan, M.C., *Spoken English: English Conversation Practice*. Vikas Publishing House Pvt. Ltd., New Delhi, 2001, p. 163.

2

English Language and Communication Skills

Mahendra Singh Dhaka

Introduction

The twenty-first century is witnessing a big boom in professional development and career profiles. Such rapid and phenomenal growth all around has never been seen or experienced in earlier times. To keep pace with the professional advancements which are taking giant leaps, the first and foremost requirement of the job-seekers is to develop professionally to the extent that they are able to match the personality requirements of the employers. One of the major personality traits in great demand is effective and excellent communication and listening skills. Although communication skills are not hugely dependant on any particular language but anyone aspiring to excel today in any professional field must possess a reasonably good command over English language. It is the key to success; it is the 'bridge' which has to be crossed to reach greener professional pastures. Globalisation and expansion of the sphere of professional career profiles and activities in education and administration, management, science and technology, commerce and industry, environment and medicine, computing and internet, international affairs and international cooperation, etc. have opened the flood-gates of new vistas to potential professionals. All these have placed ever increasing demands on the learning of English language. Gone are the days when the earstwhile communist world used to keep all their activities behind the iron curtain duly bound by the red tape. Today all the countries of the earstwhile Eastern-Bloc are encouraging their people to interact with the world in English language and replace the typically communist closed collar and high neck coats with the western suits and ties. The compulsions of modern life guide us to accord the highest priority and a supreme effort to teaching and learning of English language.

Teaching and Learning of English Language in India

The Past and Present Status. English language is being taught and studied in India for over two centuries and despite the fact that the British ruled us for two hundred years, Indians are still far away from learning to speak and listen effective English language. English is one of our official languages; it is the link language. It is the medium of teaching in most professional courses and degrees. English is the language of almost all of our selection processes—whether for admission of students in professional courses of I.I.Ms., I.I.Ts., M.B.As., M.C.As., Medicine, Hospitality industry or for any sphere of employment of our corporate sector, national or multinational, as well as officers of our defence services. Even then the average Indian student is not able to either learn English or communicate in English to a reasonable level of proficiency and fluency. The weakness persists and it shall stay as long as the teaching and learning methodology of English will continue in its present form in our schools, colleges and universities.

Whither English Language Teachers? A proficient faculty is the fountainhead, the essence of quality instruction in any field of education and this is where India's greatest weakness lies with regard to teaching and learning of English. Do we have proficient teachers of English language today in schools and colleges who are competent to teach all the four components—reading, writing, speaking and listening? Do we have an ideal syllabus? Do we have the workshops and laboratories in schools and colleges to teach reading, speaking and listening? Do we have a uniform methodology to train our English teachers? Last but not least, do our regulatory bodies and policymakers have the courage of their convictions to accept that India needs to create a huge modern infrastructure in our schools, colleges and universities to produce proficient teachers who can then teach English language to the millions of students of this country? As far as communication and listening skills of students are concerned, any training for proficiency in these skills is completely dependent on teachers who ought to be proficient in all the four elements of the language. If our education system and teaching methodologies have failed to produce teachers who are proficient in all the four elements, then how do we expect our students to be proficient in speaking and listening skills of English language?

How Do We Treat Teaching English Language? Schools, colleges and universities in India do teach the reading and writing of English language. However, testing a student is done only in written English. No fora exist for testing the students in the reading, speaking and listening elements. This is so because these elements do not form class room schedules; they are neither taught, nor practised compulsorily and hence not tested. If a student or for that matter any one, is good in the written expression of English language, he is considered to be a brilliant student. But when it comes to the proficiency in communication and listening skills, the majority of students find themselves struggling with English language. Not only their spoken English but their listening prowess is also poor. Such a poor state is not due to the students' inability alone; there are several deficiencies and causes which need to be addressed by the authorities. For example, in India, different states commence teaching English language from different classes at school level, every Board of Secondary Education has a different syllabus for the same class, different colleges and universities pursue different syllabi at graduation and post-graduation levels and hence have different standards of knowledge of English language. Each professional course like management, engineering, medicine and others lay different levels of emphasis on the learning and use of English language. There is just no uniformity anywhere in any aspect of the teaching and learning of English language. Is it not a shabby treatment to English language which has the largest following in the world, which is spoken by the largest number of people after Mandarin?

Take the example of the common admission test for engineering courses. Majority of universities conduct this test with a choice to the candidates for answering in English or Hindi because the questions are in English as well as in Hindi. This is so because most of the Boards of Secondary Education have Hindi or their regional language as the medium of instruction. However, once the admissions are made, the students have to study their engineering courses in English because the medium of instruction in Bachelor of Technology courses is English; their books are in English, all their examinations are in English and all their seminars and workshops are in English. Obviously, the students will face huge difficulties in their studies because over 95 per cent of them have studied in Hindi medium upto the senior secondary level. The effect of the problems which first year students face is so bad and distressing that "only seeing is believing". This is a big dichotomy. They genuinely do not follow the teaching in English where as they have to study their four-year engineering degree course in English. The most startling fact is that the subject of Professional Communication (English) is part of their syllabi in B.Tech. only upto the first year. After that they are supposed to fend for themselves to learn English language if they have to achieve a reasonably good standard of the engineering graduate degree or effective communication skills in English.

As a testimony to what has been said above, a small survey was undertaken by this author in an engineering college of western Uttar Pradesh in August 2007, i.e. when the first year students were about three weeks into their first semester. The observations and results are tabulated below:

Disciplines of Bachelor of Technology

Details of Students	*M.E.*	*E.C.*	*E.I.*	*C.S.*	*I.T.*	*Agri.*	*Total*
(i) Total No. of students in a class	59	59	59	59	59	60	355

(Contd...)

(ii) No. of students present during survey	48	44	48	50	55	59	304
(iii) Students from ICSE/CBSE	02	11	10	04	02	–	29
(iv) Students from U.P. Board (Hindi Medium)	44	33	37	46	53	59	272
(v) Students from Board of other states	02	–	01	–	–	–	03
(vi) Students who can converse in English	02	04	06	01	03	–	16
(vii) Students who cannot understand a person speaking in English	17	28	29	11	15	56	156

The above figures clearly show the following trends which generally exist in almost all professional colleges and institutes in the region and are quite alarming:

(a) Hundred per cent students in the first month of their first semester are not attending classes. This indicates that the most probable reason is that they do not follow the teaching and hence facing lack of interest.

(b) Students from Boards with Hindi medium far exceeded students from English medium schools of I.C.S.E. or C.B.S.E.

(c) Number of students who could converse in English is indeed very small; almost negligible.

(d) Fifty-one per cent of total number of students and almost 95 per cent of Agriculture Engineering students could not understand anyone speaking to them in English. Only God Almighty knows how these students are going to cope up with their studies for the next four years!

Before blaming the students for being poor communicators in English, let us not forget that proficiency of teachers at school as well as at college level is a major stumbling block in providing quality teaching and learning of the language. Barring a few dozen private public schools of very high repute and a few reputed colleges, teaching and learning of English language faces the same situation in almost all state funded schools, colleges and even universities as well as the plethora of professional institutes even in the private sector. English language syllabus does not include oral and practical laboratory education nor any evaluation in the reading, speaking and listening skills is conducted. These are conducted for Physics, Chemistry or other technology subjects but not for English language. Today, teaching and learning of the language with emphasis on spoken English and listening is sadly restricted to only the commercially established private organisations like the Career Launcher, T.I.M.E. Group, Hero Mind Mine and others. They are restricted to mainly the metros. Their numbers and capacity barely caters for only those who can bear their high costs. Corporate executives, electronic media personnel and only a handful of desperate but rich students can benefit from such coaching centres. The average student is not even aware of the existence of such coaching centres. Nor can he afford them. This is the ground reality, a stark truth. What we need for the benefit of English language, therefore, are well-trained teachers, need based syllabi and the creation of the basic infrastructure in every school and college throughout the length and breadth of the country. Such arrangements should be aimed to teach and learn all the four components of English language, i.e. reading, writing, speaking and listening.

Current Scenario in Colleges and Universities

Today, India has approximately 500 universities. The National Knowledge Commission headed by Sam Pitroda has demanded 1500 universities by the year 2015. Prime Minister Dr. Manmohan Singh, in his Independence Day speech in 2007, had declared to open 30 Central Universities, 8 I.I.Ts., 7 I.I.Ms., 1600 I.T.Is. and other institutions of higher learning. All this sounds very good but will the government be able to place a check on the downward slide of English language when the new institutions shall open up? Will the old and the new temples of learning be able to do justice to the teaching and learning of English language? Let us have a look at the current scenario of English language with regard to its effect on the communication and listening skills of the current population of students in colleges and universities.

Undergraduate Students. My visits to several colleges and a few universities of Uttar Pradesh have revealed the inability and helplessness of the undergraduate students to converse in English. The numbers vary only by a fraction between colleges in urban areas and those in the rural or semi-urban areas. Students of professional courses are no doubt a shade better than their counterparts in the traditional degree courses of B.A., B.Sc. or B.Com. A total absence of any type of extra-curricular activities involving English speaking was most distressing in these colleges while the professional colleges do conduct some activities where the students are required to participate in English. The most concerning aspect of today's undergraduate student is that due to his poor background of English speaking, he is shy of taking the initiative to develop spoken English. His teachers neither possess the desired skills in spoken English themselves and hence unable to set a personal example nor are they able to motivate their students to make efforts to develop proficiency in English language. The teacher as well as the student only hopes to sail through, somehow, through the obligatory English language tests which form part of the syllabi. This indeed, is a very sad state. A very large majority of undergraduates lack the will to take the initiative to develop their English language and their speaking and listening skills. My visits to several colleges and professional institutes also established the non-existence of any effort on the part of the institutes to develop these skills in their undergraduate students. To cap it all, the students themselves are shying away if an institute or college makes an effort to arrange some event or a workshop for participation by the students. It is sad to note that there are students of traditional as well as professional courses who acquire their degree without participating even in a single extra-curricular event involving spoken English. When asked to attend a free workshop on spoken English arranged for first year students of a B.Tech degree course in a local institute, the following survey speaks for itself.

Day	Disciplines	No. of Students Asked to Attend	No. of Students Who Actually Came to Attend
First	(a) Electronics & Communication Engg. (b) Electronics & Instrumentation Engg.	118	30
Second	(a) Computer Sc. Engg. (b) Information Technology	118	16
Three	(a) Mechanical Engg. (b) Agricultural Engg.	119	14

The above survey clearly indicates that today's undergraduate is foolishly shying away from ground realities and does not possess the courage of his convictions to accept the fact that he is shockingly poor in English language, particularly spoken English. Another example is when a simple questionnaire of one page of personality development could not be attempted by the N.C.C. cadets in a camp of senior division, belonging to five degree colleges because it was in English and the answers were sought in English. Students of a degree college in Pachmarhi (Madhya Pradesh) when asked to answer a similar questionnaire in English responded to the questionnaire mostly in Hindi. Such is the fate of English language as far as undergraduates are concerned.

Post Graduate Students and Research Scholars. I took upon myself to interact with a large number of postgraduate students of M.A., M.Sc. and M.Com. disciplines as well as those pursuing professional courses like M.B.A., M.C.A., M.P.Ed., M.Ed., and a few dozen research scholars too. While a majority of the girl students were willing to respond in English to express their views on subjects like student politics, dress code, the fate of English language, etc. the boys preferred not to speak much. My aim was to assess their response to my conversation with them in English language. Most of them responded only in a mixture of English and Hindi while hardly five per cent were able to speak in English notwithstanding their poor pronunciation, local accent and a poor grammar. It is not that these scholars have weak vocal chords but it is their poor proficiency in the English language which kept them silent. These standards of communication skills in English language from post graduates and research scholars are a poor reflection and should just not be acceptable. The results showcase the English language in general and proficiency of spoken English in particular, rather poorly.

Performance of Professional Students. At Campus Selections a first hand experience of three engineering, one M.B.A. and M.C.A. and one Hotel Management Institutes of Western Uttar Pradesh is sufficient to guage the standard of communication and listening skills among the students. My experience of heading a commercial institute of languages engaged in spoken English coupled with the experience of the above stated organisations has compelled me to take a plunge to expose the poor standards of spoken English displayed by the students at campus selections. It is a general practice in professional institutes that the training and placement officers make an effort to arrange practice sessions for group discussions and mock interviews prior to the campus selections. The response exhibited by the potential candidates can only be described as sad and depressing. In almost all the institutes the students were found to be careless though overconfident in their total attitude and approach towards any practice. Most of them wanted to appear directly in the G.Ds. and interviews conducted by the companies without attending practice sessions as they felt that they would crack the interviews easily. However the results were shocking. Some of the rejected students did not even find it worthwhile to know the results. The success rates have only been five to eight per cent while all the candidates had scored more than 65% in their semester exams. It is a tragedy that today's student, particularly in colleges from rural and semi-urban background, neither realises on his own nor is he being forced to realise that he is indeed very weak in important aspects like personality projection and communication and listening skills as well as in spoken English.

Communication Skills in English Language in Young Faculty. My experience of the last nine years of interaction with the young members of faculty of several professional institutes has revealed that their prowess of communication skills in English medium is rather poor. Many of them are so weak that neither they can converse fluently nor they can write an application of even half a page without grammatical mistakes. Believe me, it is not an exaggeration. When it comes to teaching the syllabi in English, they do so by mixing Hindi words. They have a very potent excuse saying that the students do not follow the teaching wholly in English language. While the statement is sadly true but does that mean that the faculty have a licence not to be proficient in spoken English when the medium of teaching and learning is in English? The picture is unfortunately grey and grim but a more sad part is that there is hardly any effort by the young faculty to develop their communication skills in English language. Their poor soft skills is the prime reason that they shun and shy away from partaking or guiding or even supervising any events in their colleges involving speaking in English. The scenario is the same in most urban areas and almost all colleges and institutes in rural or semi-urban areas.

Need for Formal Training in all Elements of English Language. There is a dire need for the regulatory bodies and authorities controlling the academic syllabi whose obligations include to ensure proper and formal training of teachers of English language in every school, college and university. Such training must be uniform and should include all the four elements—reading, writing, speaking and listening of English language. If this does not happen then the quality of teaching and learning English language shall continue to be as pathetic and embarrassing as it is at present. The proficiency of the language among the students shall also remain poor and most of them shall remain deprived of high profile jobs despite possessing degrees with first division marks. Ground realities with respect to non-availability of suitable and above average faculty with good proficiency in spoken English, compel the managements of colleges and institutes to select sub-standard faculty otherwise the shortages shall persist. Many a time, persons with no acumen, temperament and interest for teaching but possessing the required academic criteria also present themselves before the selection panels for teaching jobs. Due to huge deficiencies, many of such candidates get selected as teachers. They accept even very low offers because they are unemployed. The authorities like the U.G.C., A.I.C.T.E. and the policymakers in state and central governments need to take up the challenge of developing the desired infrastructure of laboratories at all levels of academic institutions to first train appropriate English language teachers who must acquire excellent standards in reading, writing, speaking and listening skills of the language. Only then can we hope to ensure that future generations of students shall possess the desired levels of communication skills to match the demands of modern selection processes. Until then, the students shall have to continue to struggle and suffer for want of proper facilities to develop their soft skills.

A Broad Framework for Training. The aim of training in teaching and learning the English language for facilitating the development of communication skills should be to raise the level of proficiency in reading, writing, speaking and listening in all students who attend schools and colleges. Such proficiency should be the optimum requirement by the time the students graduate. For achieving this aim the broad framework be designed at the following three tiers:

(a) Formulation of uniform syllabi, teaching and learning parameters and the methodology of the implementation of the broad framework in all schools, colleges and universities throughout the length and breadth of the country. Such a step shall entail not only a very serious effort to develop the syllabi, parameters and methodologies but also to formulate the steps to ensure obligatory adherence to the same by all academic institutions throughout the country.

(b) To train an excellent crop of teachers, proficient in all the components of English language. Preferably, this should be done at a few regional centres under the strict and watchful eye and control of the U.G.C. and A.I.C.T.E. Uniformity in standards of the teachers for schools, colleges and universities respectively should be the hallmark of this tier.

(c) To implement the uniform syllabi, parameters and the methodology of teaching and learning English language for each class in all schools and adopt the same syllabi at graduate and post graduate level in all colleges, universities and professional institutes of all disciplines. Such a step will result in uniform standards of teaching and evaluation at all levels. The students are bound to achieve the desired proficiency levels by the above implementation effort.

Solutions and Recommendations

While the teachers' training needs to undergo a complete transformation, it is equally important that learning and teaching of quality English speaking, listening, reading and writing has to be given equal weightage. The testing and evaluation system should also be revamped. Oral (verbal) tests in reading, speaking and listening are inescapable and must be included as seminars, workshops, debates, group discussions and laboratory based tests and all should count towards percentage of marks with equal weightage to all components. Parents, guardians, teachers as well as schools and colleges must guide, encourage and motivate students to learn quality English speaking and listening. On their part, the students must realise that they need to put in a huge extra effort towards learning the English language. They genuinely have no choice. Fifteen minutes of loud reading of a good English newspaper and fifteen minutes of watching and listening to a good English news TV channel daily, should be included in the daily routine for atleast six months. Students must restrict their conversation to only English once they are on the campuses of their colleges and universities. Making speeches in front of a mirror, recording the same on an audio tape and then playing it for correction by the teacher or a friend shall bring a lot of self-confidence in public speaking. Taking up a spoken and listening English course in a commercial language centre for about three months is strongly recommended. Such a step shall enable the students to achieve at least a workable proficiency. Changes and extra efforts are needed by all levels—from the highest, i.e. Ministry of Human Resource Development, National Knowledge Commission, the U.G.C., the A.I.C.T.E., etc. at the Central government levels, to the education ministries and Boards of Secondary Education at the level of the state, managements of schools, colleges and universities and down to the parents and students. The teachers in particular must move beyond the textbooks and ignite a spark to fire the imagination and create a will to learn among the students otherwise the story of the survey recorded in paras 9 and 10 shall sadly continue to repeat.

Conclusion

It goes without saying that no matter how intelligent and knowledgeable a person may be, no matter how many degrees he may possess, he shall not be successful in getting an appropriate job until and unless he possesses excellent and effective communication and listening skills. English language must be the medium in which the teachers and students alike need to develop their communication skills. There is an urgent need to develop uniform syllabi, create infrastructure for laboratories and workshops for English language and change the teaching and evaluation system giving equal weightage to reading, writing, speaking and listening right—from the schools to the level of universities. Thus, proficient teachers should first be trained and made available to schools, colleges and universities across the length and breadth of the country. Only then the students can benefit. Organisations like the Ministry of HRD, N.K.C., A.I.C.T.E. and Boards of Secondary Education have to act positively to place the whole system in its correct prospective.

3

The Communicative Approach to English Language Teaching

Karan Singh Yadav

The aims of teaching any language can be broadly indicated by using two familiar terms of 'Reception' and 'Expression.' While reception includes skills of listening and reading, expression stands for speaking and writing skills. The teaching of English in India has seen many ups and downs since its inception. It has been seen as a relic of the colonial past, as a vehicle of enslaving the mind and culture of India, something which should be done away with at its earliest. But at the same time it is seen by millions as a vehicle to prosperity and opportunity. Without going into the details of this peculiar love-hate relationship with English language in India, my paper shall be devoted to the problem peculiar to the studies of English in Indian colleges, which has made our students practically 'unsellable' in the global market. We shall ponder over the fact why despite the best efforts of many of my colleagues in colleges, we are churning out thousands of students from our educational institutions who are not only unable to get employment anywhere but are practically unemployable? Further, the paper shall discuss how the communicative approach to English language teaching can be successfully used to remove the imbalance caused by our present approach to English language teaching. Trying to keep the technical jargon to minimum, I shall also briefly examine the Communicative Methodology and how this approach can be put to use in our classrooms.

The poor standards of spoken and written English language skills have always been a matter of great concern for the academicians as well as government. The poor standard of English language has been noticed and commented upon by various commissions and study groups from time to time. The report of a study group appointed by the Ministry of Education, Government of India is a sad commentary on the predicament of English in India. The report points out, "The standard of English is deteriorating very fast in our schools and colleges [...]. Scripts are assigned marks by University examiners not for what the examinees have said but what they meant to say. The English language has itself a ghost life in India."[1]

The teaching of literature has been given priority at the cost of English language as a means of communication. The aims of English language teaching have been kept unusually high. The syllabuses of English in our universities and colleges even for U.G. courses have been literature-oriented. The texts meant for graduate and under-graduate students include masterpieces of Shakespeare, Milton, Goldsmith and poems and prose writings of Dryden, Pope, Blake, Bacon, Addison and other great writers of English Literature. The prescription of these texts in the syllabus of B.A. tends to ignore the fact that English is not the mother tongue of Indians. As early as in 1917 Principal Barrow of Calcutta Presidency College, admitted before the Sadler Commission of Calcutta University:

> When students come to college, they cannot follow lectures and they cannot read even quite simple English with ease. The curriculum is quite pretentious—Wordsworth, Milton, Arnold, etc. This may not seem ambitious but the fact is that students at the end of eight years are still without any command of modern English. Their vocabulary is extremely thin. They know hardly anything of the idiom or rhythm of the language. In this condition they are set to study 'literature' which depends for the success of its appeal on choice of allusions to Bible, to European Mythology and legend, and to English life and customs and history with which these

> boys are almost totally unfamiliar. (Their aim is to acquire) the bare literal meanings of words and phrases and allusions. To suppose that the reading of literature in this manner has any value whatever is absurd.[2]

As such our teachers of English in our colleges are expected to perform two functions at the same time—they are supposed to teach fundamental elements of the language and conceptual content of the prescribed texts. Prof. Dun, too, voiced the dilemma of an English teacher in these words: "The teacher found himself obliged to attempt two tasks at the same time—teach the basic elements of the language and also the advanced literary texts set in the syllabus. Since the two jobs existed at such widely different levels and since his own security of livelihood depended upon seeing the students safely through the examination somehow, the teacher of English settled down to become an examination coach, teaching the students how to arrive without traveling."[3]

The design of our syllabus is not according to the present objectives of teaching of English. The overemphasis on the study of literature strains the students who are hardly able to understand and appreciate the alien culture and life presented through the literary texts. The immediate need of the most of the students is to develop their command on language used in everyday life and to enrich their stock of words used in communication. To teach language through literature is a very lengthy route and is unsuitable to the second language learners. According to Halliday, McIntosh and Strevens the neglect of language and linguistics in English studies has encouraged "a process of self-annihilation in which more and more literature has been accompanied by less and less language ability until in many overseas countries the study of 'English' in the sense of 'English Literature' has become a practical impossibility in the present educational circumstances."[4]

The Communicative Approach to English Language Teaching can effectively answer some of the problems mooted above. Communicative Language Teaching is defined by K. Johnson and K. Morrow as an approach which "recognizes the teaching of communicative competence as its aim. It is on this level of aim that such a language teaching distinguishes from more traditional approaches where the emphasis is on teaching structural competence."[5] Communicative competence can be defined as the effective use of language in the social context. It is the ability to say the right thing at the right moment.

Communicative Model of Teaching

Communicative Task 1	*Drill/Structures*	*Communicative Task 2*
Students communicate using whatever language skills they possess	The teacher provides new forms and drills	Students make use of new forms

The teacher provides a communicative task to his students who are asked to communicate as much as possible with whatever language tools they possess. If the students are not able to keep the pace of communication due to lack of linguistic support, the teacher must provide them the tools and give them drills to internalize the new structures. The students are again asked to communicate using their newly discovered structures. We can deduce four principles of Communicative Methodology:

(a) **Know What You are Doing:** The teacher must prepare some goals before entering the class. These goals may be in the form of some language operations, and structures which should be realized before the end of the lesson and the learners should be able to perform functions which they could not do at the beginning of the class.

(b) **The Whole is More Than the Sum of the Parts:** The ability of the students to handle isolated elements of language is not considered a goal in this approach. What is required is the development of the ability in the students to produce strings of sentences and ideas in the spoken form.

(c) **To Learn It Do It:** Only through practice in communication mode, the language in its spoken form can be learnt. And the teacher achieves it by motivating and giving stimuli to the students to indulge in the communication.

(d) **Mistakes are not always a Mistake:** During the communication the teacher ignores the trivial mistakes of grammar and pronunciation as long as he considers the student to be on the right track. Too frequent interference and correction might be counterproductive as the student may be discouraged which may hamper the whole communication process.

Role of Teacher in Communicative Language Teaching

In a communicative Methodology a teacher has twin roles. He acts as a facilitator in the communicative process between the participants in the classroom and at the same time acts as an independent participant in the group. Thus the teacher acts as an organizer of resources and as a resource himself. Michel P. Bren and Christopher N. Candlin while emphasizing the role of teacher in the communicative Methodology assert: "In guiding and monitoring the teacher needs to be a 'seer of potential' with the aim of facilitating and shaping individual and group knowledge and exploitation of abilities during learning."[6] A teacher must recognize the difference in potential of students in the class. He should not have too rigid control over the communicative process. He should be ready to concede that "different learners learn different things in different ways at different times, and he needs to be patiently aware that some learners, for example, will enter periods when it seems that little or no progress is being made and that, sometimes, learning is typified by silent reflection."[7]

Concomitantly, while designing a Communicative curriculum, flexibility and practicability should be the watchwords. We must be aware that "there can be no such thing as an ideal and uniquely applicable language teaching curriculum since any realization of the curriculum must reflect a realistic analysis of the actual situation within which the language teaching will take place. To cope with this requirement of appropriateness to situation, the communicative curriculum has to be proposed as a flexible and practical set of basic principles which underlie a whole range of potential communicative curricula."[8]

The Communicative, approach to English Language Teaching has been successfully adopted by various countries for second language learners. It can be effectively used to counter some of the tendencies which have crept silently into the teaching of language such as apathy on the part of the teacher, lack of response on the part of the students and too much emphasis on literature at the cost of spoken language, etc. In the present day world the immediate need of the students is proficiency in the spoken form of language, to which this approach contributes a lot. It will not only check the rising tide of unemployment among our rural youth, but will also equip them suitably to face the challenges in the era of Globalization, Liberalization and Privatization.

NOTES

1. Quoted by Ram Kumar Sharma, *Problems and Solutions of Teaching English* (New Delhi: Commonwealth Publishers, 1989), p. 18.
2. S. Nagarajan, "The Decline of English in India: A Historical Perspective," *College English*, 43/7 (November 1981), p. 63.
3. *Ibid.*, pp. 665-66.
4. M.A.K. Halliday, Angus McIntosh and Peter Strevens, *The Linguistic Sciences and Language Teaching* (London: Longman Group Ltd., 1966), p. 184.
5. K. Johnson and K. Morrow, *Communication in the Classroom* (Essex: Longman Group Ltd., 1981), p. 10.
6. Michael P. Bren and Christopher N. Candlin, "The Essentials of a Communicative Curriculum in Language Teaching," *Innovation in English Language Teaching: A Reader*, David R. Hall and Ann Hewings (eds.). (London and New York: Routledge, 2001), p. 17.
7. *Ibid.*, p. 18.
8. *Ibid.*, p. 24.

4

Changing Paradigms in English Language Teaching: Methods of ELT to Integrated Course Students

K. Balachandran

A close study and observation of the performance of the students who have joined, five year integrated course after twelfth, is very discouraging and shocking. When they are asked to read the English text in the classroom, they falter; they don't know how to pronounce even simple words. Their reading skill is very poor. Alright, if their writing skill is better, it would have been satisfactory. Even their writing skill is beyond redemption. (1) Why this sorry state of affairs? (2) Who is responsible for their poor performance? (3) Who will redeem them from their deterioration? (4) Do we need innovation in English Language Teaching? (5) Do we need innovation in Instructional materials? (6) Are the learning processes good and effective? (7) How is the learners' perception? (8) Do we need a new Agenda? (9) What are the remedial actions to be taken for the success of the various programs initiated? The paper analyses all these aspects objectively with a view to help all sections.

A. Paradigm: What is Paradigm?

Paradigm is a model or example. A conceptual framework within which scientific theories are constructed which is consistent with it but may need completely revising as evidence challenging the factual accuracy of some aspects of its accumulating. Do we need changes in ELT? Emphatically no.

B. Objectives of ELT

ELT should bring good changes in the lives of the students. Equipping the learners with communicative skills, handling the English language effectively while performing different language functions; helping them to develop their cognitive and affective faculties promoting the skill of reading the text intelligently and imaginatively, enriching the active and passive vocabulary of the learner; to develop communication and comprehension skill for further learning.

C. Recommendation of N.S. Prabhu

For ELT various experts have been giving their own suggestions. Prabhu (1995) enlists quite a few: classical scholastic procedures, grammar translation method, direct method, structural method, communicative language teaching, reading methods, task-based language teaching, etc. "These teaching methods have been tried and evaluated. Some of them have been praised, adopted and then rejected to try new methods that promised successful learning by learners" (Sandhya Rani Sahoo, 73).

(1) **History of the Students' Knowledge of English Language and Present Scenario:** Students with high hopes enter the portals of a college or University after their senior secondary exam. But all those who join the five year Integrated M.A./M.Sc./M.Com. course are not fully equipped either with the reading skill or writing skill. When probed about their performance in the high school and higher secondary school, it was negligible, unproductive and almost nil. Somehow they cram to pass in the examination. Except in the reputed and Matriculation schools, teaching of English is unimaginably poor.

In the past, whether the students go through their English texts at least detailed texts are questionable. Whether the teachers ask them to study the texts or not, they may give answers to the questions. Some may even ask them to buy 'such and such' guide and learn by heart what is printed there. The school head also, it seems, should have been allowing their school students to copy in the annual examination either from the texts, notes or from good performance students papers or by some other means—dictating the answer openly or writing them in the black boards in order to get minimum 50% pass for the school, lest they should be answerable to the DEOs and other educational authorities. Sometimes the schools get cash award of Rs 10,000 from the Govt, if there is 100% pass at the 10th and 12th levels. Even in the well-reputed schools, always, 100% pass is not possible, unless they practise some kind of unfair means. The students who are reared up in an uneducative atmosphere, after their entry into Govt. College/University still live in their dream world of copying and passing by hook or by crook.

(2) When an English teacher enters the class with all high hopes of imparting knowledge he/she is shocked to find the student's level of grasping, reading, writing skills and their classroom behavior. For the poor performance both the teachers and the students are responsible. All the teachers at all levels are not doing the best. Some do the best; some do better and some, bad. Similarly the students who strive, they fare the best; those who try just so so, fare better; those who don't strive fare bad. This kind of teachers and students are mainly responsible for the poor performance of the students at school, high school, higher secondary, collegiate and university levels.

(3) It is the teachers and students who have to do their level best. Teaching and learning is not one sided affair. It should be the unified effort of both the teachers and students; both should strive for better results and outcome.

(4) There is no special need for innovation in ELT. The existing method itself can be followed but with patience and more involvement to plug the holes here and there. If fully and properly implemented the present methods will bring amazing changes.

(5) Instructional materials are in plenty when compared to the days of the past. The only thing to be done is the proper

use of the materials to inspire the students to utilize them and dedicated teachers to impart the needed English language education to the students.

(6) The learning process is good in the students who score good marks. It has to be rescheduled in the case of students who fail miserably. The learning process should be made interesting so that they can reap more harvest in the learning of English.

(7) The learners are of three types: slow learners, medium paced learners and fast learners. Very many factors decide this division. Yet the students have to compensate and adjust themselves to the fast-Learner's methods.

(8) Any agenda for English language teaching generally is well conceived. But it has to be implemented properly. Students should be more hard working to achieve the decided results. Similarly the teacher should take more interest in the welfare of the students, especially in imparting English language. All the instructional materials are available in the market are not standard materials. Regarding this, students can get the advice from experienced teachers. These aspects have to be taken for consideration. They are:

(i) **Learning a Second Language:** About learning English language, Balachandran writes:

> Learning a second language (for example, English) is a load to the below average and slow learning children. It is not a load to the above average and talented children. It is not a load to the above average and talented children. It becomes a load because of very many factors. (1) The children should be active to learn English. If it is not so, if they fail to evince interest in it, it becomes a load. (2) Teachers are also mainly responsible. If they take much pains and interest, even an ordinary student will become bright in learning English. If the teachers are careless, it may affect a student's future. (Balachandran 130)

(ii) **A Committed Teacher:** A committed teacher is the backbone of the educational system. About this Balachandran opines:

> A committed teacher is the treasure of a society. He is an asset to the institution, to the student community and in turn to the Nation. Refer to world famous leaders in India. They might have had their education from illuminating teachers and famous institutions. In this type of atmosphere, learning is a pleasure. Teaching is also pleasurable. Both the teacher and the students engage themselves in a happy learning process. The students always very eagerly wait for their teachers; the teachers also very anxiously wait to meet committed students. Here learning is considered to be a happy pastime. (Balachandran 130)

(iii) **Falling Standards:** Standard is the most important aspect in any activity. About this Balachandran comments:

> Standards have been falling down as the London Bridge is falling down! When there is deterioration of standards, how can we expect good and efficient students to come out of the educational institutions? Out of ten students only three or four are with appreciable standard. Because of the internal assessment system, they get good marks in assignments, which is nothing but copying from the text or notes at home and submitting them for marks. (Balachandran 132)

The methods of ELT are discussed under the headings below:

(I) Textbooks and Materials

Globalization, Liberalization, Urbanization have all come. Yet English is still a foreign language to most of the students and a section of teachers. Regarding the prescribed textbooks, they are good ones, no doubt. Subject experts and enthusiasts take care of writing and prescribing activities. Availability of the text is also not a problem nowadays because the Tamil Nadu Govt., has been taking the heavy job of printing in advance and sending them to various schools. Even free supply of textbooks to students is done. Then where lies the problem?

(II) Instructional Materials

Regarding the available instructional materials Sandhya Rani Sahoo writes, "The textbook is the only important source of information and knowledge available to the teacher as well as to the learner" (Sahoo 77). The teacher and the taught have to heavily depend upon the texts. But today the practice is completely different. Bazaar guides and that too guides which are 'easy' are preferred, which don't have standard. "The approach should be multi skilled activity-based and leaner-centered" (Sahoo 77). The teacher and the learner should be active participants in the classroom—the teacher is a senior student and a student is a junior student. Is it not so? "This kind of interaction gives the students the opportunity to use the language appropriately to boost their confidence, self-assurance and competence to use English effectively according to the demand of the situation" (Sahoo 77). The instruction of the teacher should stimulate thinking to formulate their own new ideas on the subject.

(III) Classroom Activities

Executing anything is somewhat difficult. It is not enough if good food is served in a feast; it has to be tasted and eaten, only then it can be appreciated. Similarly for the books—they have to be studied by the students; used by teachers. But what is the reality? Most buy or get the textbooks. Many touch them! A few read them! Even before the text is started, the guides are there in the bookshops, written by 'experienced teachers'. The textbooks should become teachers' and students' 'Bible', but in practice the so-called 'guides' have been occupying the prominent place in their curriculum.

Do the students read the text in the class? The answer is "No". Jain writes, "The student is to be taught to read, write, speak and to understand. These cover the entire gamut of language learning" (V.K. Jain 62-63). The students are not given much more practice to read, write and speak English in the class is the main reason for their very poor performance in English. Only for 'namesake' everything is done. This practice continues at the college/university level also. Teachers in their 'boot and tie' very rarely ask their students to read the text in the class; the teachers don't listen to the students' reading and pronunciation. When they read, if they listen, mistakes can be rectified.

(IV) Composition Classes

Composition hours/classes are the bygone practice of the 20th century. In the 21st century no composition hour/class is allotted. In those days, two hours were earmarked every week for this work; students used to write textual essays, general essays, precis, comprehension, grammar exercises, translation, etc in the specially meant composition notebooks; the class during the session was supervised by tutors and the notebooks were corrected by them. The tutors were very experienced people like retired Headmasters from reputed schools. The very next week the corrected compositions were distributed to the students; they came to know about their mistakes. Spelling mistakes were rectified five times on the left hand side of the composition note, sentences once. This facilitated them to rectify their mistakes and they did not commit the same mistake. Is this practised today? About composition classes Balachandran writes:

> There used to be one hour composition instruction and regular composition classes for two hours every week. And for correcting notebooks, there were tutors who did their work with commitment. In the next class, the students had to make all the corrections meticulously on the left hand side of the notebook. This kind of rigorous practice helped students immensely for their constant standard. (Balachandran 132-33)

(V) Assignments

The composition class which was once in vogue is now replaced by assignments. This is done at home without the help of tutors/lecturers. They are submitted on before a prescribed date. A student with five papers will have to submit five assignments at a time. During a semester one has to write 45 assignments—three assignments for each teacher who handles the paper (subject) concerned. All these assignment notebooks mount on the table of the teacher (the students invade the room of the teacher concerned) concerned. He or she rust ticks at one place in each page (as a mark of he has seen that page and not studied; if studied there will be correction of wrong words or sentences) and towards the foot (end) of the assignment marks like 9/10 if he or she is very generous and 5 if the evaluator is a strict person and in between 5 and 9, if the teacher is a moderate evaluator. So virtually no correction will be done in the notebook by the so-called Lecturer/Reader/ Prof./Asst. Prof./Associate Prof. (No Tutor is appointed nowadays—the post has been abolished for the detriment of the students; new post called 'Guest Lecturer' post has been created. What they do is the same work done by the Regular teachers. The guest Lecturers don't do the correction work.) When the students receive their assignment notebooks with high marks (9/10) (Without knowing their standard and without going through what has been written), they praise the teacher; scold him who gives moderate marks as a miser; and curse him if he gives fail marks. The assignment notebooks will be attractive, specially made, different colours for different subjects. The day when the teacher really corrects the students' assignments, asks them to read the text in the class will be the golden lettered day in the career of a student.

(VI) Students' Seminars

This is an annual ritual. Towards the end of each semester every student has to present his/her seminar paper. This rarely takes place—teachers with good intention of improving the students' performance will conduct this. If a particular paper is taught by three teachers, all the three should conduct the students' seminar. Each teacher will have one-third of student strength for presentation in his/her hour. Because of academic jealousy and internal politics, teachers who have good standing will not be entrusted with this work. Teachers, who support blindly the HOD, will be entrusted with this work. So students will neither be inspired nor guided by experienced and reputed teachers. The students lose the golden opportunity of presenting, listened to and corrected by the senior teachers. The teachers, who don't have either the drive or the impetus, sometimes conduct and sometimes don't conduct. They just receive the seminar papers and all are given 5/5 marks irrespective of the content in the paper and presentation methods. Is there an ideal student seminar? Yet in well reputed institution the students outwit, excel their own teachers. If this is conducted in the true spirit, students' knowledge of English language and ELT will be very high and boost their confidence in addressing, appearing before others for presentation.

(VII) Slumbering Association

Inaugural function of the English Literary Association takes place with much fanfare. Some VIPs address the students and go. Towards the end of the semester/year, valedictory function of the English Literary Association is also conducted; once again some VIPs address the student gathering. In between there is no any activity. This is meant to improve the speech/conversation/ debating skills of the students. Fortnightly meetings can be conducted in which student's performance will be judged; indirectly all their skills will be developing. In due course, say in two or three years they will have good training and when they come out they may be fit for any job with much experience or training.

But what is the reality? The teacher who is in charge (generally Vice-President) of the English Literary Association is very busy during every weekend—frequenting metropolitan cities to earn more money (as though they don't earn) by taking classes in the Distance Education/Open University system. This is not a mistake. Every week they neglect their own regular students (because the teachers who are not preferred for this work, take care of the regular students) and inculcate very precious to the enrolled students outside the cyampus! The thing is, one should not be at the expense of others.

(VIII) Students' Evaluation

Are the teachers' performance periodically evaluated by students? This is the practice in the foreign universities and not in India. Very rarely this is done here. During the NAAC visit this is done and that too without the knowledge of the teachers. The office people hand over the questionnaire and the students who have seen the rigidity of the Dept. Head normally doesn't write anything true; they are indirectly threatened for any abnormal, negative comments. For the best teacher, mediocre teacher and 'so so' teacher the ranking is the same; or because of the influence of the HOD the best teacher gets 'good'. The hopeless teacher gets the 'best' ranking. Nowadays teachers know how to 'size up' their immediate boss and other people in their academic hierarchy by any means. Their dress and make up matters much for them; their honeyed words to their colleagues bring them good impressions. Above all give them coffee party/chicken party/drinks party to size up their shortcomings. Are teachers in a Dept. really united? How much politics are there? The day when the student's fearless evaluation comes, the Indian system of Education will stand erect until that it will look like a backbone bent old man only!

(IX) Learning and Teaching: Two-way Process

Instead of making the class a 'Teacher Monologue' session, (normally this is the practice) he/she can ask the students to read the text and then he/she can explain/explicate. So, they participate in the learning activity. In the case of teaching One-Act plays, dramas the students can be asked to assume the role of characters in the text and read (rehearse). They will be in pair or more than that in reading. This kind of dialogue/conversation will whet their appetite and will improve their understanding capacity better; there will be interaction among them and enhance their competitive spirit. Tonal variations, correct pronunciation, facial expressions, gestures will be every helpful to understand and appreciate a text. Students in reputed institutions enact even scenes from Shakespeare plays and some time even from Canadian literature. This offers them the self-confidence in their students' life and it moulds them to become efficient teachers in their life who can speak and write good English.

(X) Enriching the Students' Vocabulary

A student with a rich vocabulary of English can write and speak faultless English. Enhancing their vocabulary alone will give them the confidence to write and speak better English. For this, reading the detailed textbook and non-detailed texts is a must. This is in print (in the syllabus) but has not taken place in the practical world. When the xeroxing facilities have become easier and cheaper, still a section of students hesitate to get this (buying texts) done. They spend much for other items but not for texts!

(XI) Dictionary/Thesaurus Reading

Do we find the habit of dictionary reading among the students? It can be English to English, English to vernacular, vernacular to English, vernacular to vernacular Dictionary. Daily this practice has to be undertaken like brushing the teeth. Students have interest in recent film cassettes to be seen on the T.V. and song cassettes on tape recorder. Many students don't even have a dictionary but many have cell phones! English has become the "Principal medium of Education at University level and the language of administration at the centre and in many of states" (Sahoo 71). "English has a great socio-functional purpose in a multi-lingual and the new socio-cultural environment of India" (Sahoo 72). Why, even Thesaurus reading will bring good changes in the lives of students. Every student should have a Thesaurus. How is the condition? Discouraging!

(XII) International Intelligibility

Students from reputed and matriculation schools have good command over English; pronounce words properly. By their efforts and training, they achieve the approximation to the British Standard Pronunciation. All cannot master the British RP (Right Pronunciation). Even though International intelligibility can't be achieved "approximation of the above standard can be tried out" (Jain 64). He argues that even if this is not possible at least "within India the model of GIE (General Indian English) which is the desirable model to achieve intelligibility within India would suffice" (Jain 64). Jain further asserts: "The school teachers of today don't know better pronunciation. They are also not aware of RP. In such condition, it is futile to hope that students would catch the right pronunciation. Only the BBC programmes and Doordarshan news readers may help in forming the habits of speaking English correctly" (Jain 64).

How many students are (why teachers too?) listening to BBC, Doordarshan and AIR news bulletins? One in thousand? "International Intelligibility of spoken English should be the learner's aim" (Jain 64-65). Do the students converse in English at least in the college campus, if not, at least in the classroom and when they happen to meet their teachers? Vernacular languages play an important role even while teaching English Literature. English Literature taught through vernacular language is much appreciated by the students and they say, "Now it is very clear; understandable sir".

Some students' grasping capacity is low. This can be rectified if they read English newspapers daily, half-an-hour in addition to the reading of English textbooks.

Conclusion

The above mentioned problems discussed and remedial measures suggested, if followed the atmosphere in the classroom will definitely change for the better. Students will have a new life in the annals of their higher education, especially in the learning of English language. English is no more a foreign language but part and parcel of every student who wants to have national and international acclaim, personal and societal approbation, individual and collective uplift. It is not in other's hands; it is in their hands only! Self-confidence and striving will lead them to success; Laziness and lack of confidence will lead them to their doom. So decide what you want! Rise! Strive! Succeed!

REFERENCES

Ray Mohit K. (ed.), *Studies in ELT, Linguistics and Applied Linguistics,* New Delhi: Atlantic Publishers & Distributors (P) Ltd., 2004.

Balachandran, K.; "Is Learning a Number of Languages a Load", *Studies in ELT*, pp. 129-33.

Jain, V.K., "Teaching of English in India: Problems and Prospects", *Studies in ELT*, pp. 63-68.

Prabu, N.S., *Second Language Pedagogy*, New Delhi: O.U.P., 1987.

Sahoo, Sandhya Rani, "Innovation in ELT and Instructional Materials: An Indian context," *Studies in ELT*, pp. 69-82.

5

E/IT & ELT—A Few Possible Considerations of Interface

Krushna Chandra Mishra

In "Literature and Cross-culture Communication" [Forum—*Special Issue: The Art of TESOL, Part-2*, Vol. XIII, Nos. 3-4, 1975] William F. Marquardt made the following points the significance of which I feel is immense for purposes of the present seminar on Language, Communication and Technology (CIEFL Regional Centre, Shillong. 16th Nov, 2001) primarily because of two vital considerations; first, the North-East Indian English Teaching situation, while broadly conforming to a pan-Indian pattern and order, deserves special attention in view of the fact that the demographic composition in its diasporic distinctiveness makes a genuine demand for it, and next, this region uniquely enjoys the co-existence, among the English teaching fraternity of people coming from various states of India with distinct English-use cultures. Marquardt agreed that "there should be primary emphasis on the language as a means of oral communication" (p. 185) and to this end he wanted to suggest: "since the course in English as a second or foreign language seeks as a primary goal to help the student learn to communicate in a variety of situations, the chief problems in deciding on the literature to incorporate into such a course are: (1) selecting works of literature that will give the student this skill of communicating in the shortest possible time, (2) devising the best sequence for teaching selected works, and (3) teaching the chosen works effectively" (p. 185).

His techniques for presenting literature as a way of increasing the students' linguistic skills are as follows:

1. Asking questions that requires student to use key structures and words of the text in his response.
2. Drill in transforming idioms in the text into non-idiomatic equivalents, or the reverse.
3. Drill in transforming sentences into underlying kernel sentences, or the reverse.
4. Drill in substituting vocabulary items in sentence frames taken from the text.
5. Drill in paraphrasing selected sentences in either written or spoken form (*ibid*, p. 187).

Teaching English Literature in India in general and in North-East India in particular offers a situation of cross-culture communication. The teacher's role in teaching in such a context assumes complex challenges of a highly unpredictable order. Audrey L. Wright (in the article-initial techniques in Teaching English as a second language, in *Forum—Special Issue: The Art of TESOL*, Part-2, Vol. XIII, Nos. 3-4, 1975) is worth following in this case. Says Wright.... Today language is taught essentially as a tool of verbal communication and "in a world where English plays such an important role in the fields of international relations, science, commerce, and the humanities", "great patience and considerable skill are demanded of the teacher who would foster in his students' the necessary art to master a new set of communication habits, those of the English language" (p. 337). The tips Wright gives are as follows:

1. "Use English in the class-room in preference to the students' language,...the aim being to enable your students to understand and to speak English automatically without having to 'stop and think' or to perform laborious mental translation before responding to or in English," (p. 337).
2. "Don't let your students involve you in lengthy explanations, arguments, or lectures because that will help them 'get down to the serious business of mastering a new

set of language customs'. And...the students should be permitted to do 75% of the talking" (p. 338).

3. "When a student makes an error, either in pronunciation or in structure,...immediately produce the correct form and have the student report it after you several times... letting the lesser errors pass..." (p. 338).
4. "Introduce a new structure orally. Convey its meaning by the gestures, pictures or paragraph context. Let your students hear the structures a number of times, then have them repeat it many more times. Write it on the blackboard for them, and have them written it. Be sure they understand and are able to use the new structure correctly before you go on to a new material" (p. 338).
5. "...Approach repetition drills with interest and enthusiasm...maintain a lively pace, calling now a single student, now on the class as a whole to repeat. ...keep in mind that you are seeking to develop in your students automatic control of the patterns of English, a result which may be achieved through constant repetition practice" (p. 338).
6. "An excellent lecture of the substitution drill ['to use a great variety of words within a limited number of grammatical patterns, and hence be able to express in English a variety of concepts' (p. 338)] is that it may be readily adapted to any proficiency level, from complete beginner to very advanced, and is a more challenging and varied type of practice than the simple repetition drill" (p. 339).
7. "Give plenty of drill on question forms, and then have your students ask questions of each other...within the framework of a basic pattern.... Such drills provide good comprehension and oral production practice; however, they require the teacher to do 50% of the speaking.... Most students enjoy asking questions in English. In so doing, they are using the foreign language as communication tools to gain further insight into the environment" (p. 339).

8. "Know approximately what structures and what vocabulary items you intend to teach. Divide the semester's work by the total number of teaching hours and decide what you will teach in each class period, not forgetting to allow ample time for review.... Be flexible in amending your plan to suit the needs of your particular students, but remember, it is possible to make alterations in a plan, whereas it is not possible to build successfully without a plan" (p. 339).
9. "Be creative in your use of a textbook, exploring its materials in a variety of ways.... Don't use it as a crutch, or as a teacher substitute. The essence of language is two way communications" (p. 339).
10. "Help your students by praising their good performances and their progress. Ask the harder questions of your better students, compliments will make your students do their best, and when a real desire to learn exists, half of your job is already done" (p. 339).
11. "Let your English class be an enjoyable experience for you and your students. Use humorous stories, anecdotes and example sentences liberally in your teaching. Tell an occasional joke in English, simplifying structure and vocabulary as necessary. Your relaxed enjoyment of the teaching-learning function will surely evoke a corresponding enthusiasm on the part of your students, making the teacher student collaboration a fruitful one" (p. 340).

Beyond what is given above, it is pertinent to add a student's eye-view of what makes a good teacher (Sneha Enos, *What Makes a Good Teacher? Ibid*, p. 245):

- A good teacher ought to know more than just what's in the book.
- He should not act superior and order us around like servants.
- He has to keep control of the class.
- His lessons should be organised and he should return one paper while we're still excited and are what's in them.

- A good teacher should be young, or young at heart.
- He has to like teaching us. It's easy to tell if he doesn't; you know (p. 344) .

Jayasudha T. (in her "Dynamic Tension: A Teaching Strategy?" in the *Journal of English Language Teaching* (India), Vol. xxxiv, No. 2, March-April, 1999) dwells on the importance of English in India of our days as follows:

> For more than two centuries English has been playing an important role in our educational as well as national set up.... The study of English has enriched the Indian languages and literatures. All the Indian languages have freely borrowed words from English and have coined words and phrases on English models to enrich their vocabulary. The continued use of English, even after Indian independence for the following purposes seems to have been recognised by all.
>
> 1. As a National link language.
> 2. As an International link language.
> 3. As a library language. (p. 93)

In his presidential address Prof. S.K. Desai during the All India English Teacher's Conference held in Madras (December 1990) observed:

"...English is the language of trade and commerce and science and technology, the language of opportunity. To put it in a different way English is a language of modernization, of worldwide mobility as well as upward socio-cultural movement. The bourgeois, the direct or indirect shapers of India's destiny, therefore, cannot afford to have an ambivalent attitude towards English: they want English, which is for them not merely a window upon the world but a door through which they can transact with the world." (As quoted in R. Daniel Jayakumar's "A Study of the Attitude of the English Teachers of the Higher Secondary Classes towards their Work" in the *Journal of English Language Teaching* (India) xxxviii/4, 2001, p. 22).

On the place of English in India controversy and compulsion Kailash S. Aggarwal provides a historical perspective as follows:

> India has been characterised as a 'sociolinguistic giant' (Ferguson, 1966) because of the multiplicity of languages and dialects spoken in our country. With independence, Hindi has been continuously designated the "official language of the Union of India". However, due to opposition to the domination of Hindi in all official domains from non-Hindi speaking states, English has been retained as the 'association official language'. Initially, English was to be retained for a limited period of fifteen years, but subsequent executive and administrative measures seem to have perpetuated the place of English as an associate official language (in his article: "Educational Technology in India: Stating the Obvious Cape" in the Dibrugarh University *Journal of English Studies*, No. 13, 1998-99, p. 85). He further continues: "Because of the peculiar tensions of Indian societal multilingualism, the growing Indianization of the English language (aided by its successive legitimation by native English speaking agencies), and because of the recognition of English as the 'language of opportunity', as a 'window on the world of knowledge' and 'the only viable link language' in the country, the elite-controlled policymakers and language planners have found it wiser to retain English as the medium of instruction in higher education." (*Ibid*, p. 87) (emphasis-kcn).

Prof. S.K. Desai in recognition of the 'unquestionable and unassailable place of English in the socio educational milieu of India' (Jay Kumar 2001, JELTT (India) 38/4, 2001, p. 22) expects: "...the real socio-cultural and educational need is that the student who passes the secondary school examination ought to have a fairly good command over English so that he need not wrestle with the language later on in his graduate studies, studies in science and technology, medicine and engineering, or in using it as a library language for higher studies in humanities" (R. Daniel Jaykumar in his article referred to above) (emphasis ours-kcn). But as against this Aggarwal (1998-99) observes: "...the college and university students in the country display a wide variation in their proficiency levels in English. One of the primary reasons for this wide gap is that at the school level they study either through the medium of English (mostly elite, urban groups) or they study English only as a subject (mostly in rural areas and lower class/caste/ethnic groups). Between the two poles, the range varies from the near-native command of spoken and written to the minimal comprehension of the spoken and written media of education. It is necessary to point out here that this pan-Indian generalization may not totally hold line for the North-East where, in large parts of tribal areas, missionaries set up English medium schools in remote, rural areas" (in *DUJES* (13), 1998-99, p. 86). The author as the observer of the scene prevailing in Arunachal Pradesh would like to draw attention of the scholars that educationally one of the most backward state of the North-East India, Arunachal Pradesh offers more or less a situation where more struggle may be the need if containing an alarmingly growing trend of unemployment hopefully is to be contained in the coming years. At best one could hope that the state with English as its official language and the medium of instruction at all levels as education with commitment and vision and with campaign to arrest drop-out rates at all levels and with provision for teacher training especially at the primary and middle school levels in reasonable time may come at par with the other advanced states of the North-east India on one hand and the tribal India as a whole on the other. English teaching vis-a-vis development and social change though is not the immediate dwelling theme of the paper, it deserves a brief mention especially to underline that educational planners and development analysts do have definite responsibilities to take note of the growing need to recognise that an over increasing English using educated youth population in the state is the crying demand of the day because the emerging job market holds enough and genuine promise to engulf a self employing entreprenimially clamouring clientele for its fast picking up tourism trade in the region. And it is here that language, communication and technology could be the most enrichingly interlinked to make their individual as well as combined promises work.

Observes T. Jayasudha (1999) in Indian context that "one crucial aspect that teachers of English as a second language often ignore is the communicative aspect of English" (JELT (India), 34(2), 1999, p. 95). She holds: "English at the general level is to enhance the communicative competence of the learner..." (*ibid*, p. 96). She passionately feels for innovation in the teaching-learning situation and suggests: "Teaching is not just a mechanical process.... Each teaching-learning situation is unique, calling for innovation on the part of the teacher, untried and individual responses to new circumstances, the courage and willingness to venture into new methods, to experiment to dare. All the skills, knowledge, experience, attitude, understanding and emotions of the teacher comes to be focussed on to the one moment in which the learning may be successful. Once past, the opportunity may be lost the moment should be flexible, not set by any textbook or manual of teaching, it should be inspired. Teaching as an event, a fusion of enthusiasm, of adaptability, at reacting on the spur of the moment. Learners too have to become enthusiastic. Enthusiasm comes from encounter, interaction—either person to person or learner and material interaction. This interaction is like the "spark" between two stones, which fires the imagination, illuminates new fields, motivates the learner, gives power and throws light on new ways of looking at reality. An inspired teacher easily gets interaction from students, such interactive learning requires three contributions from the learners: to use their experience, to exercise their learning abilities, and to practice" (*ibid*, pp. 96-97, emphases added). Numan (1986) studied a number of 'Communicative' class-rooms and found that, in fact, there was very little happening in these classes which could be called 'communicational' language use (Rani Rubdy, "Barriers to Implementing Innovation and Change" in *CIEFL Bulletin* (New Series) Vol. 9, No. 1, June, 1997, p. 83). Also Rubdy (*ibid*) reports Goodland (1984:123) on the study of 1000 elementary and high school classroom in the USA and the conclusion that while individual teachers only yield impressive results in difficult circumstances, the overall picture that emerged was only too familiar:

- the dominant pattern of classroom organisation was still whole class teaching;
- the interaction was determined primarily by the need to maintain orderly relationships among twenty to thirty people in a confined space;
- students essentially worked alone within a group setting;
- the teacher was the main determiner of activities;
- there was remarkably little evidence of joy in learning, and the emotional tone of the succession of lessons that made up the students' school day was remarkably uniform. [*CIEFL Bulletin* (New Series), 9(1), June 1997]

In context of the above, it is well noticeable that communicative focus in teaching, though it happens to be quite important and its promises and actual help in real life teaching-learning situations, is hardly in sight. As a result, large-scale failure in English use and production is confronted. Kundu (1990) has painted the picture of English teaching and learning in Orissa where after about 1200 hours of conscious teaching of the language about 90% of the students miserably perform. (Dr. J. Nath "Whither English in Arunachal Pradesh?" in the Echo of Arunachal: 1993) speaking of the Arunachal Pradesh college-level students' performance laments as to what could be done so that English-using scene among the students would pick-up. Mishra et al (2000) have expressed concern that Arunachal University take appropriate measures to see that students after completing graduate degree level education find themselves in a comfortable 'bread winning' position. UGC guidelines in the post-NPE, 1986 scene have been quite forceful in requiring the universities in the country to come up with application/use/function-based teaching of English with less of conscious and disproportionate literature-thrust. Roman Jackobson opined that poeticity is only one of the functional varieties of the language (Jayasudha T., 1999 in JELT (India), 34(2), p. 96). The suggestion is that in language teaching literary language use should be given a fair and limited consideration. The need to recognise the importance of developing communicative competence in the language teaching classes is now a rich case to be considered. Dr. Rathi Jarfer in her key note address on "What Ails ELT in India Today?" at the ELTAI bi-monthly meeting (reported in JELT, 34(5), Sept-Oct, 1999) pleads that the English-learning student needs be given communicative competence in English as it means developing the sense of the students' self-esteem. On the issue of use of Technology in ELT in India she holds: "Setting up of infrastructure is, I agree, expensive and time is at a premium for every teacher. I don't think technology can enter the classroom in a seamless fashion without changes dam the line. From the infrastructure to new instructional materials, from teacher training to implementive methodological shifts to a change in assessment and testing. Overhauling the system to bring it in line with the demands of the times is what we should be aiming it" (p. 190). Dr. Mangalam Neelakantam in the panel discussion on the same topic holds: "At the tertiary level what concerns language teaching is problems with appropriate expressions. Lack of reading habit and taking textbook as the Bible leaves little choice for learners in the use of English" (p. 195). Ms. Lalitha on her part suggests: "First and foremost let us consider the amount of exposure. Students studying through mother tongue medium have very little exposure to the language (i.e., English). They are exposed to the language only for 40 minutes in the class in a day. Secondly, the difference in the cognitive abilities. According to Felix, the learners come to L2 learning at a later stage and therefore with different cognitive abilities, young children may have very special mental capacities, which are specifically attuned to language learning and only these have been applied to the learning of the L1, they are not available in the same way for the L2. In India, the teaching of English starts at different stages. In some stages, it begins in std. III, in some std. V and in some std. VI. Naturally, the cognitive abilities differ" (pp. 197-98). R. Karpaga Kumaravel (in his article, "An Investigation into the use of Mother-Tongue by the Teachers of English in the Higher Secondary Schools", in *JELT* (India),

34(5), Sept-Oct, 1999) comments on the Indian English Language teaching scene in quite succint terms: "Although the need for adequate and effective language instruction is stressed in principle, in practice, language teaching in India is in a deplorable state. Research studies have shown that the students' level of achievement in the language skills is extremely poor" (Karpaga Kumaravel, 1999). Languages are taught in the same manner as content subjects. The result is that in all languages, including English, the goal of enabling learners to develop communication skills remains unfulfilled. Few opportunities exist for language learning in the average English classroom. For many learners, there is little or no exposure to English outside school. However, even in school, only one period a day is available for the teaching/learning of English thus severely restricting exposure to the language. To make matters worse, even within the limited time available, teacher's resort to use of the mother tongue. Further, as a result of poorly conceived syllabuses, large classes, lack of proper training, teachers tried to focus on rules of grammar and isolated words and sentences—there is little if any, attempt to engage the pupils in interaction, to involve them in natural communication. The result of such teaching is that even after 6-10 years of English, the students are unable to use the language in communication... (pp. 210-11).

As against the above analysis of the Indian background to teaching of English as a language (Foreign or Second Language), it is worthwhile to consider as to how technology could be used to help change the situation for the better. Prof. S.K. Desai once held "denial of English in India means denial of education" (Karpaga, Kumaravel, *ibid*). It is in order to ensure that English is provided to all our students at all levels of education so that by the tertiary level encounter with English students experience comfort, ease and confidence in all naturalness of use of the language in social interaction situations. That will go to add to their personality and self-esteem. In the job market also they can then thereby present themselves effectively to the satisfaction of the employers. Their success stories will in a powerful way then help motivate their subsequent batches of students to English language learning with interest, zeal, involvement and positive opinion of the subject.

Here the observation as also advice of Aggarwal (1998-99) needs be very rightly appreciated: "...ET (educational technology) is not primarily the establishment of new physical resources, or the introduction of new machines and gadgets. Nor is it being able to telecast more and more tumid (Countrywide Classroom) programmes through INSAT. It is first and foremost bringing a new way of thinking to the task of teaching and learning. It is the organic integration of human and material resources to maximize learning. The acquisition and adoption of communication technology media (computers, television, radio, tape-recorders and other machines and gadgets) is only a small step in the overall approach to education. The efficacy and efficiency of the educational programmes depend not so much on the medium (be it language or ET) used but the way it is used and the purpose it is used for, we must keep our feet on the ground and the long-term educational perspective in mind if we mean to make any meaningful advance" (DUJES, p. 878).

In language teaching classroom situations it is expected that each addition of hardware must support in an integrated way to the teaching-learning process so that a climate of faith could be established and cynicism of the reactionaries and traditionalists among teachers who with suspect and decision look upon innovation of any order be to a great measure satisfactorily taught. The language teaching-learning process is a skills-building and upgrading project depending on where—secondary, post-secondary, tertiary or university level—it is in operation. But at each level in a cumulative order and further an interrelated successive higher order the language skills are to be developed and strengthened in the students. Intrinsic as well as extrinsic motivation levels of the students will have to be very keenly and doggingly guarded. Performance-based reward and encouragement system will have to be neatly followed. Feedback-based prompt support-service for correction or remedial supervision will have to be guaranteed. Natural contexts, social situations, group interactions and nourishing refreshing and propelling language-use environments will have to be created in which adequate and worthwhile communication could take place. For planning, executing and testing purposes language-based activities with capability to engross, absorb and interest the learners to later gainfully help tap their aptitude and personality resources will have to be developed. The teacher development via and with the students' development will have to be innovatively ushered in. In formal and informal contexts in spoken as well as written medium, communication tasks will have to be most successfully transacted involving students. In all such situations pilot survey, promotional, testing, evaluation and consolidation projects technology will have to be used in a big but definitive ways.

Further, integrated language-skills teaching project may require the teacher to do the most difficult and challenge-spewing job. Since ET does not necessarily mean high-tech and high-cost gadgetry, it is quite in the fitness of things that low-cost high-effective audio-visual aids like black-boards, picture-cards, radio and tape-recorders and the like (Aggarwal 1998-99, p. 83) could be most creatively and successfully used. Since, further, employment of educational technology is to aid and accelerate the effectiveness of the teacher's handling of his job, it is important that as per the teaching plan and the teaching-objectives and aim worked out by the teacher, he needs independence to decide as to when, where, how, how much, how often and why or to what specific result, in terms of clear, tangible and testable learner achievement in performance tasks, which of the gadget he will use. This autonomy factor is crucial to the success of teaching of language even in the 'literature for language, way (Mishra 2001). Aggarwal (1998-99) suggests that ET must "identify scientific and technological equipment for their optional use and to work towards a clear specification of aims. A comprehensive statement of aims and goals for a teaching learning course 'has to be based on (a) an analysis of the learner's background, their entry behavior, including their specific needs, interest and abilities; (b) an analysis of infrastructure, including human and material resources available for use in the educational institutions; and (c) an understanding of the country's needs and expectations from the taught, at the end of a course (*DUJES*, pp. 83-84).

The opening decade of the 21st century, also the opening century of the 3rd millennium, introduced grandly as the knowledge century has in India been welcomed as a great hope booster for the one billion plus population. Education in the years to come to the teeming school-going tens of millions is certainly going to be an unmanageable proposition if care is not taken to switch over to the technology-aided teaching. Information revolution is now greatly picking up. Rural pockets are now being linked by electronic super-highway of information in a big way. English as a second language in its functional aspects at this crucial juncture of the rural transformation needs to be handled in the schools and colleges with the teacher making all out efforts at ensuring participatory learning an enjoyable as well as experientially confidence-enriching project and a success. To this end, let the country's English language teaching commùnity wake up so that the promises that a technology-savvy new world in its proper collaboration in the mission of empowering the learner irrespective of his location makes could really be a success and a matter of joy with teaching of English turning into a credible bread provision undertaking. And achievement for the English teacher of the ESL situation where his contribution to enabling the learner of English to bargain effectively in the emerging job market in the expected way will never more be questioned. I/ETELT interface in its possibility holds key to emancipating the teacher from the bondage of his professional commitment (Note: additional references including those and explicitly, referred to in the article especially, N. Chomsky's article "Deep Structure, Surface Structure and Semantic Interpretation" and G. Lakoff's article "On Generative Semantics")

BIBLIOGRAPHY

Bloomfield, L. (1933). *Language,* New York: Holt, Rinehart and Winston.

Chafe, W. (1970). *Meaning and the Structure of Language.* Chicago: The Chicago Univ. Press.

Chandra, S. (1992). *Aspects of Linguistics and English Language Teaching.* Delhi: Doaba House.

Chomsky, N. (1975). *Reflections on Language.* New York: Pantheon Books.

Firth, J. (ed) (1995). *Studies in Linguistic Analysis.* Oxford: Basil Blackwell.

Gazdar, G. (1979). *Pragmatics.* New York: Academic Press.

Katz, J. (1972). *Semantic Theory.* New York: Harper and Row.

Kundu, M. (1990). *Correction of Errors.* Monograph ELTI, Bhubaneshwar, Orrisa.

——, (1993). *The ELT Manual for Inspecting Officials.* ELTI, Bhubaneshwar.

Mishra, K.C. (1999). "The Survey of English Studies in the North-East India: Defining the Approaches", Paper Presented at the UGC National Seminar held at C.I. College, Bishnupur (Manipur) on 1st–2nd December, 1999.

——, (2000). "Integration or Disjunction: The Discourse of Development in Arunachal Pradesh in Transition". Paper presented at the UGC National Seminar held at Govt. College, Bomdila held on 17-18 October, 2000.

——, (1996). *Correction of Errors in English: A Training Course for the Teachers of English in India.* Unpublished Ph.D. Thesis (Utkal Univ., Bhubaneshwar, Orissa).

——, (2001). "Autonomy in the English Teaching Class-rooms of India" (Paper presented at the Dibrugarh University 13th UGC Refresher Course in English).

6

Linguistic Realities in Second Language Education

Pratibha Gupta

Linguistic and cultural diversity of Ranchi (State capital of Jharkhand) can be matched by Indian sub-continent, as people residing here represent a wide range of cultural variety and enjoy at least more than ten languages. Among them most important ones are: Hindi, Nagpuria, Sadri, Kurux, Santhali, Mundari, Ho, Maghi, Urdu, Bengali, Oriya, English and Maithili. Dominant language used in day to day life and market place is Hindi and Nagpuria. Apart from it many tribal languages are also in common use. This region is a linguistic paradise. It has heterogeneous identity—that is an amalgam of people belonging to different castes and tribes. Around 44% of population are SCs and STs. Even among tribal people, there are thirty tribes who speak different languages as mother tongue. These tribal languages belong to three distinct language genealogies: Astro-Asiatic, Dravidian, and Indo-Aryan. They not only differ in formal and structural system but also in their scripts. Parameters of shared space, norms and frequencies of interaction may prove inadequate in several cases. About ten to fifteen per cent of total population is immigrants from outside and it gives Jharkhand region a cosmopolitan status. This group speaks wide and varied range of languages.

All this has resulted in an impoverishment of local residents. Due to collapse of the traditional modes of livelihood, they could not sustain in the wake of industrialization and commercial progress and inflows of an alien like culture. In industrial labour market their demand is reduced drastically and these factors ensue restlessness in local masses. On one hand tribal languages started encountering the basic question of existence, identity, and development. But on the other hand, there has been an upsurge of language loyalty (reflected in the movement on the demand of tribal languages as a medium of instruction in primary schools), which might save tribal languages from attrition at the heavy price of blocking development and prosperity. The rapid social changes, uniform educational opportunities, linguistic practicality and desire for better socio-economic conditions, have not been conducive to tribal language's development. It promotes language shift towards dominant state languages and resulted in an identity crisis among neoelites. The duel phenomena of language shift and language loyalty can be witnessed in action at the same time space in Ranchi area. The gravity of identity crisis can be felt in their feeling of inferiority complex and low self-esteem.

Many of the affluent tribal immigrants had completely forgotten their mother tongue. In some of the families there is imposition of virtual prohibition against tribal languages. They justify it in terms of pragmatism, as Hindi and English are considered to be more viable options for their economic well being, education, job opportunities, etc. Only those who are rooted in one place use their mother tongue, particularly the very poor and rural mass confined to the interior villages and engaged in traditional occupation. In semi-rural and urban pockets there is infrequent use of tribal languages, Sadri and Hindi whereas well to do and educated masses use Hindi and English with a token use of tribal languages at home or with interaction with poor villagers. Most of the time, even church services are held in Sadri or Hindi.

There is a call for the use for tribal language in primary education, but only a few schools provide this facility in primary education. At middle and high school tribal languages are not media of instruction of any subject. Apart from it, even poor parents do not have real desire to send their wards to these schools. Prevalent linguistic situation promotes the elite languages and it leads to adoption of these languages only. In spite of tribal students' strong feeling of their mother tongue as a symbol of ethnic identity this type of language configuration negatively affects their language learning process. It creates bewilderment and confusion among students. No single language gets firm footing leaving behind a bundle of underdeveloped languages. They are Jack of all but master of none. The situation is very complex and to protect their self-image they adopt repression mechanism. It causes conflict and frustration, which further worsen the situation.

Tribal students of Jharkhand area belong to a wide and diverse community (30 tribes) and speak different languages. These languages belong to different language groups (discussed earlier). They differ not only in formal and structural system but also in their scripts (many of them are oral and do not have scripts).

These are the linguistic realities under which tribal students of the area are put to learn English. They have to adjust themselves not only with other cultures but also with other language systems (Hindi, Nagpuria, Sadri, etc.). English comes to them not as 2nd language but as 4m or 5tn language. Hence there is a strong element of unwillingness and embarrassment in attempting to produce the different sounds of other language. It overrides whatever physical and cognitive abilities they have. This self-consciousness is combined with lack of empathy with the English language and culture, (e.g., no identification with its speakers or their customs). It is due to a kind of negative feeling—affective filter. Very often he may shink back due to the fear of loosing his social identity. These negative thoughts distract their attention and begin to impair the ability to concentrate and organize thoughts logically reflected in poor performance.

Contrastive hypothesis of language acquisition affirms that acquisition of 2nd language is determined by the structure of an earlier acquired language. Here languages learnt by them are, their mother tongue and other languages used in market place are in an under developed condition and Hindi is in developing stage. In such condition when English is introduced, they find themselves in baffling situation where they do not have any developed language either mother tongue or Hindi to held solid basis for the learning of a foreign language. Linguistic multiplicity very often creates confusion not only to the learners but also to the teachers, as not a single language is properly developed to help the learners. This is accepted by 69% of the learners. It puts negative impact on their process of adjustment in learning other languages.

The cognitive categories like time, space, deixis, etc. are quite different in two languages. English is neither similar in script (except Santhali) nor in its formal system, hence it appears to them as a foreign language. They find difficulty at every linguistic level, right from phonology to semantic level. Mean score 2.32 shows their difficulty as regard with medium of instruction. They cannot follow instructions given in English (even) in mission schools. The following table shows achievement level of tribal students in English:

Table 1: Achievement Level of Tribal Students in English

S.No	*Name of Schools*	*Percentage*	*Mean*	*SD*
1.	St. John's School, Ranchi	21.05	6.07	2.72
2.	High School Bariyatu, Ranchi	8.42	10.88	2.55
3.	Girls High School, Khunti, Ranchi	17.64	2.6	2.00
4.	Boys High School, Khunti, Ranchi	30.58	4.96	1.81
5.	Raj High School, Ratu, Ranchi	16.47	2.00	1.51

As acquisition of a language is very much determined by the structure of an earlier acquired language (Krashen 1981). In tribal students' case there is not a single language which is fully developed creating lots of confusion and reflected in their level of achievement. It negatively affects the area of auditory discrimination power, visual graphic correlation and comprehension of cultural issues in particular.

It is obvious that use of multiple languages in an area creates problem to its users. It creates not only confusion and bewilderment but also very often promotes identity crisis among its users. Even in educational planning its impact is very crucial. Introduction of too many languages at the same time without providing enough time for the development of a single language exposes them to many psychological problems. In the process not only their language learning is impaired but they are gifted with personality disorders also. Hence in planning for language education it is important to look for the language configuration, language attitude, and language use of the area, as too much ambitious planning may seriously degrade the language learning process.

7

Second Language Development in Flood-Prone Area

Pratibha Gupta

The geo-morphological features of North Bihar expose the area to regular visit of flood in the form of natural calamities. It stays for approximately one to two months but its aftermath can be felt for further two to three months' duration. Its impact on the socio-economic status of the inhabitant is devastating. During this period they not only face problems of lodging, board and food but are exposed to health hazards too. Many of the areas are inaccessible during this period causing total chaos in the region. They live under stress and strain and are easy prey to fear complex and psychological trauma. These climatic conditions change their lifestyle as well as their attitude towards life. Under these environmental condition students of the area have to continue with their studies. Damaged school buildings, hostels and irregular presence of teachers further worsens the educational conditions.

English is taught as a second language in the schools. Hindi got the position of first language in the school curriculum. In the acquisition of first language, code of language goes hand in hand with the socio-cultural knowledge of the learners. But in learning the second language learners do not follow the same model as it lacks the appropriate and necessary language environment around them, demanding more prolonged and regular time period for consolidation. Flood has not only devastating effect on the socio-economic condition of the people but it retards language development as well. The unevenness of language development is the sole product of the language context provided by the area and irregular pattern that learners have to use and hear particular structures in certain contexts.

Language capacities are not only dependent on what the capacities reside within the child but the relative contribution of the nature (biology of learner) and nurture (social world in which the learner resides). It is through responses to specific stimuli that language competence is attained (Skinner 1957). For proper 2nd language development, regular and prolonged practice is required. But learners facing regular flood in the area do not get opportunities for regular language activities and sustained educational support either from parents or teachers. English being second language needs more regular efforts for proper assimilation of the language items. Prevalent educational condition grievously affects 2nd language learning process. It not only retards growth of English but impedes 1st language development as well.

Development of verbal behavior depends upon the appropriate stimulation and opportunity, which enhances cognitive faculty of the learner. Cognitive factors are responsible for the process of learning to read and write. Piaget (1950) looks at cognition as a system of living and acting operation that strives for equilibrium or balance between what the individual knows and what he perceives in the world around them. The process of language learning involves conditioning of the learners and depends on the factors like drive, cue, response and reward. These factors, which facilitate language learning and development of cognitive faculties, are absent due to prevalent environmental conditions. Instead they are pushed to fear, anxiety and problems of adjustment. It slackens their interest in 2nd language learning resulting in nipping their drive force in the bud. The area lacks favorable 2nd language learning conditions, both inside and outside class. The ethno-linguistic vitality in terms of status, demography, and institutional support facilitates the cognitive development but these factors are not conducive in the present circumstances. Attitude of the learners towards 2nd language, is one of the important factors, which directly influences proficiency level of the learners. It serves as motivational support. Since attitudes are formed through interaction with one's social environment, making a direct link between socio-cultural milieu and the motivation to acquire a L2 attitude serves the desire and effort in the process of acquisition of language. Short-range motivational props as fear of failure and desire to do well in school do not have the staying power to maintain the consistent levels of motivation over prolonged disruption of time and diverse opportunities to develop proficiency. On account of regular interruptions due to climatic conditions they develop casual attitude towards the target language.

Linguistic

Attitudes Motivaton Achievement

Non-Linguistic

Attitude determines the degree of motivation, which is responsible for their language achievement. Language achievement may be both linguistic and non-linguistic. Language achievement further strengthens their language attitude. The habitual pattern of thought and the way the world is perceived and categorized determines the output. Interrupted process of learning makes the language boundaries fuzzy and very often there is lack of a common defining element. Hence there is varied and wide-ranging responses. Comprehension is largely a matter of syntactic and semantic processing. Learned helplessness deteriorates their power of concentration and they find themselves unable to assimilate and process learned language items in proper way. Reading comprehension is difficult for 71% of respondents.

The scores obtained from 40 learners of class 8th in Patna district on various components of reading-writing skill show that there is significant difference in vocabulary, visual perception, and auditory discrimination skills whereas on copying skill difference is marginally significant. Mean achievement of 48% of learners is 9.02 in vocabulary. 39% of them have mean achievement 5.52 in visual perception. In auditory discrimination 61% have mean score 6.18. In copying skill 61% have mean achievement 8.52.

Table 1: Statistical Differential in Reading Writing Skills

Parameters	*Categories*	*Flood Affected*		*Non-flood Area*	
		Mean	*%*	*Mean*	*%*
Reading-	Vocabulary	9.02	48	12.92	67
Writing	Visual perception	5.52	39	8.47	67
Skill	Auditory discrimination	6.18	61	9.12	56
	Copying	8.52	61	9.14	73

It is clear that displaced and rehabilitation pattern of life and psychological mental makeup affects their cognitive development. It impairs their reading-writing abilities, which is basic to any educational activities. They are not only under achiever in English but they are lagging behind in general education too. Shah (1981), Sharma (2000), Swaroop (2001) have also reported that reading-writing abilities are positively correlated with the cognitive abilities of the learners.

Hence they need special attention to their problems and new teaching methodology is required for the proper development of study skills.

REFERENCES

Shah, J.H. (1981). "A Comparative Study of Some Personal and Psychological Variables and Reading Comprehension." *Journal of Education and Psychology*, 59:2.

Sharma, Lata (2000). "Cognitive Development as a Function of Reading Writing-Skills." *Psycho-lingua Jan.* Vol. 30, No. 1.

Skinner, B.F. (1957). *Verbal Behaviour*. New York Appleton-Century-Crofts.

Swaroop, Jyot et al. (2001). "Perceptual Abilities as Correlates of Age, Sex and Locale." *Psycho-lingua*. Vol. 31, No. 2, July.

8

Exploring Classroom Strategies in the Wake of E/IT-ELT Interface

Krushna Chandra Mishra and *N.P. Mahapatra*

Technology in a big way could be put to use in the ESL classrooms of India at all levels of education. For this, however, the teacher will have to shoulder a heavy responsibility. Knowing as he does the seriousness as well as sincerity his task means he will have to be a keen performer himself in the game of communication that language teaching basically is oriented towards. Teacher-learner-syllabus-examination on one hand and teaching-learning on the other hand as sides involved in a project which seeks to use technology made complicated as contributing, accelerating and even counterbalancing as factors which the Indian ESL teacher will have to very carefully know otherwise neither planned coordination nor effective result-ensuring success in performance situations he will visit his efforts. Knowing the task well, knowing how to do it well and doing it well then entail a high degree of alertness, mindfulness and keen involvement for the ESL classrooms to lead to the achievement of language proficiency of the learners concerned. Largely accepted today continuing to be the fact is that the ESL teaching situation in the country is in a bizarre shape. It is constantly felt to give to the job a face-lift in all glow and glitter and accompanied genuine promise and its fulfilment. This paper makes an attempt to see in relation to literature teaching, especially prose, short story and poem, as to how strategies could be innovatively and intelligently used at B.A. level classes using technological aids.

The traditional literature teacher finds it comfortable to usually offer background information about the author, his/her times and the melieu or 'deliver meta-critical textures about the text' [Sujit K. Dutta, "Predicting as a Pre-reading Activity", *English Teaching Forum* (Jan. 1994), p. 39]. Students in such cases remain "passive recipients" and the teacher hardly confronts the need, except only the moral, if at all, to bother whether they understand it or not. Moody (1983:23) very aptly evaluates the scene as follows: "the teaching of literature has faltered and students have been led busily but aimlessly through 'forest of inspired literary gossip' or cajoled into rigid and doctrinaire interpretation" [as in S.K. Dutta, *Ibid.*, *ETF* (Jan. 1994), p. 39]. Green finds that "in large teacher-centred classes, students have little opportunity to deliver enough output to be judged fairly or receive constructive feedback to enhance feelings of security and success"; and again, "comprehensible input from the teacher is of little use, if students, through lack of language practice and use, are able only to produce virtually incomprehensible output, or language so marked by gross error that it has little international viability" [Christopher F. Green, "Learner Drives in Second Language Acquisition", *ETF* (Jan, 1993), p. 2]. Traditional 'literary-critical' teaching approach with no direct inspirational concern for the students does maximum harm especially as this approach neither provides for any scope for the teacher to know the students individually in their "studial capacity" nor in "whole-person terms" and in line of Green one finds that pedagogic planning which could benefit out of an understanding of the motivational contents of the students suffers much due to the fact that student "disequilibrium" sets in and "teacher behavior" which should be affected by it never comes to any change. It could largely be because on the part of the poor students' need fulfillment on the educational front hardly takes place thereby giving them any sense of pride of achievement since what achievement is there is never perceivably served out through any teacher-student interaction worth the name. The teacher involvement remaining contained as it mostly does to lecturing from the dias in real terms in absence of student development remains unproductive and hence in the true sense passive and meaningless. In spite of it whenever students achieve any distinction it is exclusively due to hard work occasioned by a strong commitment to become something. This' could be in the sense of Maslow (A.H. Maslow, 1954. *Motivation and Personality*, New York: Harper) acute example of *maximal ego-centred development* (as in Green, *op. cit.*, *ETF* (Jan. 1993, p. 2). In a second language teaching environment where teacher's contribution needs matter the most as an initiator, organiser, manager, facilitator and coordinator, absence of active interest of the teacher in the development of the students, the learning outcome in majority of the cases has to be next to nil in its absence. And if language teaching fails to translate in learning in the learners, it fails to justify the profession. In this sense, literature-oriented syllabus doing in the hands of methodologically unsound mass of our teachers of ESL at all levels and most especially the college and university education levels means not doing language teaching in any appropriate sense. Communication in its confinement to only one side of the classroom (the dias), to only one person (the teacher) and to teacher's personalized expression (his only contribution called text-interpretation) in this case also fails largely because its very vital component of exchange and participation get thoroughly ruled out with an all-knowing and everything-doing teacher who virtually rules the classroom.

When ensuring a right level of sustained motivation is an important teacher-support in the student development programme (Green 1993, Ansubel 1965, Burstal 1975, Havell 1984, Krashen 1981, Canale and Swain 1979). Green (1993) suggests that motivation through appropriate planned teacher work be created at the pre-teaching stage, maintained at the whilst-teaching period and supported and reinforced in the post-teaching reproduction and feedback-ensuring sharing as well as feedback-led assisted or independent correction and learning-retention and retrieval programmes. However, Green

(1993) holds that "no matter how comprehensive and successful the teacher's motivation enhancement plans, certain students will, of course, nevertheless, help to provide the impetus for the learner to achieve all that he is capable of achieving in this particular field of intellectual endeavour." It is important here to observe that the teacher's task consists pre-eminently in strengthening the individual students' resolution to progress on the basis of their successful learning experiences which the teacher necessarily critically most sensibly makes use of to stress the fact that confidence-level of the participating students is boosted and contribution-level later on in terms of involvement and dedicated hard work is remarkably upgraded on every subsequent teacher-student evaluation-based interaction. Here again the teacher creates and fosters a non-threatening learning-ensuring atmosphere using his understanding of the students' background—cultural, socio-economic and the like—which play important roles in determining learning success and the rate and pace of its consolidation.

The interaction of the nature discussed above is crucial not only for what it finally produces as elaborately discussed above but its validity in its own right is due to the fact that students' lack of competence in oral-skills, a negative factor, is made to be remedied by the concomitant positive factor that as Doud (1994) suggests, "Students (in Syrian University EFL classrooms) have a real desire to speak English more effectively, not only in the language classrooms but also in out-of-class situations" (*ETF*, April, 1994, p. 42). Doud says, "I have seen students listen, read and write when asked" and this is important for the supportive, learning-ensuring and student-development-minded teacher. This asking in Doud's 'When asked'—appendage provides the hinge on which student-participation in actual production-performances depends.

As can thus be realized, interaction is crucial to motivation-creation as also to spurred-production activities and in itself interaction is the key to occasioning learning-outcomes. Language teaching, especially in Indian ESL classrooms, has to integrate objectives of literature-teaching to those of language skills development goals. In this integration literature initially might appear to be getting subordinated to language teaching. However, much subordination is in the least not offending because literature that in its production uses skills of the highest language sophistication order in considered social and cultural expressions in skills necessary to appreciate it requires that kind and level of linguistic sophistication in proficiency terms on part of the students. Such sophistication could come after years of sustained language use with keen partaking in the business of the society and the culture in which the students grow.

Though literature-heavy Indian university syllabus for the degree level programmes may take years to admit a change in favour of a total language-skills-development-oriented one, due especially to the fact that for the entire period we have been doing English in India, we have been doing it for literary appreciation purposes—for purposes of aesthetic pleasure, for transportation into worlds away and above the mundane and the ordinary daily life's world, for purposes of search of the rose without thorns and its inevitable pricks. Our cultural mooring has been that way geared to expect for the unachievable, the impossible. Though in itself enough and worthily grand and lofty and immensely comforting and convincing as a goal ultimately to be achieved by the leisure-passing and pleasure-seeking amongst us, who traditionally and historically could be linked up to royal or *zamindari* ways of life, it is painful to go for such an attitude today because now is the day of the sweat of the brow that alone in a highly competitive world could ensure the bread for the millions of the hungry in the country of a billion-strong population. Educational planning could hardly afford to keep on harping on to literature-only-song of the syllabus-designing committees. Pragmatics of our day suggest that we switch over as early as we can to the 'language-first' and also 'language-as-fast-as-could be' mould for there alone the pricks of the thorns of the roses, and perhaps a rosy life, lie, and we cannot afford to be foolishly ignoring any more that roses, if at all, have to be with pricking thorns only. In the job markets of our times we definitely see the survival is the rule for the strongest among the educated seekers who know well how to sell themselves, sell their candidature. Language skills of interpersonal communication being the only factor as proof of labour and success in every profession the educated take with them and the employers look for in the candidates, it is time that communication orientation, interaction focus is insistently brought into our classrooms.

For reading comprehension development the task of the ESL teacher is not only to ensure that understanding of the matter, though immediately a powerful goal in itself, does live with the motivation to perform well at the post-reading test-phase writing communication. The discovery approach put in use at the comprehension achieving stage through planned question-answer based communication could be sustained with care so that the successful answers in the oral production stage are reproduced in the writing section. Here, however, fluency and form, content and accuracy aspects need be carefully balanced with revision of the answer-text at all the stages of grasping and planning the response, pruning, sequencing and organizing it to suit the objective or the long-answer type questions, and rewriting, reformulating, providing omissions-by-slip due to haste and anxiety and final revision of the product (i.e. the answer-text) in hand for correction in grammar or usage sections.

Teaching through listening, speaking, reading, understanding and reproducing in writing at the testing phase is a complex communication-rich exercise. The complexity grows with the teacher being required to put in his best while carefully evaluating the qualitative significance of the material he is offering, with adequately simplifying and abridging the matter wherever necessary to suit to the local demands and now and then relating the text to the learner's store of experience. The teacher of literature in the Indian situation could meet the demands of language teaching objectives by adequately grading the matter in terms of difficult ideas and complex expressions. Verily the teacher here as an advanced reader in his explanation of the text to the students with lower order linguistic excellence and application and limited range of contact with the factual world of the writer's encounter which he has as per his guiding vision transformed into the fictional has to make reading skills available in the appropriate and timely order to his students and in a step by step manner lead the students to identify the original world of the writer's encounter or an approximate replica of it and students come to contact such a world their negotiation of the meaning of the text will be possible.

Technology in a big and powerful way can be put in use to achieve such a goal—making the understanding heart of the students spontaneously bursting out into rhapsody-making in keen and powerful expressions in explaining the world floating in front of their sparkling eyes—bearing in endless joy of achievement and aroused by the insightful and interpretation aiding, comprehension-occasioning teacher whose involvement in the task of using of simple language to explain expressions involving structural complexity and ambiguity of meaning, etc. now becomes the resourcefulness and confidence of the jubilant young students whose success spurs further future successes at understanding and interpretation of texts—also of the literary nature. Listening, speaking, comprehension projects could be now helped by use of audio cassettes, videos, television, computer and writing and writing correction programmes can now be fruitfully and time-savingly be done with computers. At advanced levels net-surfing for library-exploitation services on an effective scale can be recommended. If technology lessens the efforts in the hands of the intelligent user and enhances the scope of his achievement and thereby confidence and enjoyment thereof, classroom successes in teaching-learning programs involving language use for literary appreciation and for a thousand other practical life's purposes will never elude us any more even in our fund-starved student-support service programmes.

REFERENCES

Arnat, V. (1987). "Six Writers in Search of Texts: A Protocol Based Study of L_1 and L_2 Writing", *English Language Teaching Journal*. 41, 4, pp. 257-67.

Bustall, C. (1975). "Factors Affecting Foreign Language Learning: A Consideration of Some Current Research Findings", *Language Teaching and Linguistics: Abstract*. 8, 1.

Coolie, J. and S. Slater (1987). *Literature in the Language Classroom*. Cambridge: Cambridge University Press.

Dutta, S.K. (1994). "Predicting as a Pre-Reading Activity", *English Teaching Forum*, Jan. 1994, pp. 39-41.

Green, Christopher F. (1993). "Learner Drives in Second Language Acquisition", *English Teaching Forum*. Jan. 1993, pp. 2-5 and 11.

Gueye, M. (1989). "Computers for EFL in Developing Countries: Problems and Solutions", *CALICO Journal*. 7.1, pp. 77-85.

Krashen, S.D. (1981). *Second Language Acquisition and Second Language Learning*. Oxford: Oxford University Press.

Moody, H.L.B. (1983). "Approaches to the Study of Literature: A Practitioner's View", *Teaching of Literature Overseas: Language-Based Approaches*, ed. C.J. Brumfit. English Language Teaching Documents 115. Pergamon, British Council.

Munby, J. (1978). *Communicative Syllabus Design: A Socio-Linguistic Model for Defining the Content of Purpose Specific Language Programmes*. Cambridge: Cambridge University Press.

Nunan, D. (1988). *The Learner-Centred Curriculum*. Cambridge: Cambridge University Press:

Rodger, A. (1982). "O Where Are You Going? A Suggested Experiment in Classroom Stylistics", *Language and Literature*, ed. R.A. Carter. London: Allen Unwin.

9

Relevance of Introducing English as a Subject from the First Standard

Mallikarjun Patil

A headline like "English is a Global Language" may surprise us often. But it is a truth that English is a global language today. Why one may ask. The answer is that it is a language of higher education, science and technology, a link-language wherever there is a multi-lingual society. The need of English is acute particularly in the globalization era. David Crystal argues, "English will put us in touch with more people than any other language of the world." As per the recent statistics, English is the language most widely taught as a main foreign language in over 100 countries, such as China, Russia, Germany, Spain, Egypt and Brazil. English language has been used as the first language, second language, and foreign language and as an official language all over the world. It is said nearly one-fourth of the world's population is already fluent or competent in English. That means English speakers are more than 1.5 billion people, exceeding the Chinese speakers (1.1 billion).

What makes a global language is a political hegemony more than the simplicity and internationality of a language. As we know, once Sanskrit was a pan-Indian language because of Aryan hegemony. Hindi has replaced Sanskrit today. The ancient Tamil was a south-east Asian language for more than 500 years, solely because of Tamils' enterprise. Latin was a leading language because of the hegemony of Roman Empire in the first millennium A.D. Once the rulers go the language goes with them or it remains (as in the case of English in India and other countries) if it is a language as a paragon, on account of its implicit aesthetic qualities, clarity of expression, literary power, or religious standing. Sanskrit, Hebrew, Greek, Latin, Arabic and French are among those which at various times have been landed in high terms and English is no exception.

The reasons why English is a global language today are many.

English Language is Easy and Beautiful to Learn and Use

The general characteristics of English are that it is extraordinarily receptive and it has an adoptable heterogeneousness. A second outstanding feature of English is its simplicity of inflexion. Its relatively fixed word-order is its third hallmark. It is a direct language and for which it uses prepositions. The next quality of English is the development of new varieties of intonations for expressing shades of meaning which were formerly indicated by varying the shapes of words. These features have made English so much strong and popular that today it is spoken by the largest number of people all over the world. In 1848, a reviewer in the British periodical *The Athenaeum* wrote: "In its easiness of grammatical construction, in its paucity of inflection, in its almost total disregard of the distinction of gender excepting those of nature, in the simplicity and precision of its terminations and auxiliary verbs, not less than in the majesty, vigor and copiousness of its expression, our mother-tongue seems well adapted by *organization* to become the language of the world."

Why English as a Global Language? A Historical Context

'Why is English the global language and not some other?' There are two answers to the question: one is geographical—historical; the other is socio-cultural. We know that Europeans, particularly the English explorers explored several lands and settled down there, becoming the conquistadors. Socio-culturally, the western civilization and culture reached the people of the second and third worlds through the agency of English, in the highest. The English separatist church people emigrated to America, facilitating English mass emigration to the new continent. A similar story holds true of Canada, Australia, New Zealand, the Caribbean Islands, South Africa, South Asia, particularly India, the African colonies like Sierra Leone, Ghana, Gambia, Nigeria, Cameroon, Liberia, Kenya, Tanzania, Uganda, Malawi, Zambia and Zimbabwe and south-east Asia and the south Pacific, particularly Singapore, Malaysia, Hong Kong and Papua New Guinea. Braj Kachru, the US linguist says English has spread around the world rapidly. He says nearly one-third of the world population knows English, though only a proportion of these people have some command of English. It is estimated that the users of English as L1 are 337,407,3000 and the users of English as L2 are 235,351,3000 in 1995.

Why English? The Cultural Foundations

John Wallis says, "Because there is clearly a great demand for it from foreigners, who want to be able to understand the various important works which are written in our tongue." And he goes on: "all kinds of literature are widely available in English editions, and, without boasting, it can be said that there is scarcely any worthwhile body of knowledge which has not been recorded today, adequately at least, in the English language."

If John Wallis wanted English for the English of knowledge it had. Richard Mulkaster wanted it for patriotic reasons. He said in 1582: "I love Rome, but London better. I favour Italy, but England more. I honor the Latin, but I worship the English." The poet Samuel Daniel speaks of the blessings of his tongue:

> And who in time knows whither we may vent,
> The treasure of our tongue, to what strange shores,
> This gain of our best glory shall be sent,
> To enrich unknowing nations without stores,
> Which worlds in the yet unformed Occident,
> May come refined with the accents that are ours.

The Earl of Chesterfield wrote in 1750 about the rapid growth of English. "I have...a sensible pleasure in reflecting upon the rapid progress which our language has lately made, and still continues to make, all over Europe."

Isaac Pitman in the *The Phonetic Journal* states:

> We may esteem on this basis that in the year 2000 the most important language will be spoken by the number of persons as under:

Italian	53,370,000
French	72,571,000
Russian	130,479,800
German	157,480,000
Spanish	505,286,242
English	

a. Europe 178,846,153

b. United States and non-European British dependencies 1,658,440,000

a + b = 1,837,286,153

Similarly William White said later that 'English is the language of the future.' It is said English language has found itself 'in the right place at the right time.' What makes English a world language is that it facilitates an access to knowledge.

Why English? The Cultural Legacy

English language is used in the former colonies as a cultural legacy. Those who hated the English ruler then did not mind to retain their tongue. India is an example. In fact, some countries replaced French and other languages by English as they found English to be a better language. In this regard, the statistics of Union of International Associations' Yearbook sounds pleasant. As it reports there were about 12,500 international organizations in the world. A sample of 500 of these showed that 85% (424) made official use of English for more than any other language. French was the only other language to show up strongly, with 49% using it officially. Thirty other languages attracted occasional official status, but only Arabic, Spanish and German achieved over 10% recognition. Of course, other European languages to achieve a satisfactory progress are French and German. It is said, "The overriding impression is that wherever in the world an organization is based, English is the chief auxiliary language."

Today there is an ongoing controversy in many parts of the world over the issue whether or not they must use English. For example, Sri Lanka adopted English and when it got freedom from the British it removed English from use. But it has adopted it once again in view of globalization. Asian countries like China and Japan are making use of English very much. There are thousands of English teaching schools and colleges in these countries today. Just recently (refer to the article "A Time for Englishes", *The Times of India,* dated 10-11-2006) the Cambridge educated Singaporean Prime Minister Lee Hsien Loong made English a lingua franca of Singapore. What more; many European countries, once rivals to English and England, have adopted English as one of their market languages. In fact, English is already an international language as it is used by the world organizations like UNO. We often hear of jobs of teaching English in all African and Arabian countries. By the by, India adopted English right from the time of independence and the use of the language will be there for unlimited time thanks to the Tamil agitations against Hindi and the north. What more English is a pan-Indian language, an official language, a link language, a library and literature language (one must know Indian English writers are making a very good progress in their English writings with Booker Prizes), science and technology language, an international language, a commerce language. *The Times of India* observes in the article referred above: "It is the language of power and without it India may miss the globalization bus. As a result, more and more states are realizing the need to bring back English...." This is wonderful. English is a language of emancipation and empowerment. Our freedom fighters if they are with us really can tell us that Indians could succeed in getting their freedom mainly because of their English education. That is to say Macaulay was paid back. In Karnataka where there is a great controversy when the government decided to introduce English as a subject in its schools, the dalits said, 'please do so,' for they think it can be a weapon for their advancement of learning. They think that, as Indian freedom fighters used English education for our freedom, dalits can use it for their advancement. Nothing wrong in it. Long ago, Savitribai Phule said, "By learning English casteism can be destroyed off" Dr Ambedkar said, "English is the milk of lioness." In fact, he wrote his *Annihilation of Caste* in English.

To be precise, there is an ongoing controversy whether English may be studied as a subject right from the first standard. Yet it is difficult to answer the question rather positively because the so-called Kannada intelligentsia is mistaking and misinterpreting the issue. There is politics of caste, language and culture. The whole issue is mired in confusion and paradoxes. After a similar kind of politics of all dimensions, many Indian states have introduced English as a subject right from the first standard. For example, in the state of West Bengal English was not so much. The CPM which had banished English from the state-run schools had to eat crow and admit it was wrong. In 1991 the same government appointed a review commission which suggested introducing English from the first standard and Buddhadeb Bhattacharya did it so in 2004. In Maharashtra, English was made a subject from first standard from 2003 after it realized that not many of its 3,00,000 sixth graders could make a sentence making use of the word 'friend.' Gujarat also realized the importance of English from 2004. It felt lack of English hindered talent and investment flows. It knew Gandhi's strict 'Swadeshi Theory' kept the state off the IT tide. *The Times of India* writes about the English scenario in Karnataka under the small caption: WE DO NEED ENGLISH EDUCATION.

"The damage began in 1994, when the state disallowed setting of government English schools. Reason: promoting Kannada. Result: lakhs of kids kept out of knowledge revolution happening in their backyard. Ironic that a state dubbed as a knowledge hub, boasting of highest revenue from IT, still has lakhs of students who cannot speak a single sentence in English till they are eight years old. But nearly 90% bureaucrats sent their children to English medium schools while grandsons of politicians went to foreign universities. Kannada-medium schools are quietly teaching English. Realizing this, the government has now ordered closure of all these schools. With the 1994 order pending before the Karnataka High Court, it seems only the judiciary can come to the rescue."

....

Now the point is that why Kannada patriots hate the introduction of English from the first standard or the introduction of more number of English medium schools in the state. There are again several reasons, political lobbies, prejudices of caste, culture and language and the like.

First of all, the Kannada patriots in the fashion of Tamil and French patriots, do not want either English as a subject from the first standard or more number of English medium schools in the state. Their reason is that if this happens Kannada language, culture and Kannada's dignity will be smashed up. It is true much of this will happen. English may dominate education, job market, much of cultural matrix and what not if we believe international linguists with foresight, Kannada may, within a thousands years, be out of use. As a professor of English, as a Kannada native speaker and as a creative writer in both the languages, I think the Kannada people need not worry of this, because, the introduction of English as a subject from the first standard will not affect them significantly. The state is introducing it just as ONE SUBJECT not as a medium from the first standard. What will happen if, as a subject, English is taught? Simply our poor, village and needy children will learn English as a second language and will benefit much. Let them become aware of modernism, multiculturalism, globalization and their benefits. Why should they be deprived of benefits of modern life when they are living in modern times modern benefits are used by many of our brethren here and abroad. Why should we keep them in dark about the benefits of the modern times. Let's share and care for each other. Let there be Sarvodaya and Viswamanavate. After all, why should not we worry much about Kannada, for it is just a language. Even language is an item of trade. If it is lost when we gain English or Hindi, or even both, we will not lose much. Why all the worry about our culture? People who have read Indian cultural history must know Pali and Prakrit are gone. So many other languages have disappeared. Does it mean that their descendents, cultures, ethos and mores have disappeared? Such things are there with us in their essence. Actually we must know that English is not England's language. It is a Germanic (Anglo-Saxon) language. C.L. Wren says three-fourth of English is from different sources ranging from European languages to Asian languages. English has a great *capacity to absorb words from other languages and cultures.* The language loves all and all people love English. (Emerson says if you love all people all people will love you) Latin and French were the languages of so many counties in the past. So were Tamil and Sanskrit the languages of Far-Eastern nations centuries ago. After all, America is a bastard country! English is its main language. Americans with English as their lingua franca created a great miracle—American Dream. What is more important?—our life or our namesake culture? Of course, life means culture. Lord Macaulay argued that the benefits of English would be of far reaching consequences for Indians. O! it is amply proved. Where would we be if we had not adopted English? Just think of the benefits of IT, BT, Knowledge Industry, the use of science and technology. William Walsh, a Commonwealth scholar, says, "English has an amazing capacity to express an immense span of sensibility." I remember my childhood-saying that English is like a donkey. If we trust it can carry us around the world. Indeed, our Sanskrit and their Latin are gone. Well then does it mean Indian culture is gone? No. If we use English more it does not mean we lose our culture. Our culture is like our breathing. It will be with us wherever we go. Maybe less or more. It is like our very shade and it will follow us faithfully. Our culture may change. It does not matter even. The change is always for our good. Here culture is more important than language. The latter is needed for the preservation of the former. What of our people abroad? Do they lose their culture? If they lose their culture do they die. Or if Kannada patriots think they lose their culture why do they not return home? Goethe and Rabindranath Tagore said this very gossip about patriotism is NONESENSE. Indeed, it is not necessary, when we are living in a global world. Now the whole world is converging into a brotherhood.

Another important reason is that the children of the age three to six cannot learn English without causing damage to their mother tongue. But the psycho, socio-linguists like Helen Doren and Hocket, have studied the issue carefully and they say that children of age group three to six can learn one or two languages easily, provided that proper educational environs are there. The child of this age is already a 'linguist adult.' Dr Lenneberg observes that, "There is a clear basis for 'regarding the age of four or five as something of a milestone in language acquisition.... If a child is not exposed to a human language during this period, the innate capacity will atrophy and the ability will be lost forever." Klein writes the second language may be acquired before the completion of learning the first language. Michael Halliday whose lecture I attended at CIEFL Hyderabad in 2000 said, "children may learn two or even more languages simultaneously if they are exposed to them.... Neurophysiology confirms that it is about the age of eight or nine that maturation begins to render it somewhat more difficult to learn a language."

There are rich benefits for polyglots. They will be very rich with different language experiences. It is said the more languages we learn the more knowledge we will gain. More people, more culture we will know. Our cultural outlook is widened. The thing is that we should learn more useful languages properly. We should at the same time, live like natives in terms of our way of living (Samskar). After all culture is the way we live and civilization is the things we use.

10

English for the Socially Disadvantaged: A Skill Focal Model of Remediation at Tertiary Level*

K. Ponni

English is not a subject but a condition of existence. To quote George Sampson, "The lesson in English is not merely one occasion for the inculcation of knowledge; it is part of child's initiation into the life of man" (Sampson 24-25). The significant importance of English is strongly felt by the learners as the way of their future; they crave to learn proper English. "It has a great socio-functional purpose in a multilingual and the new socio-cultural environment of India" (Sandhya Rani Sahoo 72). It has to become a part of their natural habit. The term 'Socially Disadvantaged' may refer to the socio-economic background of the low income group parents who have failed to provide the intellectual stimulation to learn English. It is meant that the basic institutions like family, school and society haven't taken the proper care in the second language acquisition. In the primary and secondary levels, these socially disadvantaged students form an attitude that English is an unwanted burden of Bunyan's Christian. Though they have passed their secondary and Higher Secondary English by hook or by crook it remains an unfulfilled desire to acquire competency in English. At tertiary level they are language blind

* Paper presented in the Third International Congress on English Grammar, organised by the Sona College of Technology, Salem, Jan. 23-27, 2006.

or English dunk. On the part of a college English teacher it is a venture to square up the entrants.

Reviews by the researchers express that the primary and secondary part II English syllabi are well designed and enlisted with almost all the grammar topics. But the objectives are not attained because of so many factors including uncongenial classroom climate, single teacher primary school situations, illiterate parents, uncaring society and so on. Uninitiated basic skills are the impediments to comprehend secondary level competencies, taught by non-English teachers. All these make the second language not only foreign but alien. Obtaining pass mark in English becomes their only aim and they seek shortcuts to circumvent. The responses of the students reveal the following strategies:

- The English textbooks are not taught; studied, explored or mastered to attain the objectives.
- Role memory of the prepared summaries for the selected lessons.
- Improvisatory answering to the grammar questions during evaluation.

Being assured a pass mark in English by their strategies, the linguistic behavior is at the square root level of the expected competency, where the teacher does not have a footing. A Bridge Course becomes a dire need for the students to get an access on to the direction to cope with the English syllabus at tertiary level.

The avoidance attitude of the students towards part II English classes will be changed into a real quest for correct English, through this fridge course. Getting pass marks in English would be a natural outcome by this process, because a socially disadvantaged student is unable to get his degree since it is a Himalayan task for the learner to pass English, even though he might have passed in the core subject with high marks.

A crucial period in the life of the learner is wasted just to get pass marks in English. Learned helplessness has become the attitude of the learners and 'drop-out' is the resultant behavior in many cases. There is no spider in the vicinity of these Robert Bruces to instill hope in them.

The school curriculum consists of syllabi starting from the initiation to the higher order reading, writing along with negotiation skills. The survey proves that all the language items are not taught in the class. In the course textbook of twelfth standard for the academic year 2004-05 the units end with a note to the teacher to refer to the handbook for the passage to teach the given items of language skills. But the students are not taught with the handbook. The syllabus covers all the skills in a graded pattern with the specifications of the techniques of teaching with the aids like graphs, maps, diagrams, flow and pie charts, line-drawing, etc. The twelfth standard English starts from 'stress shift' to interviews' to cater to the needs of the students. But it is a dead capitalor a wasted investment or an unhandled tool for the socially disadvantaged, which forms up rust instead of framing the young minds.

The college English teacher has to remove the rust of wrongly framed linguistic behavior and the resulted psychological hindrances like frustration, lack of confidence, etc. Their minds have to be ignited towards self-actualisation. The poor performance is the cascade effect of low income group parents and the related economical, emotional, environmental and intellectual factors. The socially disadvantaged students are denied of their right to learn L2 with all its contents.

Even though the state is the backbone of the educational systems in a democratic country, the relationship is very mechanical and materialistic. Some of the vital issues like the spirit of the school, the ideals of education and methods of teaching are beyond the expansion of education, and are in the increase. But the acquisition of the knowledge in English remains elitist and urban oriented. So it has become a social problem. Walsh and Furfey define social problem as a 'deviation from the social ideal remediable by group effort'. Since these socially disadvantaged students pose the 'deviation from the social ideal', remediation can be sought by 'group effort'. Here it has to be taken by the institution concerned.

A college English teacher gets a conglomerated group of entrants who studied English in so disproportionate a manner that one or more of the four skills of the L2 have been totally or partially neglected. The defective acquisition takes into task the capacities of a language teacher. The process to make them unlearn the vicious linguistic habits demands a constant vigilance. A multiple line approach is needed to make them realise their flaws and practise real skills.

The technophilic educators may insist on multimedia language laboratories, computer-aided teaching and other latest technological developments. But for the socially disadvantaged student community for which even an audio system is a rarity, the teacher is the only possible boat to cross their sea of troubles in learning English. The English teacher's role becomes vital and the teacher-learner relationship is so crucial as a facilitator. The late adolescent stage of the learner requires a friendly and not an authoritative or an autocratic teacher. The supply must meet the demand.

Harold E. Palmer opines that the good language learners "appreciate teachers who are systematic, logical and clear, but prefer to treat them as informants rather than to rely on them." (Palmer, p. 549). But in this context the students completely rely upon their teacher. It is the teacher's ability to design and manipulate the learning environment with learner friendly behavior, contextually appropriate strategies and positive psychological stimulations. A stress-free classroom to build group rapport, a friendly teacher who respects learner autonomy, and reinforces learner's self-esteem consistently, an earnest learner with an aim to earn the competency and possible teaching aids are the pre-requisites for this clientele. The approach is eclectic.

The Skill-Focal Model

An evaluation of the responses of the entrants to the specially framed questionnaire shows that an English word gets so many different spellings. For example the word "labourer" gets spellings like "lapurare", "larber", "laburare", "laboar", "labpoer", "labar", "laburare", etc. The word "government" is spelled as "government", "governament", "govertment", "ganment", "garmend", "govtment", "govnment", "govertment", "goverinont", "gournment", "gounnamend", "govtmant", "governament" and so on. The word "uneducated" is spelled very strangely like "unegecated", "anagecated", "enejikated", etc.

A careful analysis of these spellings leads the researcher to arrive at the following reasons for these misspellings:

- L1 interference
- Negative influence of the social climate
- Guessing without ever having learnt the spellings
- Defective pronunciation habit leads to defaulted spelling
- Very limited vocabulary.

The limited vocabulary of the entrant does not permit an English teacher to use his own vocabulary for the bridge course. There is an impending danger that the student may not understand the meaning of the word. The hardships of the teacher may prove futile.

Instructional materials constitute an important element in the teaching-learning process. The methodology is skill-focal, need-based and learner-centred approach. The enriched bridge course is purely innovative. This model consists of four phases with four stages in the third.

This model consists of four stages and third stage's each student with the equivalent meaning in the target language and L1.

- Compilation of individual lexicon
- Compilation of institutional lexicon by the language teacher
- Instructional material for LSRW competence
- An apprenticeship to attempt a comprehensive exposure to all the skills.

Phase 1

An entrant who has ample time in the beginning of the course is instructed (with guidelines) to prepare individual lexicon and submit it within a week. The guidelines may be:

1. Words have to be arranged in the alphabetical order.
2. Only the known content words have to be included.
3. The equivalent meaning in the L1 and L2 have to be specified.

The failure to understand the teaching is caused by the learner's limited vocabulary and the teacher using words out of the learner's lexicon. This individual lexicon shatters the hurdle and comprehension is ensured.

Phase 2

Individual lexicons are collected and the teacher compiles common lexicon which serves as a base for the entire process. Since a college in a rural area gets only socially disadvantaged students this common lexicon becomes the lexicon of the institution. In all the four stages of Phase 3, the teacher has to restrict his vocabulary usage to the words selected from this lexicon.

Advantages

It is a bold enterprise on the part of the teacher to entrain them with their lexicon. It enables the teacher to make use of vocabulary from this lexicon in framing the syllabi for the four skills and in the classroom activities.

Phase 3

Preparation of Instructional Material for the Language Competencies

LSRW order is a natural process for a L1 learner but for a L2 model adult learner this model envisages better performance. According to this skill-focal model, listening, stimulus causes both speaking and reading responses simultaneously and in turn, they become the stimulus for the response of writing skill.

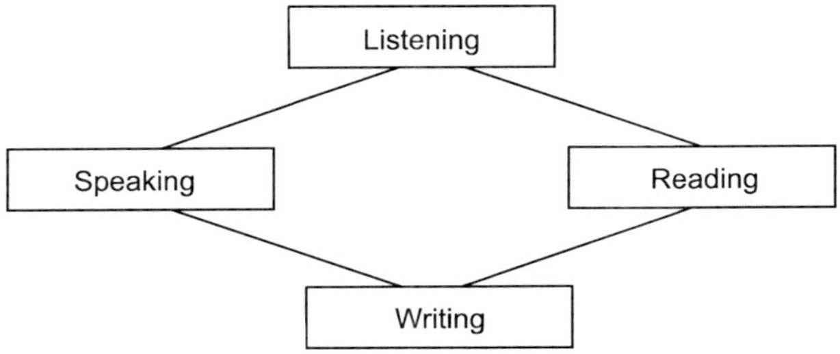

The skills are taught with the linear steps of initiation learning and connection. Audio system is the only electronic aid used in this model.

Stage I: Listening

Language teaching starts with listening. The auditory stimulus initiates and ignites the propulsion, towards second language acquisition. Harold E. Palmer says that "when we listen with understanding what someone is saying...we go through a process called "inner articulating" we articulate mentally, our speech muscles, without necessarily moving, are stimulated by the nerves communicating with the speech centre of our brain".[1]

Syllabus

An audio text with graded items of phonetic symbols words, minimal pairs and dialogues, along with the corresponding printed text.

Method

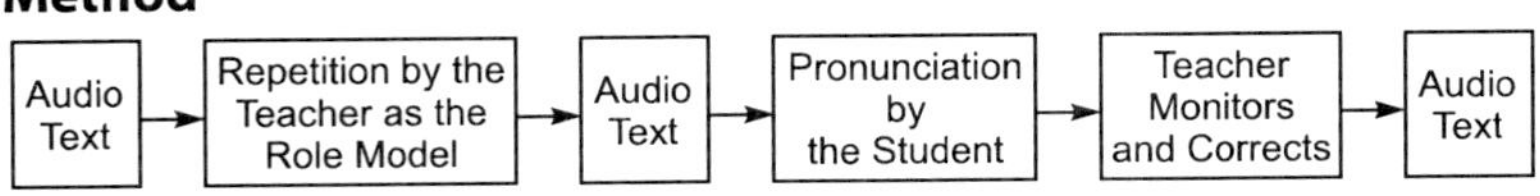

These steps can be repeated to the demand of the student.

Drill

Each student pronounces the printed text aloud when other learners are the listeners.

Evaluation

1. Monitoring the pronunciation.
2. The receptive capability is tested by asking them to write the words by learning the audio text.

Home Work

Writing minimal pairs for the sounds.

Advantages

In a sense this model proves more advantageous than even the natural process since the printed text is supplied along the audio text. Double stimuli of two sense organs namely ear and eye simultaneously cause double responses of speaking and reading directly and the skill of writing indirectly. They understand the phonetic system of the L2.

Stage II: Speaking

Palmer argues that, "Learning to speak a language is always the shortest way to learning to read it or write it..." (Prilwer 15).

The already initiated skill of listening power gives a better prospect for speaking. Since the reader has had the ear training, of the sound system of L2 already assimilated non-verbal behavior is strictly prohibited.

Syllabus

A list of questions to elicit responses in a graded manner from words, phrases to single sentences. A list of answers to the questions in a separate sheet.

Method

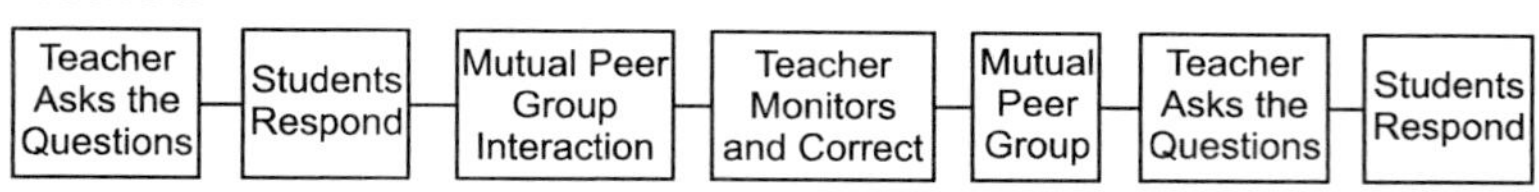

Drill

Mutual peer group consists of two students. When A questions B answers and vice versa.

The list of questions and responses are repeated with the monitoring of the teacher.

Evaluation

Similar questions are asked to elicit responses with proper pronunciation.

Home Work

Imaginary situations are given and students write dialogues for them. In the next class the mutual peer group presents it in the class.

Advantages

Unconscious assimilation of the pattern and usage is the positive outcome of the mutual peer group drill. As the learners have a suppressed longing to speak English, the internal motivation would instill the interest to speak. The process would be speeded up by writing dialogues.

Stage III: Reading

It is a process of using the sensory perception of eye and ear as well as the mind to understand the literal as well as the conveyed meaning of the writer. According to Venkata Iyer, "Reading and understanding is a relationship between the conscious and the subconscious, like the mother and the child".[2]

Syllabus

Selected lessons from the course books of the Primary English, History and Environmental Science.

Method

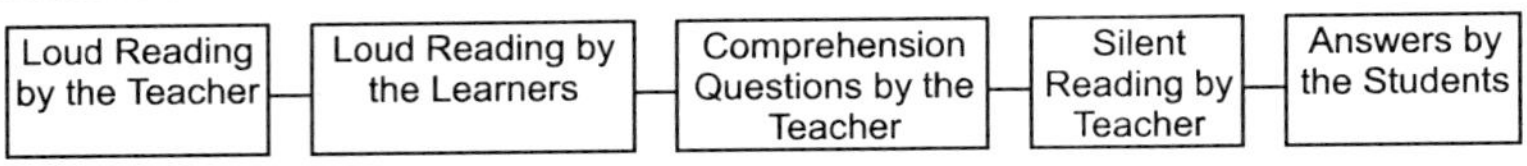

Both loud reading and silent reading are practised.

Drill

Loud reading by the selected learners makes others passive learners. (Silent reading is insisted to answer/comprehension questions). Teacher monitors and corrects pronunciation, pause and other techniques of reading.

Evaluation

Pronunciation is evaluated during loud reading. Silent reading is insisted to answer the comprehension questions.

Home Work

Printed texts of children's stories are supplied. Reading and re-reading is insisted till they comprehend the meaning.

Advantages

Loud reading causes catenizing which means, "learning to recognize or to produce a chain of sds or syllables as an integral whole, irrespective of all considerations of meaning." Silent reading causes semanticizing which means. "Forming a perfect association between a word and that for which it stands" (Palmer 21). Reading competence ensures speaking and writing.

Stage IV: Writing

The observation and initiation of the previous stages of the third phase along with the power of imagination procure the ability to write. The joint action of the previous stages provide ample scope to write on their own.

Syllabus

Popular children's stories of the learners' culture and a list of examples for basic grammar terms.

Method

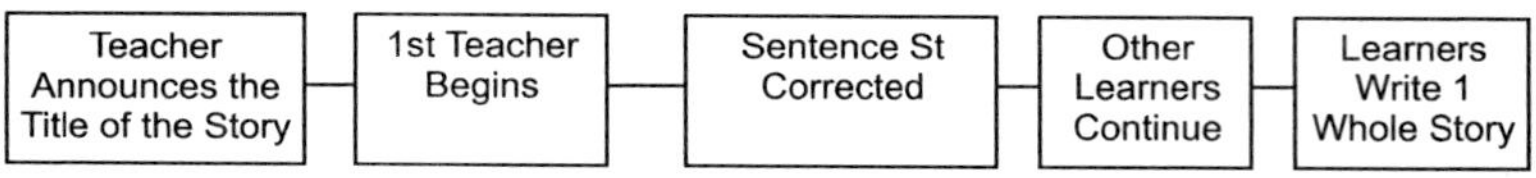

Drill

Children's stories, riddles, conundrums and other popular stories are stimulated in the class and the students write them.

Evaluation

Hints developing and precis writing skill is evaluated through.

Home Work

Topics like the autobiography of the learner and the biography of the learner's parents and grandparents may be given. This may enhance his self identity by reliving the learners own, parents' and grandparents' past which would inscribe his family culture into his.

Advantages

The previous linguistic experiences are recalled and somehow gain the power to express spontaneously with comparative ease and correctness. A flow of self-expression is instilled by the homework. Palmer is of the view that "Both vocabulary and grammar must be assimilated in association with living subject matter" (Palmer 5). The channel of the instruction material transmits the skills upward and learners are stimulated to gain the mastery through constant practice.

Phase 4

An Apprenticeship to Attempt a Comprehensive Exposure to All the Skills

The congnizance of the four stages of Phase 3 has to be ascertained. The learners have to be simulated to transfer their acquired skills to the requirement. "Language students need language as a whole: there is little point in teaching them the grammar...if they cannot pronounce it, do not know the vocabulary and cannot join conversation" (Vivian Cook 205).

Syllabus

Homework of the writing skill and the learners' write-up of their personal experiences in learning L2. L1 is strictly prohibited.

Method

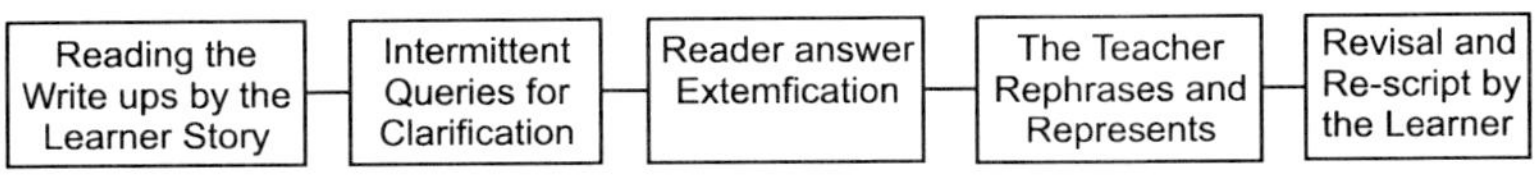

Drill

The learners come out with their doubts in L2 acquisition. Other learners try to clarify. The teacher helps.

Evaluation

Mock-Interviews and picture interpretation can be conducted to ensure the application of the acquired skills.

Advantages

This phase is a kind of reinforcement to weigh the output. The teacher tackles the individual learner differences. The bridge course accomplishes with this phase of apprenticeship.

This bridge course ensures learning of the skills of English through initiation practice and evaluation. The acquisition of the skills makes them on a par with the other learners at tertiary level. This serves as an ignition to motivate them to learn other paralinguistic behaviors. Apart from achieving their educational aims these learners would form a stimulating intellectual group environment which would be recorded in their family institution and society. Future generations from socially disadvantaged areas may be booned with a conducive climate to acquire second language competences during their primary and secondary levels. The objectives of the school curriculum would definitely be achieved. The future entrants of tertiary level will be equipped with the language skills even without undergoing this bridge course.

The learning assumption of this proposed model is the self-expression of the mind's intent. Self-learning would be the ensuring development in the process of L2 acquistion. Vivian Cook suggests, "some consciously accessible learning strategies that the language as a thing of its own" (Vivian Cook 108).

Libraries and competitions can develop meta-cognitive abilities. Simplified versions of the classics would enhance their competence. Compulsory library attendance, announced prizes to the students who read the largest number of books, holding inter-class and inter-departmental competitions, develop both the modes of language.

The increasing demand for proficiency in English makes the role of an English teacher pivotal. The teachers can enrich this model with their own instructional items in consideration with the contextual needs to equip the learners enough. Computation of such well-knit software into the cognitive domain of the L2 learners would be saved to facilitate them to meet today's competitive world and tomorrow's brave new world. That would render them the ability to handle L2 effectively, while performing different language functions.

A committed college English teacher becomes the stimulator to energies the student community, and a propeller to thrust their potential onto the upward social mobility. A careful utilization of this model would make the Utopia of L2 competence a reality for the socially disadvantaged.

NOTES

1. Harold E. Palmer, *The Oral Method of Teaching Languages*, W.H. Effer and Sons Ltd., Cambridge, England, 1955, p. 21.
2. Venkata Iyer, *Dynamic Reading Skills*, Sterling Publishers Pvt. Ltd., New Delhi, 1986, p. 5.

WORKS CITED

Ahuja, Ram, *Social Problems in India*, Rawat Publications, Jaipur, 1997, Rpt. 2001.

Cook, Vivian, *Second Language Learning and Language Teaching*, Arnold, New York, 1996.

Balmer, Harold E., *Oral Method of Teaching Languages*, W. Heffer and Sons Ltd., Cambridge, 1995.

Sahoo, Sandhya Rani, "Innovation in ELT and Instructional Materials: An Indian Context", *Studies in ELT, Linguistics and Applied Linguistics*, Mohit K. Ray (ed.), Atlantic Publishers and Distributors (P) Ltd., New Delhi, 2004.

Sampson, George, *English for the English*, Cambridge University Press, London, 1985.

Venkata, Iyer, *Dynamic Reading Skills*, Sterling Publishers Pvt. Ltd., New Delhi, 1986.

Walsh, Maty E. and Paul H. Furfey, *Social Problems and Social Action* (3rd Ed.), Prentice Hall, Englewood Cliffs, New Jersey, 1961.

Yule, George, *The Study of Language*, Cambridge University Press, Cambridge, UK, 1997.

English Reader, Higher Secondary Second Year Part II—English, Tamil Nadu Textbook Corporation, Chennai, 2001.

A Report on the First Orientation Programme for University and College Teachers, Academic Staff College, Pondicherry University, Pondicherry, 1988-89.

11

Pedagogical Implications in Using Multimedia Language Lab

Pushp Lata

At the onset of the new millennium recent innovations in information technology have raised new hopes for accelerated development and change in modern education system. Computer-assisted language learning has become the trend in foreign/second language teaching. As Gousie (1998: 55) states, "In the fast-moving 1990s, a variety of new technological tools have appeared on the scene. No longer were we swept by a wave of methodology; we were swamped by a tidal wave of Computer-assisted technologies. Suddenly the capability of incorporating laserdiscs, hypertext cards, CDs, CD-ROMs and the Internet into our syllabi became a reality." Instructors of foreign/second languages are now faced with a myriad of new multimedia tools unheard of just a few years ago. In the case of language laboratories as an auxiliary tool for EFL/ESL teaching and learning, more and more institutions happen to be setting up or updating laboratories so that they may be provided with such multimedia facilities. Thus the key factors contributing to this new hope are moves towards increasing impact of new technology, decentralization, students' autonomy and a change in the behavior and perception level of students. These moves have brought about a radical change in the roles of students and teachers.

Keeping in view the changes occurred in the second language teaching the aim of this study is three folds: (i) to explore viability of multimedia and Internet in language teaching, (ii) students' adaptability in learning English with the aid of multimedia computers and the interaction pattern between students and multimedia computers, and (iii) pedagogical implications of using multimedia lab and internet.

In order to focus on the above stated objectives it is of paramount importance to delve deep into fundamental questions such as what are the similarities and differences of language teaching and learning between a traditional classroom and a multimedia language lab? Are there any changes in the roles of teachers and students when they are in a different teaching environment from traditional classroom? What are the implications of using a multimedia computer language lab in teaching English language?

What is a Language Laboratory?

The Language Laboratory is essentially an audio-visual aid, which has various devices such as CDs, audiocassettes, and videos to impart instruction or information for learning English language to the user. The user, who is a student in this context, uses the devices under the proper guidance of his teacher. Interactive computer network allows students to test the result of learning without the risk of being punished for any mistake that he may commit while learning. Learning takes place in a conducive environment for it is free from undue pressure and fear which students normally experience otherwise in the classroom. Thus computer-assisted language learning in language lab reduces the anxiety of students and makes a positive learning environment.

Setting and Operation

The multimedia lab shares some features with the traditional audio-lingual language lab. In both the settings teacher is present but teacher becomes a sort of guide in the lab rather than an information reservoir as he is expected to be in traditional classroom. The teacher can broadcast the teaching materials by playing audiotapes, videotapes, or CDs. Students can practise individually or in pairs or teacher themselves can make the students do the software packages under his guidance in the lab. Here all the computers/desktops (20 to 60) are networked. There is a master console for the teacher to monitor the learning of the students if he feels it is required. In addition, the computers in the MLC are wired together in a Local Area Network. This means that the computers can share software and files and be controlled by an administrator. The server is operated exclusively by the programmer consultant and director. As a monitor, teacher should be aware of the setup of the network but are not in any way responsible for maintaining it.

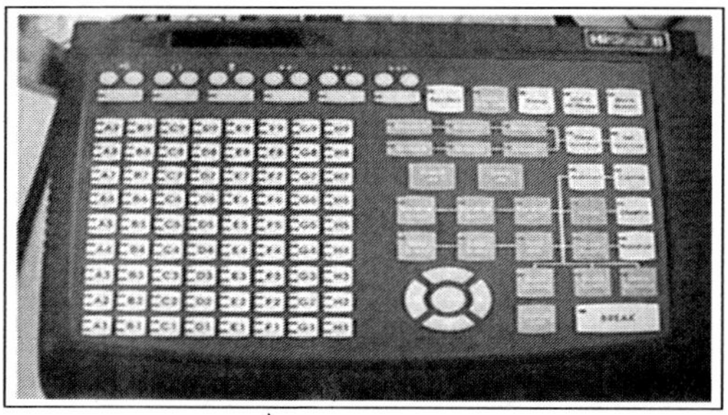

The lab encourages both collaborative work and the development of multimedia materials by both faculty and students. Interactive Teaching Approach and computer-assisted language learning have increased responsibilities, creativity, productivity and team work. The research combining the two fields is not common so far, which makes this study vital and pertinent.

The instructor in a classroom is merely equipped with only desks, chairs, and a large blackboard. A traditional language lab does not have the function of video on demand. Students can choose an English teaching program they are interested in and learn on their pace of learning. The English learning program will just serve the student's desired goal of learning. In one sense, students easily get the individual attention from the computer. Second, the function of a multimedia lab is multiple. It cannot only assume the role of a traditional language lab, but also offer teachers with more powerful teaching tools with the aid of modern computer technology. It permits the student to have his own pace of learning and monitor and evaluate his own performance if he is doing individual practice.

The successful and effective use of the lab depends heavily on the organization of material stored in it and the awareness of the proper operation of the equipments and the software. Computer-assisted language learning material should have both the type of simulations: instruction-oriented and fun-oriented (Huang 1997). Their categorization depends on their primary purpose, the nature of computer-human interaction. The dramatic increase in the use of electronic and computer-assisted language learning systems, including Internet has compelled the use of a new range of learning resources. The excessive use of information technology has brought a sea change in the needs and the learning attitude of students. There is a need for such material that can be used for knowledge building and have fun while learning. The multimedia lab and Internet help in using e-learning and develop soft skills, which is the need of the hour.

Teaching and Learning Gains

- Multi-media objects and internet are powerful pedagogic concepts, adding value to materials through integration of different media, portability.
- A digital multi-media environment may have profound effects on teaching and learning. It makes the computer into a virtual machine: text, audio, video, text tools (including proofing tools, concordancers), voice recognition (English) and CALL are available, while internet connectivity provides access to authentic L2 materials, machine translation, dictionaries, glossaries and software.
- Authentic use of technology to facilitate local processing of global resources.
- These aids help us meet the student expectations and act as a showcase.

Change of Roles for both the Teacher and the Students

The roles of teachers and students have apparently undergone a change. The teacher assumes the role of a coordinator or monitor. In multimedia language lab the teacher must realize that to some extent he/she has been shared with the computer. Computer never intervenes in a teacher's teaching. The major fear is if the teacher does not play his own role in the desired manner, perhaps this tool may become the master. Thus if a learning-oriented computer software is used in a multimedia lab, teacher has to be aware that students no longer depend on him as the only source of knowledge. The computer software will "teach" students the knowledge that teachers are supposed to teach. As a result, a teacher must transform his role and coordinate teaching learning in the lab. He has to coordinate the flow of communication between the teacher and the student as well as between the student and the computer.

On the other hand, breakthroughs in technology have made possible for students to be in contact with multimedia simulations of the target language. Teachers are introducing multimedia software as a means of exposing their students to native and rather realistic activities of the target language. Students now have the opportunity to interact with simulations of residents of different communities and as a result realistic input takes place. In the traditional classroom students are more willing to pay attention to the teacher lecture.

	Traditional Classroom	**Multimedia Lab**
Teaching tools	Chalk, blackboard, audio tapes	Local computer network, video on demand.
Teaching materials	Textbook	Interactive computer Software
Communicative activities	Imaginative role-play	Computer-simulated environment
Student-teacher	Direct communication and more "intimacy"	Indirect communication and less "intimacy"
Student-computer	Not available	Interactive

Students should elevate their learning motivation and independence on learning. They should use the learner autonomy they have got and not to misuse it. Students' higher motivation is reflected by the interest of participation. They can take the help of the teacher and not be dependent on their teacher for explanation as most of the software packages have inbuilt self-instruction and self-evaluation.

Determinants for Successful Operation of Lab

Williams and Burden (1997) have identified four key sets of factors which determine the successful use of language lab. First, the choice of appropriate computer software that fits into the setting of a multimedia lab, is one of the keys to success. As discussed above, the setting of a multimedia lab is different from a traditional classroom. Computer software is not used at all in a traditional classroom. Textbooks and audio-tapes are the main teaching sources. They are still very helpful teaching tools in a multimedia lab. However, the medium of teaching ought to go along with the computers. Chalks and blackboard are obsolete. The computer is the most appropriate teaching tool in a multimedia lab. Accordingly, using computer software in a multimedia lab should be fun and interactive learning process—teachers, learners, tasks and contexts. However, none of these factors exists in isolation. They all interact as part of a dynamic, ongoing process.

Second, orientation is important. The problems come mainly from two aspects. One is the computer software itself. One extra job that students have to do is to learn how to manipulate the computer software. For the first few weeks, students have to become familiar with the manipulation of the computer software so that they can begin to make use of the software. Teachers should be aware of the possible frustration resulting from the unfamiliarity of computer software. The student's difficulty in the manipulation of the software usually undermines the students' interest in the class. The computer software is completely new to students. Consequently, negative interactions between students and the computer proved to be very frustrating for most students. Alexis and Trollope (1985) warns that "less threat and anxiety were as an advantage of simulations, but the opposite can also be true, because simulations call for intensive interaction among participants, and the results of decisions and suggestions a student may make are immediately apparent to participants. Simulations can be more threatening and more anxiety provoking than traditional lecture methods" (p. 185). They are required to do experiment and play with it. However, the teacher's assistance will help them smooth out the difficulty and they will be able to engage themselves in all communicative activities by using computer software.

The other is the technical problem in the management of the multimedia lab. For most of teachers, it demonstrates a major challenge. In a multimedia lab, the management demands not only the fundamental knowledge of computer, but also the advanced knowledge of computer, which is almost impossible for the majority of English teachers. In other words, you need to be familiar with the operation part of computer software you are using in the class, answer students' technical questions, and diagnose the temporary shutdown of computer. In comparison with the work in a traditional classroom, managing a conversation class under the communicative framework in a multimedia lab is relatively demanding.

The Implications of the Multimedia Computer Language Lab in Teaching

As discussed above, the setting of a multimedia lab is different from a traditional classroom. The role of interaction in the foreign language curriculum is increasing with influential works like the one done by M. Warschauer and D. Healey (1998) about software-related research in CALL such as the amount and type of interaction at the computer and attitudes toward computers and CALL. Interaction is intrinsic to success, effective instructional practice in any teaching learning situation. The implementation of interaction-based activity can be perceived as an art (Sims 1997) because it requires a comprehensive range of skills, including an understanding of the learner, an appreciation of software engineering capabilities, the importance of rigorous instructional design and the application of appropriate graphical interfaces. In fact, language is the key mode by which we learn the social principles of our cultures and through which we organize our verbal thinking and regulate our actions. In the lab the students' social relationships promote their mental abilities development and language learning and it underlines the importance of peer support for any form of learning.

The program works best with individual users, but it proves to be a Herculean task to use it for pair work and group activity. It may be a fiasco if not well planned and thought out. Since the use in the classroom situation would be dependent upon the availability of computers. The video clips could be listened to by the class as a whole, with the instructor exploiting the authentic and contextual language situations and/or preparing the learners for further practice in peer discussion and group discussion.

Many teachers and administrators feel uncomfortable with technology. They rather than having a friendly attitude, are quite antagonistic towards them. Even there are times when they get scared of it. In that case, the best way to overcome this fear is facing it by solving as many multimedia exercises as possible. Computer literacy is very important for teachers of English.

The major problem that I have observed is most of the schools and colleges manhandle all the CDs or DVDs they have. They do not properly number them and catalogue them, so that the person in charge may find it difficult to locate the material when asked by the teacher or any other user.

As it is concluded by Huang, Shih-Jen (2000) interactivity between multimedia games and users is more balanced than the interactivity between instructional multimedia and students. In the language lab interaction, teachers appeared not to be at the center of the teaching learning processes. The classroom operation in the lab is in fact based on the recent theories such as Social Constructivist Model which addresses the learner as the center of this process. Teacher finds as though his due importance in the teaching-learing setting has been plundered of. But it is not the complete truth. It is the teacher who requires to adapt to the changed teaching-learning environment. However, modern multimedia has made it possible that teachers can explain old ideas in new manners and methods. Thus if teacher becomes computer friendly, he will not only enjoy his teaching but will get the desired results from the students.

Although multimedia is more affordable and available today than ever before, unfortunately and despite the incredible advances and advantages, not very many English as a foreign language students and teachers benefit from its potential. Students can easily learn all the four skills from listening and speaking, reading and writing segments of multimedia that include speakers of the target language in authentic situations.

A major pedagogical implication could be that teachers should take action to challenge the social belief that some students might bring to the computer lab setting of perceiving the teacher as an authoritarian source of knowledge who cannot be interrupted. Indeed, teachers should be ready to allow students to ask questions at any time during the class sessions. This dynamics may foster students' collaboration and cooperation in learning styles.

As far as equipment is concerned, together with traditional cassette and video playing-and-recording facilities, the resource center contains multimedia applications including the various uses of computer programs, access to Internet resources (e-mail, chats and newsgroups, distribution lists, video conferencing, etc.). Satellite television and radio, together with DVD and hi-fi are also available. In case of extremely limited financial support, teachers will have to act both as counsellors and technicians as well. This may be the case in the early functioning stages of resource centers in various institutions.

SUMMARY

Exponential growth of information technology and its impact on education system is easily visible in the form of multimedia language labs. In spite of the fact that various myths regarding the use of computers in education system are prevalent among the pedagogues and administrators, they have become the necessary evil for the society. Moreover, this change has brought about a change in the roles of a teacher and student. A teacher has become a coordinator or manager rather than an information reservoir and a student has become a user or active member of the whole affair rather than a mere recipient. The software teaching materials are fun oriented as well as information oriented. The students find it interesting to learn with the help of colorful images graphics and sound effect. These materials often have self-assessment mechanism which doubles the fun of learning and they can maintain a self paced learning. However, the success of this technology requires a careful preparation of materials and a computer friendly attitude.

REFERENCES

Gousie, L. (1998). "New Methods and Tools for Teaching Foreign Languages". *T.H.E. Journal* 25(9), pp. 54-56.

Huang, Shih-Jen. (2000). "Communicative Language Teaching in a Multimedia Language Lab". *The Internet TESL Journal.* Retrieved from the World Wide Web: http://iteslj.org/Techniques/Huang-CompLab.htm.

Sims, Roderick (1997). *Interactivity: A Forgotten Art?* [Online] Available http://intro.base.org/docs/interact/, January 27, 1997.

Warschauer, M., and D. Healey (1998). "Computers and Language Learning: An Overview". *Language Teaching*, 31, 57-71.

GLOSSARY

CALL: Computer Assistance Language Learning.

Constructivism: An education philosophy based on the premise that students learn better when they are active participants and control their own education, in such a way that they construct in an individual way the foundations of knowledge acquisition.

Computer: An electronic machine that stores and processes data.

Collaborative learning: A learning environment where students work together to expand their knowledge and their education experience. At computer laboratories students can use multimedia to foster collaborative learning.

Interactivity: A necessary and fundamental mechanism for knowledge acquisition and the development of both cognitive and physical skills.

Media: The plural form of Medium. Media is a plural noun. There is an increasing tendency to use it also as a singular noun because of the ambiguous senses of medium.

Multiple-level Interaction in the Lab: The interaction that takes place between the learner and the Multimedia Software content, the learner and the instructor, and between learners.

Role: The characteristic and expected social behavior of an individual.

Software: Written or printed data, such as programs, routines, and symbolic languages, essential to the operation of computers.

12

English for Specific Purposes (ESP): A Developing Branch of EFL

Hitesh D. Raviya

Need for ESP Courses in India

It is a universal grievance in many states of India that the undergraduate students of various faculties are not able to communicate in English very effectively. It is needless to say that accurate developed communication skills are indispensable for the job market today. In India, with the spread of globalization and constant enhancement of international contacts in various fields, a great deal of attention is being paid to the design of ESP courses that can prepare the learners for 'accurate developed communication skills.' In this respect, Professor Dr. A.K., Singh, Vice Chancellor, Dr. Babasaheb Ambedkar Open University, Ahmedabad, Gujarat, rightly says, "The changing context of University Education in the 21st century makes it necessary to restructure the curriculum and re-orient the teachers who are responsible for curriculum transaction. In view of Globalization and the needs of 'knowledge society', the teaching of English has to shift the focus from teaching of literature to teaching of Language and Communication Skills." For many years, teaching of English was limited to translating prescribed texts in the vernacular language in the classroom! Of course, such traditional methods of teaching could not attract the students in the classroom and on the contrary it resulted in poor participation on the part of the learners. However, in 21st century, winds of change are blowing up, the spread of new direction of ELT in India demands development and designing of new course that can attract the learners' interests and satisfy their needs. It is felt that the general English course for students at the undergraduate level does not bring them to the required competence in all areas of the language at the end of their graduation. It is found that many students across disciplines are not very good at communication and generally lack the proficiency that they require to meet the growing demands of the present day workplace competencies. Students at the completion of their graduation end up having excellent technical skills, however, lacking in effective communication. Therefore, concrete efforts are required to be made to prepare the students for utilizing communication skills in an effective manner. In the light of such growing necessity for specific course content, it is felt that a course in English for Specific Purposes (ESP) can be more effective than a general English course. Therefore, the rationale of this research paper is to put forward an idea about English for Specific Purposes (ESP) Courses that may help the teachers to understand a concept of "English for Specific Purposes (ESP): A Developing Branch of EFL." Thus, it is no longer necessary to stick to the teaching of a fixed textbook when it comes to the teaching of English for specific purposes. The early 21st century has seen a paradigm shift toward communication skills in English required in various professions. I have therefore tried to take a look at "English for Specific Purposes (ESP): A Developing Branch of EFL" in this research paper. India of 21st century has called for an attention to improve communication among all citizens. In order to meet these communication needs, more and more individuals have highly specific academic and professional reasons for improving their communication skills in English. For such learners, English for Special Purposes (ESP) courses will be very useful. ESP programs focus on developing communicative competence in a specific field, such as international business, hotel management, call-centre, banking, management, technology and so on.

The Emergence of ESP

There is no doubt that a good deal about the emergence and origin of ESP has been written so far. However, the most useful and notable information about the emergence and origin of ESP is found in Hutchinson and Waters' *English for Specific Purposes: A Learning-Centered Approach* (1987) published by Cambridge University Press, Cambridge. Hutchinson and Waters (1987) note that "There are three reasons common to the emergence of all ESP: the demands of a Brave New World, a revolution in linguistics, and focus on the learner." They further note that there are two key historical periods that breathed life into ESP. Firstly, the end of the Second World War fetched with it an "...age of enormous and unprecedented expansion in scientific, technical and economic activity on an international scale, for various reasons, most notably the economic power of the United States in the post-war world, the role of international language fell to English" Secondly, "the Oil Crisis of the early 1970s resulted in Western money and knowledge flowing into the oil-rich countries. The language of this knowledge became English." The universal effect of all this expansion and growth were to put forth the pressure on the language teaching profession to 'deliver the required goods'. Thus, the second important reason for the emergence of ESP was a revolution in linguistics since revolutionary pioneers in linguistics focused the ways in which language is used in real communication. Hutchinson and Waters (1987) point out that one important finding was in the ways in which spoken and written English differ. In other words, given the particular context in which English is used, the variation of English will change. This thought was taken one step farther, if language in different situations differs, then modifying language teaching to meet the requirements of learners in 'specific contexts' is also possible. Therefore, in the late 1960s and the early 1970s there were many attempts to describe English in Commerce and Management (ECM), English in Science and Technology (EST), and English in Information Technology (EIT). One must not forget that ECM, EST, and EIT are all now a part of English for Specific Purposes (ESP). "Hutchinson and Waters (1987) identify Ewer and Latorre, Swales, Selinker and Trimble as a few of the prominent descriptive EST pioneers."

Apart from what Hutchinson and Waters (1987) refer to as the most influenced reason for the emergence of ESP, there is one more powerful reason which triggers off the emergence of ESP that is rooted in learner-centered approach of the new academic era. Since, more and more attention is given to the ways in which learners acquire language and the discrepancies in the ways in which language is acquired, learners are 'seen to employ different learning strategies, use different skills, enter with different learning schemes, and be motivated by different needs and interests.' Consequently, the needs of the learners grow equally important. This resulted in designing 'specific courses' to meet the individual needs and gave a birth to ESP.

Thus, English for Specific Purposes (ESP) has developed into one of the most important areas of EFL teaching today which germinated in the early 1960s. Its growth is mirrored in the ever-increasing number of universities either offering an MA in ESP or optional paper of ESP in MA. Many universities in India offer need-based ESP courses to the students. For example, in Gujarat, Sardar Patel University, Vallabh Vidyanagar, has established CTRLC Centre headed by Professor Dr. Javed Khan. This center offers various need-based short-term courses to the international students, doctors, engineering students, and so on. However, in India, the ESP program has shown a slow but specific growth over the last decade as a result of the globalization. The increased interest in ESP has been spurred in India as a result of the globalization of the 21st century. Many books on ESP program are being published across the world. This movement and 'rapid growth in English courses aimed at specific disciplines' is taking place of the traditional 'General English' courses in the universities at the under graduate level. "There is a clear necessity for effective English communication skills for graduates in the current globalized work environment. It is observed that students do not gain the kind of proficiency demanded in present day context where communication is beyond the mastery of reading, speaking, listening and writing.

Communication across global companies and multinationals, or even in the Call Centers require workforce that is competent in skills like negotiations, team work, oral presentations, report writing, decision making, etc." (Sheba Dayal 2007).

Means of ESP

It appears though many scholars have interpreted the concept of ESP in their own manner, still there exist differences in how people interpreted the meaning of ESP. Some people described ESP as simply being the teaching of English for any purpose that could be specified. Others, however, described it as the teaching of English used in academic studies or the teaching of English for vocational or professional purpose. Hutchinson and Waters (1987) define ESP as "an approach to language teaching in which all decisions as to content and method are based on the learner's reason for learning". Strevens' (1988) definition of ESP makes a difference between four absolute and two variable characteristics:

I. Absolute Characteristics

ESP comprises of English language teaching which is:

- designed to meet specified needs of the learner;
- related in content to particular disciplines, occupations and activities;
- centred on the language appropriate to those activities in syntax, lexis, discourse, semantics, etc, and analysis of this discourse;
- in contrast with General English.

II. Variable Characteristics

ESP may be, but is not necessarily:

- restricted as to the language skills to be learned;
- taught according to any pre-designed methodology.

Anthony (1997) makes a note that there has been considerable debate about what ESP stands for despite the fact that it is an approach which has been 'extensively used over the last three decades.' He further notes that it is not clear where "ESP courses end and general English courses begin; numerous non-specialist ESL instructors use an ESP approach in that their syllabi are based on analysis of learner needs and their own personal specialist knowledge of using English for real communication."

Dudley-Evans and St John (1998) slightly changed, revised and modified Strevens' original definition of ESP to form their own. In 1997, Dudley-Evans offered his modified definition of ESP at the 'International Conference on English for Specific Purposes' held on the campus of Aizu University, Fukushima Prefecture, Japan. At 'International Conference on English for Specific Purposes' held at Japan Tony Dudley-Evans was very much aware of the existing confusion that prevailed amongst the ESP community in the world and in particular in Japan, therefore he explained in his one hour speech to elucidate the meaning of ESP and gave an extended and modified definition of ESP in terms of 'absolute' and 'variable' characteristics. The modified definition of ESP, suggested by Dudley-Evans and St John (1998), is as follows:

I. Absolute Characteristics

- ESP is defined to meet specific needs of the learner;
- ESP makes use of the underlying methodology and activities of the discipline it serves;
- ESP is centred on the language (grammar, lexis, register), skills, discourse and genres appropriate to these activities.

II. Variable Characteristics

- ESP may be related to or designed for specific disciplines;
- ESP may use, in specific teaching situations, a different methodology from that of general English;
- ESP is likely to be designed for adult learners, either at a tertiary level institution or in a professional work situation. It could, however, be for learners at secondary school level;
- ESP is generally designed for intermediate or advanced students;

- Most ESP courses assume some basic knowledge of the language system, but it can be used with beginners.

The definition offered by Dudley-Evans and St John is visibly influenced by that of Strevens (1988). It is needless to say that in the hands of Dudley-Evans and St John, the definition has been improved significantly. In the new modified definition, we find the removal of the absolute characteristic that ESP enjoyed in contrast with 'General English' and addition of more variable characteristics. The separation of ESP into 'absolute and variable characteristics' is very useful in determining what is and is not ESP. The definition makes it very clear that "ESP can but is not necessarily concerned with a specific discipline, nor does it have to be aimed at a certain age group or ability range. ESP should be seen simple as an 'approach' to teaching, or what Dudley-Evans describes as an 'attitude of mind'."

Thus, Dudley-Evans and St John assert that "ESP is not necessarily related to a specific discipline." Furthermore, "ESP is likely to be used with adult learners although it could be used with young adults in a secondary school setting."

The Categories of ESP

David Carter (1983) identifies three categories of ESP:

1. English as a restricted language
2. English for Academic and Occupational Purposes
3. English with specific topics.

The language that is used by air traffic controllers at the air-port or by waiters at the restaurants or hotels are instances of 'English as a restricted language'. Mackay and Mountford (1978) show the clear difference between restricted language and language with this statement: "...the language of international air-traffic control could be regarded as 'special', in the sense that the repertoire required by the controller is strictly limited and can be accurately determined situationally, as might be the linguistic needs of a dining-room waiter or air-hostess. However, such restricted repertoires are not languages, just as a tourist phrase book is not grammar. Knowing a restricted 'language' would not allow the speaker to communicate effectively in novel situation, or in contexts outside the vocational environment."

The second category of ESP that Carter (1983) mentioned is 'English for Academic and Occupational Purposes'. There is an excellent diagram of the 'Tree of ELT' discussed by Hutchinson and Waters (1987). In their discussion of the 'Tree of ELT', ESP is broken down into three branches:

1. English for Science and Technology (EST),
2. English for Business and Economics (EBE), and
3. English for Social Studies (ESS).

Hutchinson and Waters further divide each of these branches into two divisions namely English for Academic Purposes (EAP) and English for Occupational Purposes (EOP). An exemplar of EOP for the EST branch is 'English for Technicians' whereas an example of EAP for the EST branch is 'English for Medical Studies'. They also note that there is not a definite difference between EAP and EOP. They are of the opinion that people can work and study concomitantly; it is also possible that in several cases "the language learnt for immediate use in a study environment will be used later when the student takes up, or returns to, a job." This argument of Hutchinson and Waters (1987) is perhaps the implied and hidden justification of rationale for classifying EAP and EOP under the same category of ESP identified by David Carter (1983). In my personal opinion, David Carter (1983) implies that the ultimate use of both EAP and EOP is nothing but an 'employment'. Nevertheless, the ultimate use may be one and the same but their means to attain the end is indeed very different.

The third and final type of ESP identified by Carter (1983) is 'English with specific topics.' In Carter's argument it is in this category where 'emphasis shifts from purpose to topic'. This type of ESP is exclusively concerned with predictable future needs of English, for instance, learners of science faculty requiring English for their postgraduate studies or employees requiring English for working in foreign companies and institutions. However, some scholars argue that this is not a separate type of ESP but rather it is an essential component of ESP programs that focus on situational language. This situational language is the result of the interpretation from needs analysis of 'authentic language used in target workplace settings'.

The Features of ESP Courses

There are basically three features which are common to all ESP courses identified by Carter (1983). He states that the three features common to all ESP courses are:

1. Authentic material,
2. Purpose-related orientation, and
3. Self-direction.

If we re-examine Dudley-Evans' (1997) declaration that ESP should be offered at an intermediate or advanced level than the exercise of 'authentic learning materials' is completely reasonable. A closer assessment of ESP materials pursue us to believe that it is sufficient to say at this juncture that use of authentic content materials, 'modified or unmodified in form', is undeniably a feature of ESP, particularly in 'self-directed study and research tasks'.

'Purpose-related orientation' is connected with the replication of communicative tasks required of the target group and setting. Carter (1983) refers to the students' simulation of a conference which involves the groundwork for research papers, articles, reading habits, note-taking, note-making, and writing. A good example of 'purpose-related orientation' is found in the management faculty. Now-a-days, many universities in India, the postgraduate students of management faculty are given special training in English for business courses in which the learners involved themselves in the design and management of an exclusive business venture like 'market research', and 'logo creation'. At the end of the course, they are required to present their final products in the presentation session. For our health science program, students attended a seminar on improving your listening skills. Thus, 'purpose-related orientation' is connected with the reproduction of communicative tasks required of the target group and setting.

The third and the last category of ESP identified by Carter (1983) is 'self-direction'. Here one must not forget that the ultimate aim of the ESP course is to turn the learners into users. The 'self-direction' takes place when the learners are given a certain degree of 'freedom to decide when, what, and how they will study'. It goes without saying that the teachers must attempt systematically to educate the learners how to learn by educating them about learning strategies and teach them how to use newly learned information in a new culture.

Difference between ESP and ESL

The most vital point that requires an attention of the teachers of English is that there is a specific notable difference between English for Specific Purposes (ESP) and English as a Second Language (ESL) which is known as general English in most of the universities in India. The most significant difference between ESP and ESL lies in the learners and their intentions of learning English. The students who want to learn ESP courses are generally adults who have already some knowledge with English language. Apart from that their main purpose of learning language is to communicate in professional skills and to carry out their specific job-related functions. Therefore, ESP courses are generally designed on the basis of an assessment of purposes and needs for which English is required. Thus, ESP focuses more on 'language in context' than on teaching grammar and language structures. ESP includes the various subjects like English for accounting, English for medical profession, English for computer professional, English for tourism, English for business management and so on. Consequently, in ESP courses English is not taught as a subject alienated from the students' real world on the contrary it is incorporated with a subject matter area which is important to the learners.

One more important focal point that is required to keep in the mind is that ESL and ESP diverge not only in the nature of the learner but also in the aim of teaching. If truth be told, as a common rule, in ESL all four basic language skills known as

LSRW, i.e. listening, speaking, reading, and writing are stressed uniformly while in ESP only those skills which are most needed by the learners are stressed and the syllabus is also designed according to the needs of the learners. For instance, an ESP program might stress the improvement of reading skills in those students who are preparing for graduate work in business administration; or it might encourage the improvement of spoken skills in learners who are studying English in order to face professional interviews or visa interviews. In fact, ESP program unites the subject matter and ELT in such a way that it becomes highly motivating and at the end of the course the learners are able to use what they learn in their English classes to their core field of study, whether it is 'accounting, business management, economics, computer science or tourism'. At the end of the ESP program the learners are able to exercise the vocabulary and structures that they learn in a 'meaningful context' reinforces what is taught and further boosts up their enthusiasm. Thus, in the ESP class, students are exposed how the 'subject-matter content' is expressed in English.

Course Designing of ESP Program

"Course Designing is a process involved in the designing of courses of study either in a formal system of education or in an informal or non-formal one." The most important point in designing ESP courses is 'to start the course-developing process with an analysis of the target group of students'. Most of the problems that arise in teaching English are more or less a result of not paying attention to learners' interests and overlooking students as a resource of essential information. In the last decade, most of the universities in India have witnessed a wide spread of ESP and as a result much emphasis has to be laid on the 'learner-oriented, instruction'. As a result, needs analysis has been given significant attention in making a particular course serve a particular group's interests.

I. Needs Analysis

Needs analysis, in broad terms, is a reference to a process used in an academic setting for the purpose of determining the social, academic, and vocational needs of a group of learners requiring the use of a language, and for prioritising these needs by making use of both subjective and objective information. Therefore, it should be the starting point for designing courses and strategies for teaching and learning. A needs analysis is undertaken by a course designer in order to find answers to questions like why is it being undertaken? Whose needs are to be analyzed? Who performs the analysis and who decides what the language needs are? What is to be analyzed? How is the analysis to be conducted? When is the analysis to be undertaken? Where is the course in English for special purpose to be held?[1] Discussed formally and extensively for the first time by Higgins (1966) toward the mid-1960s, it attracted the attention of Richterich of the Council of Europe team in 1973, Strevens (1977), Coffey (1984) and Jordan (1997), becoming more and more scientific with the passage of time.[2] It is necessary to understand how these questions, when answered, help us do.

A good needs analysis exercise almost always involves a whole list of logical steps to be followed. A needs analyst must:

- be clear about the purpose for which the exercise has been undertaken.
- delimit the student population by selecting groups and individual subjects from each of these groups at random since the entire student population cannot be involved in the exercise.
- decide upon the approaches to be adopted.
- acknowledge the constraints or limitations governing the entire exercise.
- select the most appropriate of the methods available for collecting the necessary data.
- collect the data and analyze the results before interpreting the results.
- determine the objectives that the exercise is expected to fulfil.
- take decisions pertaining to the syllabus, content, materials, methods, etc.

- evaluate procedures and results in order to undertake further study where there is not much data available or evidence in store so that the work becomes more relevant the next time the course is offered again.

II. Students Analysis

Since the students are capable of providing much more important information for teachers than only 'an expression of their needs', an improved term than 'needs analysis' might be 'students analysis'. Students' analysis offers us two types of information. Firstly, it helps us to find out learners' current level in the target and methods of learning they have experienced so far. Secondly, students' analysis corresponds to what the students want to achieve. There are various ways of finding information about students' needs and their earlier experience. At the university level, it can be done through a variety of questionnaires, reviews, surveys, group discussions, individual chats, etc. For example, the students of Business Management Faculty, i.e. students if BBA and MBA, could be asked to make a list of areas in which they can anticipate use of ESP like 'selling insurance, opening bank accounts, selling housing loans, dealing with NRI customers, translating business documents from English into their vernacular language and so on. Though the data and needs of the students are very important, there should not be overuse of it. Analysis of the students' needs does not mean that teachers are supposed to teach only what their students need. However, there is no doubt that in developing a new course, students' analysis helps the teachers to bring together the desired goals and objectives, conceptualizing the content of the course, choosing teaching materials, and course evaluation.

III. Setting up of Goals and Objectives of the ESP Course

The objectives are set up for ESP courses to achieve and an effort is made at the time of evaluation to find out whether or not these have been met and, if "yes", to what extent. Therefore, it is important for the course designers to give due thought to these before deciding on the course content. Formulating objectives for a particular course allows the teacher to draw a clear picture of what the course is going to be about. Objectives convey definite ways of achieving the goals. Clear perceptive of objectives helps teachers to be sure what material he is supposed to teach, and when and how it should be taught. Nunan (1987) gives a clear account of how one should state objectives. Depending on what is desired, objectives may sound like the following:

- Students will learn that....
- Students will be aware of....
- Students will develop....

Thus, the course designers must ask themselves the following questions and answer these too.

(i) What should the proposed course aim at and what should be its actual objectives?

(ii) What does one need to do in order to ensure the attainment of these objectives?

(iii) Should provisions be made for flexibility in the course content so that these objectives are better met?

(iv) At what precise point in the syllabus does one provide for this flexibility?

(v) How does one provide for this flexibility?

(vi) How do we ensure that these aims and objectives reflect interdependence with the subject matter and the scheme of assessment?

(vii) How the course designer can get down to the task of selecting the course content?

IV. Conceptualizing the Course Content

From year to year, with the rapid development of the world, teaching ESP courses in India has been witnessing an alteration in the needs and interests of the students. Therefore, in ascertaining a learner-centered approach there should be a modification in the selection of the content of the course. This shift will certainly serve the learners' interests and needs.

Course content is another name for what has come to be called a syllabus. A word derived from the Lain and Greek root *sillybe,* meaning the label of a book, syllabus was originally taken to mean an abstract of a programme, as of a series of lectures or a course of studies[3] usually based on a catalogue of positions taken on what should constitute a course in a particular branch of study and why? In a formal educational set up, it is taken today to mean, "An outline or brief description of the main points of a text, lecture or course. It may represent the obligatory contents of a course".[4] Conceptualizing the course content is not a context-free process. At the time of taking into account information about the students' needs, and objectives of the course, the teachers are required to resolve which aspects of ESP learning will be incorporated, stressed, included, and used as a center of the course to address students' needs.

There are many ways of conceptualizing the course content. Teachers can focus on developing basic skills, communicative competence, vocabulary awareness, etc. For example, English for Academic Purposes (EAP) course for the students who are going to participate in 'an international students exchange programme' can be conceptualized to attain intercultural communicative competence. In such courses, students develop language skills, but it is skilled through the integration of the socio-cultural component into teaching various elements of the language. It is also clear that though in such courses all skills appear divided in structural charts, but in reality all the skills and aspects of the language are intermingled in the real communication. Hence, 'they should be treated, taught, and tested as one inseparable unit'.

V. Selecting and Developing ESP Materials

"In student-centered instruction, the appropriateness of materials includes student comfort and familiarity with the material, language level, interest, and relevance" (Nunan 1987). However, there are some situations where the teachers are very much dependent on the materials and they use the same textbook repeatedly. As such, there is nothing wrong in using the same teaching materials, if everything is conceptualized through a learner-centered approach. For example, the teachers may use the same audio story which can be used for developing listening comprehension skills, cultural awareness, expanding vocabulary, and so on. In this respect, it is said "teaching materials are tools that can be figuratively cut up into component pieces and then rearranged to suite the needs, abilities, and interests of the students in the course" (Graves 1996).

After preparing the main objectives and selecting suitable teaching material, the teachers should start planning a new course. The term 'course planning' is another name for 'curriculum design'. The 'course planning' is the study and the development of the aims and objectives, and implementation and evaluation in an educational system. However, it is desirable on the part of the teachers to be flexible in course designing. The teachers should be prepared to modify the syllabus and make minor necessary changes in the course while teaching with a view to dealing with students' interests and needs in an effective manner. It is also desirable that the teachers evaluate their courses in order to improve and promote their efficacy.

The evaluation system to be used to assess performances on a course is set up on the basis of responses to the following queries: (1) Does the proposed course require formative, or ongoing and iterative evaluation during an instructional sequence, permitting mid-stream adaptation and improvement of the program, or summative evaluation, i.e. evaluation undertaken at the end of the program? (2) Does such an evaluation require setting up tasks only on the basis of the books prescribed, or does it also require other kind of tasks on related reference material? (3) How often would the learners need to be evaluated on the course? (4) What kinds of tests would be suitable for the purpose of evaluation of the course work? (5) What needs to be done to ensure that the results of the tests are reliable for determining the levels of achievement? (6) Do we propose to use the feedback from these tests to decide upon the kind of changes that would be required in the course content and, if "yes", then at what point of time? Apart from all these issues having a direct bearing on the courses, there are issues related to teacher training and institutional support that we propose to deal with here onward. All this makes a curriculum cyclical in nature. The feedback from evaluation at the end of the course should be used year after year for the purpose of reviewing and revising it. Thus, evaluation of the course is a brave step for the teacher. The teacher should be open-minded in hearing and implementing learners' comments. The different students with different needs make it necessary to change and adjust the course. Thus, course development is an on-going process.

Conclusion

It is needless to say that a course in English for Specific Purposes (ESP) can be more effective than a general English course and therefore in the era of globalization, it is no longer necessary to stick to the teaching of a fixed textbook when it comes to the teaching of English for specific purposes in India of 21st century. However, we must take a note that in India, ESP is still in its infancy. If ESP is to grow and flourish in India, it is very important that the teachers of English across India understand what ESP really represents. Only then, we will see a change in our education system. The purpose of this paper is just to shed some light on ESP course in general as it addressed key notions about ESP and has discussed the needs for ESP courses in India, the emergence of ESP, means of ESP, the categories of ESP, the features of ESP courses, the difference between ESP and ESL and course designing of ESP program.

NOTES

1. For instance, in case of Jordan (1997).
2. Higgins (1966), Strevens (1977), Coffey (1984), and Jordan (1997).
3. CTCD, p. 1367.
4. IDE, p. 332.

WORKS CITED

Anderson, R. and D. Ausubel (Eds.) (1965). *Readings in the Psychology of Cognition.* New York: Holt, Rinehart & Winston.

Dudley-Evans, T. and M. John (1998). *Developments in ESP: A Multi-disciplinary Approach*. Cambridge: Cambridge University Press.

Graves, K. (1996). *Teachers as Course Developers*. England: Cambridge University Press.

Hutchinson, T. and A. Waters (1987). *English for Specific Purposes: A Learning-centered Approach*. Cambridge: Cambridge University Press.

Jordan, R.R. (1997). *English for Academic Purposes: A Guide and Resource Book for Teachers*. Cambridge: Cambridge University Press.

Krashen, S. (1982). *Principles and Practice in Second Language Acquisition*. Oxford: Pergamon.

Nunan, D. (1988). *Syllabus Design*. Oxford: Oxford University Press.

Selinker, L., E. Tarone and V. Hanzeli (Eds.) (1981). *English for Academic and Technical Purposes*. Cambridge: Cambridge University Press.

Vygotsky, L. (1978). *Mind and Society*. Cambridge: Harvard University Press.

13

Modality, Mood and Modal Auxiliaries: A Critique

Prashant Mishra

Modality

Most of the grammarians deal with modality in terms of modal verbs. However, modality is not a formal notion, it is a semantic notion. It is "a conceptual category, a type of meaning, or complex of meanings, with various reflexes in language" (Khlebnikova 1976:3). Modality refers to certain meaning categories like question, assertion, request, ability, wish, permission, possibility, insistence, etc. These meaning categories are expressed through the use of different moods such as declarative, interrogative, imperative or through the use of modals such as will, shall, can. Khlebnikova says that modality "is expressed principally in a generalized form, in the imperative and conjunctive moods, and also in the lexical meanings of modal verbs and certain lexical units" (1976:5).

Modality is a term used by the logicians to refer to a certain way of classifying propositions. It has been discussed since the days of Aristotle. Aristotle's 'De Interpretations' and 'Prior Analytics' are said to initiate the discussion on the modal logic. His discussion of the notions of necessity, possibility and impossibility and the relations between them are said to provide the basis of modal logic. Modal logic deals with various propositions which are drawn from human attitudes and experiences from which semantic choices like necessity, possibility, impossibility, available for utterances, are derived.

The method of analysis in modal logic is based on "the proposal that a proposition can be said to be true in one particular (real or imagined) world and false in another" (Perkins 1983:6). Modality is, thus, interpreted in terms of an event or a proposition and analyzed with respect to the universe in which such events or propositions are thought of as true or false. According to Perkins in the framework of modal logic "a given event or proposition may be made relative to, or may be qualified by, a particular world view, state of affairs, set of principles, etc" (1983:9).

Lyons, while discussing various types of modalities—epistemic, deontic, etc.—treats mood as a grammatical category and favors the traditional description based on the inflected forms of the verbs. According to him, "Mood is a grammatical category that is to be found in some, but not all, languages. In traditional usage, 'mood' is applied to such subsets of inflected forms of verbs as are distinguished one from another by means of the terms 'indicative', 'imperative', 'subjunctive', etc; and we have chosen to respect this usage" (Lyons 1977:848). But he has not attempted to define modality in the above cited work. However, in one of his earlier works (1968:308), Lyons has hinted at his notion of modality. He has discussed three scales of modality—the scale of 'wish' and 'intention', of 'necessity' and 'obligation', and of 'certainty' and 'possibility'. However, the above classification of modality on three scales makes us infer that modality is a semantic term for Lyons and is expressed with the help of grammatical categories like mood and modal auxiliaries. Palmer (1979:4) too agrees with Lyons in this respect and treats mood and modality as two opposite categories—the former is grammatical whereas the latter is semantic.

Halliday (1970), who made a significant contribution to the functional paradigm, believes that a text is a product of social and cultural context from where it springs. He is of the opinion that people use language with one another in order to manage their social lives. Modality is directly related to the social functions of language. Modality, which expresses different semantic implications like permission, request, obligation, necessity, possibility, is used to perform different communicative acts. Halliday regards modality as a form of participation by the speaker in the communicative act. Modality is related to the interpersonal function of the language. A language is used as a means of social interaction and it expresses various social roles and performs various communicative functions like questioning somebody, requesting or commanding somebody or telling somebody something. Such types of interpersonal functions of language are reflected in various sentence types like declarative, interrogative and imperative and also through the system of modals. The three choices in the mood system perform various communicative functions like declaring, asking a question, making a request or giving a command. With these sentence types, modal verbs like 'can', 'may', 'will', 'must' help in expressing various social functions such as making a request, seeking permission, expressing rights, obligation and possiblity. Thus, modality is directly related to the social functions of language.

Modality, as we have discussed above, is a notional category (Khlebnikova 1963, Harries 1978, Lyons 1968) used to perform various communicative functions (Halliday 1970). Performative verbs that indicate performance of action are said to express modality and illocutionary force in language. Austin believes that a person utters a sentence not only to convey something but also to perform somę act. When a person utters a sentence like—'I promise to come back within a week'—he is not making a simple statement but is performing the act of promising. According to Austin, "a complete account of the meaning of a sentence cannot be restricted to semantic analysis as these are usually understood and that they must be extended to include information about the kind of speech act involved in uttering the sentence—that is, its illocutionary force" (Austin 1962 quoted in *Boyd and Thorne* 1969:58). In the beginning of his discussion, Austin makes a distinction between performative (short) utterances and constative (descriptive) utterances. This distinction is related to the various functions performed by language. In his 1962 work *How to Do Things with Words*, Austin says that constative utterances refer to the statements which describe some event, process or state of affairs and which can be characterised as either true or false. Performative utterances, on the other hand, instead of evaluating something as true or false, are used to do something. The difference between constative and performative utterances depends upon the difference between 'saying something and doing something by means of language'. Austin, in this way, challenged the view of the logical positivists who thought that language makes only empirically verifiable statements. According to them, language had only one function, i.e. descriptive. All the other utterances are classified as emotive. But people, like Wittgenstein (1953), who were earlier associated with this theory, soon came to realize that language utterances are heterogeneous and are determined by various social conventions. A person becomes competent in the use of language by learning to use it in different types of social contexts. Besides relating the use of language to social situations, Wittgenstein also relates the semantic aspect of a word to its use. Thus both Wittgenstein and Austin "emphasize the importance of relating the function of language to the social contexts in which languages operate and insist that, not only descriptive, but also non-descriptive utterances should be of concern to the philosopher" (Lyons 1977:728). Hence the theory of speech acts which relates modality, a notional concept, to the illocutionary force of an utterance, which is governed by various socio-cultural situations, is of great relevance to the study of moods and modals.

Modality is expressed linguistically by a number of devices like moods, modal auxiliaries, quasi-auxiliaries, adjectival and participial expressions, nominal expressions, lexical verbs (Perkins 1983). Apart from these grammatical categories, modality is also manifested in orthographic devices like punctuation, prosodic features like stress and intonation-contour (Searle 1969). Verbal categories like tense are also used in some cases to express modality. Lyons says that "reference to the future...is often as much a matter of modality as it is of purely temporal reference" (Lyons 1977:816). In

English, for example, modals like 'will' and 'may' have a temporal function besides their modal functions like prediction, willingness, intention, insistence. But most of the grammarians recognize the modal function as primary and the temporal function as secondary.

Moods and Modal auxiliaries are the two important grammatical categories which have the potential to express different aspects of modality. Modality and illocutionary force, which are influenced by various socio-cultural factors, are realized grammatically by the formal category of mood and modal auxiliaries. Moods and modal auxiliaries perform various grammatical functions like expressing modality and tense. But they primarily express different types of modality and illocutionary force. The semantic notion of modality is often influenced by various socio-cultural factors. Linguists have now realised that modals have the singular potential to represent illocutionary force in language. For example, 'He will come on Monday' can be interpreted as 'I predict he comes on Monday'. Searle regards the study of the meaning of sentences and the study of speech acts synonymous as "the speech act or acts performed in the utterance of a sentence are in general a function of the meaning of the sentence" (Searle 1969:18). This view of Searle's relates the semantic notion of modality to the functional concepts like speech act and illocutionary force. We have clearly stated that moods and modal auxiliaries are used in various languages to express various propositions. However, the meaning of these propositions is always influenced by various pragmatic forces.

We have so far tried to discuss the concept of modality and how it is related to the concepts of speech act and illocutionary force. Before going ahead in our study, we shall look at the concepts of mood and modal auxiliaries as these two grammatical categories are by and large capable of expressing different types of modality in various languages.

Mood

Jespersen (1969) recognizes three moods—indicative, subjunctive and imperative. He regards mood as a formal category which is marked by the verb forms. Mood, according to Jespersen, reflects the attitude of the speaker that forms the content of the sentence. According to him, "the imperative, like the infinitive, has the same form as the base of the verb, and the same is true of the present indicative (except the third person singular) and the whole of the present subjunctive" (Jespersen 1969:293). These forms are used to express the various attitudes of the speaker, e.g. statements and questions (indicative); a wish (subjunctive) and requests (imperative).

Myklestead (1971:243) too regards mood as a grammatical category and says, "by the mood of a verb we understand the designation by means of conjugational patterns or equivalent verbal forms of how an act or a state as expressed by the verb is to be conceived (a) as a fact, (b) as a command or request (c) as desirable, possible, contingent, doubtful, unreal". He agrees with Jespersen that mood is a formal category realized grammatically by verbal inflections. He too recognizes three moods in English and illustrates them by giving the following examples:

Come! (Imperative), He comes (indicative), May he come (subjunctive) (Myklestad 1971:243). Myklestad, thus, classifies moods as imperative, indicative and subjunctive depending upon the relation of the subject to the predicate and as conceived by the speaker.

Zandvoort (1962) also associates mood to the verb inflections and regards the third person singular form of the verb with '-s' infection as subjunctive and the same without '-s' as the indicative. He says that this difference in the form of the verb between the two is one of mood (1962:86).

Palmer (1979) regards mood a grammatical category in English as opposed to modality which is a semantic term. Mood, he thinks, is "usually reserved for inflectional categories that exhibit modality—the subjunctive, optative, etc. as opposed to the indicative" (1979:5). He dismissed the category of mood in English and even rejected the presence of subjunctive mood in the English grammar. In his scholarly work *Mood and Modality*, Palmer writes, "There is no need to be much concerned with the subjunctive in English. The only possible candidate for this is the simple form (identical with the infinitive) that is used in formal language after verbs of ordering, requiring, etc. This form has largely disappeared from English, and it can well be agrued that it has been replaced by the modal verbs, though traditional scholars may still argue for its use" (1979:7). Palmer, thus, rejected subjunctive and regards modal auxiliaries as its substitutes in English. He does not find any difference between subjunctive and simple present tense as their forms are the same.

Quirk and Greenbaum (1975) do not recognize mood as an important category in English and hence it has not been discussed in detail. They observe that "mood is expressed in English to a very minor extent by the subjunctive, as in, 'So be it then!' to a much greater extent by the past tense forms, as in, 'If you taught me, I would learn quickly' but above all, by means of modal auxiliaries, as in: 'It is strange that he should have left so early'" (1975:51). The above statement is incomplete and vague. It only makes us infer that recently the attitude of the grammarians towards mood has completely changed and as we have seen various criteria for the study of mood have failed to satisfy the grammarians.

Collins Cobuild English Grammar (1996) treats mood as a syntactic category that depends upon the order of words in a sentence. Collins's grammar holds that "the main clause of every sentence is in a particular mood" (Sinclair 1996:196). It lists three moods declarative, interrogative and imperative. For example, when we look at the following sentences:

John is an intelligent boy.

Is John an intelligent boy?

Go and bring a glass of water for me. ,

the word-order indicates that the first sentence is a statement, the second sentence is a question and the third sentence is a command. The first sentence, in which the subject is placed before the verb, is in the declarative mood whereas the second sentence, in which the main verb or auxiliary verb is placed before the subject, is in the interrogative mood. But the third sentence is an example of the imperative mood. In an imperative mood, subject is absent and the base form of the verb is placed in front of the clause.

After considering the views of some of the Traditional Grammarians, let us examine the views of some of the representative Structuralist and T.G. Grammarians on mood. Bloomfield, whose book *Language* (1933) is regarded as the manifesto of modern linguistics, mentions mode (mood) as one of the chief inflectional category discovered by the ancient Greek grammarians. However, he says that Greek linguists defined these inflectional categories not in formal terms that are identifiable but with respect to the abstract semantic implications. Discussing modes in English, Bloomfield says, "English has many modes distinguishing various approaches of an action to its actual occurrence" (1933:273). He regards mood as a formal category and chooses morphological and syntactic criteria for identifying and classfying them. Bloomfield writes, "morphologically, English distinguishes between 'real' (he is here) and 'unreal' (if he were here); syntactically, English recognises a whole series by the peculiarity of certain irregular ('auxiliary') verbs which are followed by an infinitive without to: he will write, shall write, can write, must write, may write" (Bloomfield 1933:273). He mentions indicative and subjunctive with regard to the verb of the clauses. Indicative refers to the real in clauses, whereas subjunctive refers to the unreal in clauses.

Noted linguist C.C Fries (1940) denies the existence of mood in English. He says that mood is absent in present-day English and instead of verbal inflections, modal auxiliaries are used to express various modalities. Referring to the subjunctive mood, he says, "In general the subjunctive has tended to disappear from use. This statement does not mean that the ideas formerly expressed by the inflectionally distinct forms of the verb, called the subjunctive, are not now expressed, but rather that their ideas are now expressed chiefly by other means, especially by function words" (Fries 1940:106). Some other prominent Structuralists like E.A. Nida (1964), H.A. Gleason (1965), Martin Joos (1964) do not discuss mood at all in their works. They discuss only modal auxiliaries.

T.G. Grammarians in their description of the structure of English syntax have not mentioned mood at all and represented the modal auxiliaries under the label of 'M'. We do not find any mention of the mood in the works of the distinguished T.G. Grammarians like Jacobs and Rosenbaum (1968), Lester (1971), and in *Syntactic Structures* (1957) and 'Aspects of the Theory of Syntax' (1965) by Noam Chomsky.

Halliday (1970) regards modality "a form of participation by the speaker in the speech event and is derived from the interpersonal function of language, language as expression of role" (Halliday 335). He believes that mood and modal auxiliaries are the two important grammatical categories that manifest the interpersonal function of the language. In *Language Structure and Language Function* (1970) Halliday quoting Sweet (1955) says that "subject and finite verbs are closely linked together, and combine to form the one constituent which we call mood. The mood is the element that realizes the selection of mood in the clause. It has sometimes been called the 'Modal' element; but the difficulty with this is that the term modal is ambiguous, since it corresponds both to mood and to modality" (Halliday 1970:73-74). In *Functional Diversity in Language*, Halliday writes that verbal as well as non-verbal means, like word-order and prosodic features, are used to represent modality. However, Halliday (1970:328-30) lists only modal auxiliaries among the verbal forms and does not mention moods at all.

Modal Auxiliaries

Having discussed the concept of mood, let us examine the category modal auxiliaries. Unlike the grammatical category 'mood', there seems to be some agreement among grammarians on the category of 'modal auxiliaries'. Modal auxiliaries are overtly realized in English. However, there are some differences among some English grammarians regarding the inventory of modal auxiliaries in English. In the first half of the 20th century, various auxiliaries like 'can', 'may', 'shall', 'will', 'must', 'ought', 'dare', 'need' etc. were treated separately and were not grouped together under the system of modals. Henry Sweet (1955), Jespersen (1969), Kruisinga and Erades (1960) and Strang (1962) do not distinguish a separate set of modal auxiliaries. It was in the 1960s that various grammarians like Sledd (1959), Martin Joos (1964), Twaddell (1965), Ehrman (1966), Palmer (1974), Leech (1971), Quirk and Greenbaum (1973), etc. discovered some common properties in these verbs and classified them as modals.

Ehrman (1966) includes 'can', 'will', 'shall', 'must', 'ought', 'dare' and 'need' in the list of modal auxiliaries and defines them as "that closed class of verbs which may occupy the first position of verb phrase, which may not be immediately preceded by another verb, which may invert with the subject in interrogation, and which are negated directly by 'not'" (Ehrman 1966:9).

Leech (1971) in addition to 'may', 'can', 'must', 'will', 'shall', 'need', 'ought to' also included 'have (got) to', 'am/is/are to' and '(had) better' and treated them as modals as they can be substituted by other modals and hence are also similar in meaning. Leech regards that the meanings of 'have (got) to' relates to 'must' and 'am/is/are + to infinitive' are similar in meaning to 'have (got) to' and 'ought to'. He chooses semantic criterion to describe various modal auxiliaries.

Quirk and Greenbaum (1973) list 'can', 'may', 'shall', 'will', 'must', 'ought to', 'dare' and 'need' as modal auxiliaries. They regard 'used to' as a marginal modal auxiliary as "it takes 'to-infinitive' and occurs only in the past tense" (1973:37). 'Dare' and 'need', according to them, can be used both as "modal auxiliaries (with bare infinitive and with no inflected-s form) or as lexical verbs (with to infinitive and with inflected-s form)" (1973:37). Quirk and Greenbaum define modals by following morphological and syntactic criteria. However, the use of modals, according to them, is governed by meaning categories like ability, compulsion, permission, etc.

Palmer (1986) follows formal criteria for defining modals in English. He includes 'may', 'can', 'must', 'ought to', 'will', 'shall' and marginally, 'need' and 'dare' (including might, could, would and should) in the list of his modals. According to him, modals exhibit what Huddleston (1976:333) has called the NICE (negation, inversion, code and emphasis) properties that distinguish them from main verbs. In addition to NICE properties modals also have some formal features that exclusively belong to them. Palmer lists the following formal features of modals:

> They do not co-occur: there is no 'will can come,' may shall be, etc.
>
> They have no '-s' forms for their 3rd person singular, e.g. 'He oughts to come.'
>
> They have no non-finite forms, e.g. 'to can' or 'canning'.
>
> They have no imperatives: 'can be here!' (1986:33-34).

In her work on modal auxiliaries, Jennifer Coates (1983) includes 'must', 'should', 'ought', 'may', 'might', 'can', could', 'will', and 'shall' in the list of modals. In this classification, she follows formal criterion to separate modal auxiliaries from main verbs. The first four of this list follow the NICE properties as marked by Huddleston (1976:333) and the last three follow the modal criteria (NO '-s' form for third person singular; no non-finite forms; no co-occurrence) as laid down by Palmer (1986:33-34) to exclude the auxiliaries 'be', 'have' and 'do' (Coates 1983:4). Coates regards 'have to', 'be going to', 'be able to', 'be bound to' as quasi-modals and excludes 'dare' and 'need' from her list as "the use of 'need' and 'dare' as modals as opposed to main verbs is rare and apparently on the decline" (1983:5).

Collins Cobuild English Grammar (1996) includes 'must', 'should', 'ought to', 'may', 'might', 'can', 'could', 'will', and 'shall' in its list of modals. 'Dare', 'need' and 'used to' do not find a place in this list of modals. Collins's Grammar calls them semi-modals for "they have some characteristics which other modals do not have" (Sinclair 1996:241). Modals are considered to be special kinds of auxiliary verbs used to make requests, offers, or suggestions, or to express our wishes or intentions. Modals are used to indicate our feelings about what we are saying (1996:217). Collins' Grammar extends the study of modals to Pragmatics and makes an important point that modals are also used to express politeness and tactfulness.

Referring to the use of modals, it is observed that "modals are mainly used when you want to indicate your attitude towards what you are saying, or when you are concerned about the effect of what you are saying on the person you are speaking or writing to" (1996:217). Modals are chiefly used to indicate the speaker's attitude when (s)he gives information; his/her attitude towards the things (s)he intends to do, or intends not to do; and his/her attitude to people, i.e. how (s)he affects and responds to a particular person or audience. The use of modals is situational and goal-oriented. Referring to pragmatic factors, Collins' Grammar observes, "Modals are often used to produce a particular effect, and the modal you choose depends on serveral factors, such as the relationship you have with your listener, the formality or informality of the situation, and the importance of what you are saying" (1996:218). Apart from pragmatic and registral characteristics of modals, Collins Grammar also discusses in detail the various formal characteristics of modals as discussed by Palmer and other grammarians.

Conclusion

This paper presented a critique of modality, mood and modal auxiliaries. This exercise, related to their brief historical discussion, helped us in building a conceptual background and removing many a misconception prevailing about the notions of modality, mood and modal auxiliaries. Thus, from the above discussion, we concluded that modality is a semantic notion used to refer to a number of semantic categories like question, assertion, request, ability, wish, permission, possibility, insistence, etc. Moods and modal auxiliaries are among the various grammatical means which can be used to express modality. We also observed that the concepts of mood and modality were interpreted differently by different grammarians and they even differed with each other in respect to the membership of modal auxiliaries. We further found that grammarians do not recogonize the existence of mood as a grammatical category in English. From the findings in the present paper we come to know that modal auxiliaries are the chief means of expressing modality.

REFERENCES

Austin, J.L. (1962). *How to Do Things with Words*. Oxford: Clarendon Press.

Bloomfield, L. (1933). *Language*. London: George Allen and Unwin Ltd.

Boyd, J. and J.P. Thorne (1969)., "The Deep Grammar of Modal Verbs". *Journal of Linguistics*. 5: 57-74.

Chomsky, N. (1957). *Syntactic Structures*. The Hague: Mouton.

——, (1965). *Aspects of the Theory of Syntax*. Cambridge, Mass: The M.I.T. Press.

——, (1981). *Lectures on Government and Binding*. Dordrecht: Foris.

——, (1995). *The Minimalist Program*. Cambridge, Mass: The M.I.T. Press.

Coates, J. (1983). *Semantics of the Modal Auxiliaries*. London, Canberra: Croom Lelm Ltd.

Ehrman, M. (1966). *The Meanings of Modals in Present-day English*. The Hague: Mouton.

Fries, C.C. (1940). *American English Grammar*. New York: Appleton-Century-Crofts, Inc.

Gleason, H.A. (1965). *Linguistics and English Grammar*. London: Holt, Rinehart and Winston, Inc.

Halliday, M.A.K. (1970a). "Functional Diversity in Language as Seen from a Consideration of Modality and Mood in English". *Foundations of Language*. Dordrecht: The Netherlands, 6: 322-65.

——, (1970b). "Language Structure and Language Function". In John Lyons (ed.), *New Horizons in Linguistics*. Harmondsworth: Penguin (4th Impression, 1973: 140-65).

——, (1973). *Explorations in the Functions of Language*. London: Edward Arnold (2nd Impression, 1974).

Huddleston, R.D. (1976). *Some Theoretical Issues in the Description of the English Verb*. Lingua 40: 331-83.

Jacobs, R.A. and P.S. Rosenbaum (1968). *English Transformational Grammar*. London: Blairdell Publishing Company.

Jespersen, O.C. (1969). *Essentials of English Grammar*. London: George Allen and Unwin Ltd.

Joos, Martin (1964). *The English Verb: Form and Meanings*. Madison and Milawaukee: The University of Wisconsin Press.

Khlebnikova, I.B. (1976). *The Conjunctive Mood in English*. The Hague: Mouton.

Kruisinga, E. and P.A. Erades (1960). *An English Grammar*. Groningen: Nordhoff.

Leech, G.N. (1971). *Meaning and the English Verb*. London: Longman.

Lester, M. (1971). *Introductory Transformational Grammar of English*. London: Holt, Rinehart and Winston, Inc.

Lyons, J. (1977). *Semantics*. Vol. 1 and 2. Cambridge: Cambridge University Press.

Myklestead, J.M. (1971). *An Advanced English Grammar for Students and Teachers*. New York: St. Martin's Press.

Nida, E.A. (1964). *A Synopsis of English Syntax*. Benjamin Elson (Ed.). Linguistic Series No. 4. A Publication of the Summer Institute of Linguistics of the University of Oklahoma.

Palmer, F.R. (1974). *The English Verb*. London: Longman.

——, (1979). *Modality and the English Modals*. London, New York: Longman.

Perkins, M.R. (1983). *Modal Expressions in English*. London: Frances Pinter.

Quirk, R. and S. Greenbaum (1973). *A University Grammar of English*. London: Longman.

Searle, J. (1969). *Speech Acts: An Essay in the Philosophy of Language*. Cambridge: Cambridge University Press.

Sinclair, J. (1990). *Collins Cobuild English Grammar*. London: Harper Collins.

Sledd, J. (1959). *A Short Introduction to English Grammar.* Chicago: Scott, Forsesman and Co.

Strang, Barbara M.H. (1962). *Modern English Structure.* London: Edward Arnold Ltd.

Sweet, H.C. (1955). *A New English Grammar.* Oxford: Clarendon Press.

Twadell, W.F. (1960). *The English Verb Auxiliaries.* Providence Rhode Island: Brown University Press.

Wittgenstein, I. (1953). *Philosophical Investigations.* Oxford: Blackwell.

Zandvoort, R.W. (1959). *A Handbook of English Grammar.* London: Longman.

14

The Socio-Cultural Aspects and Language Learning*

K. Balachandran

India is a land of rich social and cultural traditions. These have helped for a conglomeration of social institutions, customs, values, beliefs of different races, communities and regions. There is a relationship between Society and Education. Education involves Learning and Teaching. Education is one of the means for social development. A well-developed society is a prerequisite for educational excellence. Each (society and education) influences the other.

Education makes society and society moulds the educational system. Similarly culture makes society and society enlivens culture. Hence socio-cultural aspects play an important role in Language Learning. Learning a second language (English), in addition to one's own mother tongue is a necessity to everyone. It is easy for some and difficult for some others. Learning process involves both the teacher and the learner. Learning a language involves a link between the language forms and their meanings. The process involves (i) Form (ii) the Content, and (iii) The Association. The paper analyzes all these and other relevant aspects.

---

* Paper presented in the 'National Seminar on Second Language Acquisition/Learning' organized by Central Institute of Indian Languages, Mysore and Dept. of Linguistics, Uni. of Kerala, at Kariavattom, Trivandrum, 4th to 6th Dec. 2003.

Age is one of the prime factors in learning a language. Learning one's own mother tongue is generally believed to be easy for students. So language learning here indicates the second language learning. At present English is taught even at the pre-K.G and L.K.G. levels. Whether one's mother tongue is taught or not, English is compulsorily taught at this early age. It is due to many reasons. Parents believe that their children should be proficient in English (at the elementary and school levels). Once when they come to 10th standard or plus two level, they want their wards to get more marks in the III part subjects like Maths, Physics, Chemistry, 'Botany, Zoology, Computer Science, etc. to enable them get their B.E./M.B.B.S./ B.D.S. and other professional course seats easily. The interest which they had shown at first when their children were in the first to ninth standard, now completely changes after they come to 10th standard.

Sometimes parents (even students) think that conversing in their mother tongue is below their dignity and conversing in English brings them much respect. At times they don't write correctly even in their mother tongue because of their giving over-importance to the learning of English. So the period between three years to fourteen years in a student's life is very important in learning English. The students who learn English well during this period, have a good foundation in English and so they speak good English and write good English and get the subject groups as they like at higher secondary level and later at the collegiate level (provided they get good marks in the III part also).

The students who don't learn the second language properly during this period have to suffer at the higher secondary level and later too. This reflects in their performance even in other subjects. Students who study in their mother tongue medium, don't have this difficulty. But those who are made to study compulsorily (because of their parents' wishes) in English are the sufferers. They spend much of their time in memorizing the answers big and short. This may not help them always. That is why after the examinations they lament, "Memory failed me",

"Questions were tough", "Expected questions were not asked", etc.

Gender is a second factor which we have to consider in learning English. It is a general trend among the girl students to study with much effort and commitment. Hence the pass percentage is also higher when compared to that of boys at the 10th standard level, higher secondary level and at the collegiate level also. Boys study but the competitive spirit is still wanting in them. Since boys have very many other things to attend, they may not have much time (as girls have) to concentrate on their studies. It does not mean that boys are dull headed. When we see students who are going to higher jobs (IAS/IPS/ICS) and foreign countries, we notice that most of them are male students. The question of being a woman prevents the fair sex from preferring these two types of jobs. But today the trend has been changing slowly; it is also true. Boys are good at listening and speaking but when it is the question of writing, girls do comparatively good.

Social status (or economic status) is a third factor which plays an important role in learning the second language. If there are three divisions as (a) poor or lower class, (b) middle class, and (c) rich or upper class, it is the middle class which learns English language convincingly. The poor economic status prevents the parents from admitting their children in private (matriculation) schools, because these schools are beyond their means in the real sense. They cannot afford to spend much. Hence their children study in village panchayat, municipal or corporation schools. They are satisfied with 'whatever' English they learn from these schools. Parents who are highly ambitious and have high hopes of their sons and daughters, send them to private schools. In these institutions more importance is given to English and so they learn with much effort and the result is highly appreciable and rewarding.

The upper class forms lesser percentage and the students from this category who realize their responsibility learn the second language properly; those who do not realize, suffer. So it is the students from the middle class who are more well-equipped in the second language learning. This does not mean that there are no exceptions, (i) A student from poor class may become well-versed in English; (ii) A student from middle class may not become well-versed in second language learning; and (iii) All students from the rich class may not be well-versed in English. Exceptions are always there in all categories and this cannot be ruled out but this exception is only a negligible per cent.

Fourthly comes the factor of influence from the outside in learning a second language. This can be from (a) Teachers, (b) Classmates, (c) Friends, and (d) Relatives.

For many successful students, their teachers serve as their role models. This they may not utter openly but they cherish it in their heart of hearts. If a teacher takes good or real interest in imparting, the students get this first class learning from him. He motivates them properly and positively. Rank students, in addition to their hard work, have the support (guidance) of their teachers. Committed and inspiring teachers (in second language) are the real backbones of a well-educated society. Proficiency in second language learning is achieved if the teachers at the high school and higher secondary level are of this type. This kind of teacher is better than thousands of uninspiring and non-committed teachers.

One's classmates also play a significant role in the learning of English. Getting good name among their classmates, makes them hard working; at times, they feel like 'a cock among the hens'. Like minded students get on well in learning. Their mutual enthusiasm (friendship), helping nature, conversing habit in English, are surer ways of successful learning of English.

Another important influence in achieving efficiency in second language learning is one's friends. 'Tell me your friends! I will tell you who you are' says the proverb. One who has good circle of friends, achieves many laurels during one's school days. One who has bad circle of friends will be going in the wrong route. This kind of friendship spoils one's learning aptitude.

One's relatives also contribute constructively for achieving efficiency in second language learning. Relatives should be of helping tendency and encouraging nature. They should not be of fault finding types. Their encouraging words, "You speak good English", "You write good English", "On the other day I listened to your English oration which was good" are tonic-like to them. This may not be a major factor but even a minor factor cannot be neglected for successful learning of second language in one's learning process.

Learning a second language involves a link between the language forms and their meanings. For some students poetic form is appealing; for some this may be difficult. Some prefer prose forms (essay, fiction, short story, novella, novel). Some others prefer dramatic form (drama, one-act play). Some others may prefer science subjects and some others humanities. Everyone begins to study according to one's taste. According to his/her taste and proficiency, he/she studies and selects either poetry/prose (narrative) or dramatic form. This in future helps them to take the genre concerned for their M.Phil. or Ph.D. research (if they are students of literature).

Contents also decide one's successful learning of second language. Some like religious sentiments; some about nature; some about family relationship; some about crime and terror; some about adventure and patriotism, some about atheism, etc. As the wise saying, 'Taste differs' predicts even in selecting the contents of their study and specialization, students have their own likes and dislikes. How the students associate themselves with the form and content, make them proficient in second language learning. 'Healthy mind in a healthy body' is a meaningful maxim. So the emphasis is on both the healthy body and healthy mind. A student should have an alert mind always to observe, learn and preserve, what is taught in language classes. All the three activities are important in the learning process. If one just observes and hesitates to learn it is of no use—he is a lazy student. If one observes and learns, they are also not enough; he should not forget, remembering it, is needed. It is like saving money for the future.

A learner is a member either in the student circle (when he or she, stays in a hostel) or in the family circle (when he or she stays with his/her parents, brothers and sisters). This circle also decides a successful study of second language. Members in these circles should be helpful, adjustable and appreciable. Anything antagonistic, objectionable and negative will mar the successful process of learning a second language. For example, if he or she becomes an addict to liquor or 'Kanja, in his/her hostel (or to any other vice), the student will lose all interest in learning and his or her career will be a 'successful flop'. Congenial atmosphere (either at hostel or at home) is an added advantage for successful second language learning.

For all these, the initiative should come from the students. If they are inquisitive and dedicated, any hardship can be tackled and the target in second language learning can be achieved. If they are slackening and lazy they may dub "English is difficult", "It is a tough language", "I don't want to study/master English", "Who will read English?" It is the duty of the teachers mainly to see that the second language learning is designed as a pleasurable activity—a pleasing one to the learner also. It does not relegate the responsibility of the parents who have also a significant role in motivating their sons and daughters in learning a second language. They are the watchdogs and indirectly the beneficiaries. Hence it is the collective effort of a student, teacher and his/her parents which decide the successful learning of a second language. Let the students love their teachers and their parents. Let them love English and English will love them in turn.

RECOMMENDED BOOKS

E.G. Vedanayagam, *Teaching Technology for College Teachers*, Sterling Publishers Pvt. Ltd., New Delhi, 1989.

Rod Ellis, *The Study of Second Language Acquisition*, OUP, New York, 1994.

Vivian Cook, *Second Language Learning and Language Teaching*, Arnold, New York, 1996.

15

Linguistic Complexities and Realizations: A Tribute to Rajul Bhargava

Bernice J.M. West and *Michael H. Lyon*

Sifting and choosing authentic language styles to reflect lived experiences and analytical ideas requires the deployment of existing language forms and the generation of new approaches. The metalingustic uses of language are challenging not only to poets and linguists but also to social scientists who are concerned with the process of cultural engagement whilst carrying out research and writing in publications as authors. The present psychologists and sociologists are primarily writing up their studies of migration and marriage; of old age and health; of culture and identity; of retirement and return; of business and settlement amongst a key diasporic community namely the Leva Patels of Charotar. In pursuing these investigations we have developed and adopted a constructivist research practice.[1] This approach denotes the whole sequence by which phenomena are actively construed in origin, by what means evidence is collected and the process of reporting a firmly coordinated analysis. Thus research procedures have to be clearly plural in embracing these consecutive stages of investigation. The mode of enquiry operates in stages by following sequence. Firstly by understanding problematic processes of social and psychological construction, and then by pursuing thematic meanings in 'parallel' to actual generative events. Finally by holding all of the dual practical concerns in a close 'matching' relationship the constructivist research aims to build and transmit knowledge in a multi-disciplinary way.[2] All stages of the process are important but in this tribute attention concentrates on writing-up practices.

The opportunity of writing this tribute article to Professor Bhargava has been an intriguing experience. There is a common interest in the Indian Diapsora[3] and the construction of narrative, albeit from very different disciplinary perspectives. Bhargava's recent writings[4,5,6] have brought to consciousness a number of realizations about our own authorship namely the rich diversity of linguistic expressions used to connote meaning, the potential thematic expansiveness of the written language and the value of experimenting with form and grammatics to present a rich textural account.

In this contribution "Linguistic Complexities and Realisations: A Tribute to Rajul Bhargava" the authors use a reflexive approach. By presenting four literary forms, which move through different modes of autobiographical cultural engagement key aspects of an "outsider" perspective on India, are articulated.

1. Writing and Language: Diary Excerpts of Personal Naive Exchanges

The first set of writings is taken from personal diary excerpts and provides a somewhat solipsistic account of experiences over a 17-year period.

> I was walking behind my husband and a senior academic as we moved through his natal village. I saw a woman bent over a wood fire making unleavened bread. I stopped and tried to speak with her and ask her to show me how she did the feat. Slapping millet or wheat dough between her hands until a large circle formed which she then threw onto a hot iron plate and in a few minutes—fresh *rotis* or *chapattis* or *bakri*. I made one with her, much to her amusement and as we walked off our host explained my behaviour in terms of Christian love. (1986)
>
> When visiting friends the women have been very concerned about my colour change and the browning of my skin because of sun exposure. Some think I have

> whitened the inner aspect of my forearms and turn my arm over and try to scrape the white off. Today people asked "What has happened to your face (when it goes red and then brown)?" Several told me "You should cover it with watermelon or wear a cap". "You should stay white—it is better. Use a whitening cream—see!". (1990)
>
> Yesterday I visited the home of our servant and ate a meal which she had prepared. "You should not go there Bernice she is without caste!!" "So am I, Krishna" was the reply to my Brahminical friend. (1996)
>
> Increasingly over the years I have become concerned to understand the culture and symbolism of caste in new ways. Like class, its relations can be pathological and maleficent but at the same time fascinating and gripping. Individuals may try not to subscribe but in Indian society cultural resistance is almost impossible. Caste permeates the social structure and the minds of people. In India, caste is everywhere in all communities whether they are Hindu, Muslim or Christian. (2000)
>
> It is impossible to live in Gujarat for any length of time without becoming caste conscious. As a white European I am highly visible to an essentially rural people. In many contexts and encounters I seem to be exempted from caste maybe because of race preference. This has been brought home to me on several occasions in the form of colour preference. Caste distinctions, beliefs, and behaviours are highly visible and meant to be seen. Caste is exclusive and mean of spirit, and is sustained in the present day through notions of hierarchy, caste organisation, absurdity and occupational deformity. (2003)

The diary extracts use emotional language, draw on personal encounters and real exchanges with female friends. In the latter excerpts an attempt is made to be a little more existential but the language used is still so personalized and value embedded that the soliloquy continues in a diary form.

Bhargava[7] has suggested that language can become an "interpretant" and cites poststructuralist discourses which suggest the privileged position of language is derived from experience and subject to changing connotations. The diary excerpts illustrate the complexity of understanding caste as an outsider and illustrate bizarre experiences of personal engagement and dissonance which for an insider may be totally straightforward and obvious.

2. Social Exchange: Field Notes of Practical Observations in Language

In the article entitled "Grammatics and Diasporic Identity: The poesis of Sujata Bhatt" Bhargava[8] introduces us to the power of language to this poet who in her writings creates dialectic discourses of identity. Bhatt[9] herself in an interview for the Poetry Archive described the Gujarati language and her Indian childhood as constituting "the deepest layer of my identity". English, however is the language she speaks every day and generally writes in. The duality of her linguistic heritage and her dual identity are explored through her poetry. Bhargava addresses these potential dilemmas through an appreciation of poems from the volume "Her mother's way of wearing a sari"[10] and develops an analysis of the semiotics of language. Bhargava[11] tells us that all Bhatt's language associations are to do with her mother tongue (Gujarati). Bhatt herself explores the repercussions and implications of her divided heritage most explicitly in "Search for My Tongue"[12] which alternates between the two languages. This interest in weaving two languages together to construct a narrative demands attention to particular turns of phrase and nuances in order to convey hidden meanings. The duality may involve tensions and produce a combined language such as Hinglish which is amongrel but resolved form in itself.

The following extract from a set of researcher field notes provides an awareness of the intermingling of archaic and modern expressions with pragmatically constructed language forms in order to support or even enable active communication.

Field Notes on Cultural Engagement

The Indian English language has continually been interesting to us when working as researchers in Gujarat. Whilst many people we met and interviewed spoke English the variants ranged from what the speaker referred to as Pukkha English to the more antiquated Indian English. Yann Martell in the introduction to the "Life of Pi"[13] tells the story of being at the railway station and asking the ticket wallah "Are you trying to bamboozle me"? And his reply was "There is no bamboozlement here sir". This he cites as an example of the Indians love of words and language. Indeed after a couple of months in Gujarat we start to speak Indian English also. For to be natural in our own dialect was to invite confusion and sometimes the indignant response that we do not speak proper English. The latter can be galling. Over the years we have worked at learning the Gujarati language. Despite purchasing the infamous "Gujarati in Thirty Days"[14] (20 years ago) we still have minimal formal mastery of the language. Rather we have devised an intermediate language to enable us to communicate socially. Our oral comprehension of Gujarati speech varies. When the social context is predictable there can be considerable intuitive understanding of what is being said. Where encounters are out of the blue the language is lost and we typically revert to English or an interpreter.

Another complicating factor for us is the similarity between Gujarati and Hindi words and the peppering of the language with occasional English phrases. In the bazaar when we asked for "Half Kg Bhindi; half Kg Brinjals; ketla rupia?" We were told "You speak very nice Hindi". Gratifying but we believed ourselves to be speaking pidgin Gujarati. This example begins to illustrate part of our intermediate language. We have found a way of phonetically writing the Gujarati words which we hear in Roman script. Our first teacher Varsha from her living room in Aberdeen provided us with an

> array of phrases which allowed us to enter into social contexts and leave them graciously. We wrote down all of these Gujarati phrases with a Scottish phonetic emphasis. This resulted in strong vowel sounds and Gujarati with a Scottish accent—much to the subsequent amusement of many native Gujarati speakers. Our ability to phonetise the language into Roman script was regularly shared with others whilst conducting our research in Charotar villages. This often caused amusement and then correction of our English phonetization of the Gujarati language. People could not believe what they were hearing such as "Mane cha dudh ane kand vugurni" (I take my tea without any sugar or milk). In the land where Chai Masala (spiced tea boiled with sugar and milk) rules, asking for tea without milk or sugar was most unusual. Often this gave the license for teasing and easing the social situation with older people asking if water was wanted in the tea or just the leaves by themselves.

This description of an intermediate type of language-use provides an awareness of implicit freedom of expression and the dynamic nature of reasoning. The nature of language in culture, in expression and in exchange is never axiomatic.

3. Participatory Language: Cultural Dialogue and Development

In our narrative constructions based on the oral tales told to us by migrants we have attempted to articulate the voice in such a way as to enable readers to appreciate the meanings behind the stories.[15] Where we have been listening to accounts of the lives of our informants for a long time we have struggled to convert what the scientist would term longitudinal data from a series of interviews, conversations and observations—and to transform these into a constructed narrative. Initially in transcribing, reporting and analyzing we collaborated with the orthodox demands of social science method and produced sound research reports[16] which seemed to rob the personal narrative from the characters who informed us. More recently we have deployed alternative writing styles. The authors now aim to retell stories in such a way as to build knowledge and to allow the speaking voice to come through into the writing.[17]

Cultural Engagement: Living with Savitaben

We first met Savitaben in 1986 when we stayed in her home in the village. Her husband had invited us and introduced us to his mother and his wife. She spoke no English and we very little Gujarati. At this time her sons were completing their education as engineers. They were hopeful of going to the US but she was adamant that she would never be going and laughed when we suggested that she would. She was the Bahu and looked after most of the household, milking the three buffaloes in the byre beside the kitchen and preparing food for the family. Each day she went to the temple and bound thread around the banyan tree.

The household had a pre-determined routine which was mysterious to us. It involved waking at 5.00 am, boiling water for bathing, looking after the farm and beasts and preparing food. Her mother-in-law was 80 years old but still active in looking after herself and in carrying out some household duties. The household shrine was lit in the morning and the evening and looked after by the women.

Savitaben was curious about our conjugal relations and why I did not have gold and kept trying to ask about the number of Tolas there were. She showed me her gold locked in a metal box in a cupboard in the house which contained all the gold ornaments and jewelery she had received when she married and subsequently over the 20 years of her marriage. As a married woman Bernice too should have Tolas. A wedding ring was insufficient evidence of marital status and wealth.

She never spoke to Gopalbhai directly in company and he told us "we never use one anothers names". She never ate with us. Indeed when we were hungry we turned up in the kitchen sat on the floor and a Thali was put in front of us with food, as we finished one portion of sag aloo or dhall or puree another was put out until we reached the point of surrender.

Eighteen years later when we met her again things had changed. She called her husband Gopalbhai and he used her name directly to her, she came and sat with us to drink tea and conversed in English.

The two sisters Savitaben and Vimlaben had just returned from the USA with Gopalbhai. In their retirement both sets of couples had emigrated to the USA to be with their sons' families in New Jersey. Vimlaben's husband died three years ago. For the last five years they have been living with their children in New Jersey and visiting Gujarat occasionally. All had become US citizens and the women worked at English in order to successfully undertake the naturalization and citizenship interviews.

By now Savitaben was well into her 60s and had the experience of living in the USA. We too had changed after 20 years of regular visits to Gujarat. This time Bernice was wearing Shalwar Khamees and a mungulasutra. The necklace was worth four Tolas. Savitaben asked about this immediately when we met again. She wanted to know about Bernice's gold bangles. Bernice said "I only have one worth five Tolas!!" This caused great hoots of laughter. Some things never change!

This story told in a fairly light narrative style but at the same time introduces a number of complex socio-cultural themes: household ritual; gender relations; symbols of respectability and processes of cultural engagement over time.

Bhargava sees narratives everywhere—across all spatial and temporal dimensions and inextricably linked to one another and considers storytelling and story listening as basic ways of thinking about the world.

Articulating and reporting complex stories with authenticity as a cultural outsider is challenging. Over the years in the social sciences there have been attempts at experimentation and search for new form.[18] Methodological purists may cavil at the limitations of form and stylistics. But innovation in writing style and the use of language should not be disregarded. Literary expositions ensure that the reporting of research involving people and culture remain living documents.

4. Complex of Culture: Poetic Ambivalence

Sujata Bhatt when being interviewed said "I think there is a level of dialogue that one can achieve in writing that one cannot in speaking, and poetry of course also involves metaphor and a subtle nuance with language that one may not come up with when one is speaking.... I think one enters a very private and inner world where the most intimate things can be spoken about in a poem, or alluded to in a poem, and I think one wouldn't have that quietness or concentration in a conversation". In this final example of literary form to illustrate cultural engagement we reflect upon poetry.

The substantive content of this poem concerns love of India obsessively/critically—from inside and also, through separation, from 'outside'. What is of general interest, in this remote context of overseas writing, is how a poetic form might be useful to articulate such ideas, experiences, and (above all) feelings towards Indian culture and its affirmation.

BHARATI

Bharati, beauty, why are you so?
My love is fast and yours so slow.

Such culture-style and poise in peace.
What cosmos dreams of sure surcease.

Who holds pent achings down below
lets life-gathered waters still flow.

We dance the Gurba. All clap hands
to village smiles, while harvest stands.

Though when you're by yourself, my love
sad-sweetest smiles I see
Preparing face to greet the world
not being fairly free.

Do proper job! Beyond all health
Pure person, but no self.
How can you be, when you don't work:
an antique off the shelf?

You're safe in slowest lanes
with holy mother cow.
And sure the fastest always wins.
What smart Western know-how.

Bharati calls "We do one thing"
and saying, cast the magic ring.

Tight ritual-bound, in monsoon seas.
A monkey prays—the migrant flees.
She sits upon the golden floor
for time shall tyrannise no more.

The best is given, without a cost-
such pacts of gain should not be lost?

My missing's keenest in the night
(and busied labours past
When seeling dark scarfs up the will)
you call me back at last.

Let us define the form first; then examine its operation, in linguistic analysis. Poesy is a piece of contrived culture and also a neatly worked-out communication. The poet is universally recognizable as a word-smith with a very distinctive task:

(i) To make a language piece and form which is relatively removed and self-contained—as it follows very coded rules—preferably (but not necessarily) in considered writing;

(ii) Yet which bears an analogical relation to other meaning-worlds for the reader by means of powerful devices—metaphor, simile, allegory, etc.—which make key language allusions transferable, and the meanings transformable, by both parties.

(iii) A poem's form registers the special 'inner' authority of its language rhythms and endings; its verse-organization and cultural claims to be (metaphysically) real.

Perhaps the "Bharati" poem presented requires some personal reflection by its author amounting to an analysis, or confession, of the poetic means and values employed?

In this case, the love-theme is mainly one of ambivalence which is declared to be so because of separation: resulting from the pleasure of participation and the pain of parting and absence. The critical mixture, and tone, in personal loving, however, also indicate and reflect a fierce sense of frustration in culturally arrested participation. The poem is pent by good appreciations: of attractions, beauty and village fulfilments.

But the chiding male voice, in this one-sided dialogue, introduces severe reservations as the part-outsider (with knowledge) and English critic from a doubtful vantage point about the modern unacceptability of woman's role (in pleasing and employment); regarding the peculiar Indian sense of time (cosmic, valorised and 'unpunctual'); and in respect of ritual bonds (in temples and dances)—which may be external and unintelligible—certainly hard of intimate access. For these cultural exchanges do not depend crucially on words: they involve more fundamentally body-language and fulfilments; participations and beliefs; cultural competencies and high values.

In fact the crucial meanings taken out of poetry depend on the readers perceptions, interests and needs. What is important for cultural research, and social scientific interest, is to understand this reception/reader end of the whole poetic process.

Devotees might see poetry as wonderful in dealing with all of these things too: believing that poetry is an apotheosis for the whole culture; possibly our common culmination in writing, the offering of a set of transcendent meanings, to be universalised and appropriated. However, the importance of the non-language values (mentioned above) also suggest that this claim for exaltation might well be greatly exaggerated. The language skills and appeals identified above as culturally powerful, also have their dark side. Poetry-haters, especially small boys, resent the induced euphoria of contrivance and any false sentimentalisation of feelings. As Bhargava[19] wisely says: words can be enemies, as well as best friends.

Three correlative aspects for the abuse of poetry-in-culture may be identified:

(a) The **autochthnonous,** neat, format can be a convenience packet for manipulators and consumers—in most propaganda and advertisements—in deceptions and jingles.

(b) As **surrogate**-realities, poems are shallow language-devices and may convey, or open up an over-easy alternative world of cushioned comfort. So, for casual readers (or hearers) they can serve to gratify escapist impulses, fantasisation indulgences, heroic dreams and wish fulfilments which need not, indeed should not, be taken seriously.

(c) **Poetic reader-reception** involves a privileged opportunity to select (and to avoid) poetic communications freely. The ability to transform the understandings in personal application—is culturally open and free, even comparatively 'wild' in literature and extraordinarily irresponsible in psychology. The gems that refract all meanings, cannot (without engineering) provide readers with a clear focus on the relevant value.

If the presented poem can reach urban Indians, who are more 'modern' and potentially critical of village traditions, or appeal to Diasporic Indians whose dual identities are fraught with feeling and sub-liminal in the working out of language and consciousness—so much the better. If indigenous Indians perceive how the outside world understands their cultural peculiarities, this could be interesting when India becomes a hegemonic power. Authorially, however, more immediate considerations are driving pressures for relief after personal disruption and the management of pain; researcher-reservations about repeated distancing and memories of close friendships; also a craving to return to the beloved ancient New World.

Final Thoughts

The more mundane, ordinary or 'plain' types of language materials which we have considered so far—solo diaries, observational notes and memos, recorded sequences of dialogue, etc.—have modest aims which serve an appropriate, controlled and practical purpose. These more prosaic materials, as recorded in writing, are more clear in reference; more tied down in context, memory and conveyance; more accountable, in scientific terms, to the reader; and, therefore more specific about their audiences' knowledge, purposes and validations.

Written language, both from an authorial and a readership perspectives, has been conventionalised into many purposes into types of sub-cultural or literary material. We feel that there need be no single hierarchy of worth between the considered array of literary forms and types of language [such as diaries, memos, transcriptions, reports and poems] since they serve a clear plurality of purposes and a variety of receivers. Each cultural set should be sufficient to itself and valuable in its own relatively pragmatic terms.

As Bhargava[20] says "Language makes meaning by transforming meaning". From our perspective the craft of the author is to use language, form and style in order to participate actively in this transformation process.

NOTES

1. M.H. Lyon and Bernice J.M. West (2004). "Patel Migrants: Pioneer Narratives of Self-identity" in Sharma Pal and Chakrabati (Eds), *Contextualising Nationalism*

Transnationalism and Indian Diaspora, New Delhi: Creative Books.

2. B.J.M. West and M.H. Lyon (2007). *Cultural Care and Indian Elders: Hindu Spiritual Life in the Ashram Spirituality and Health International* 8, pp. 135-47.
3. See contributions in R. Bhargava and Shubshree (Eds) (2004). *Of Narratives and Narrators*, New Delhi: Rawat Vedam Books.
4. R. Bhargava (2004). "Grammatics and Diasporic Identity: The Poiesis of Sujata Bhatt" in Sharma Pal and Chakrabati (Eds), *Interpreting Indian Diasporic Experience*, New Delhi: Creative Books.
5. R. Bhargava and Shubshree, 2004, *Ibid.*
6. R. Bhargava (Ed) (2002). *Indian Writing in English: The Last Decade*, New Delhi: Rawat Vedam Books.
7. R. Bhargava, 2004, *Ibid.*
8. R. Bhargava, 2004, *Ibid.*
9. S. Bhatt Recording made for *The Poetry Archive* on 1st September, 2005 at The Audio Workshop, London and produced by Richard Carrington.
10. S. Bhatt (2000). *My Mother's Way of Wearing a Sari*, New Delhi: Penguin.
11. R. Bhargava, 2004, *Ibid.*
12. S. Bhatt (2002). *Search for My Tongue*, New Delhi: Penguin.
13. Yann Martell, *The Life of Pi.*
14. Gujarati in 30 days.
15. M.H. Lyon and B.J.M. West (2004). "Constructivist Writing: Working with Patel Tales" in Barghava R and Shubshree (Eds), *Ibid.*
16. M.H. Lyon and B.J.M. West (1995). *London Patels: Caste and Commerce*, New Community 213, pp. 399-419.
17. B.J.M. West and M.H. Lyon (2007). *Ibid.*

18. The early work of John Berger is one of the best examples.
19. R. Bhargava, 2004, *Ibid.*
20. R. Bhargava, 2004, *Ibid.*

16

Ebonics

J. Samuel Kirubahar and
Anita Evelyn

Origin of Ebonics

Ebonics, translated literally, means "Black Sounds". Historically, in psychology, it is referred to by the name Black English. 'Ebonics' is a way of communicating used primarily by African Americans. In the beginning, black people lived in Africa and there were no black people in America until the slave trade began. Blacks in Africa spoke thousands of languages, often wildly varying from village to village. During the age of imperialism, traders from Western Europe communicated with the natives of their colonies via simplified languages collectively known as Pidgin, which mixed a European vocabulary with a native grammar. Many different forms of Pidgin have been devised and the forms of pidgin used in West Africa and the South Pacific are the most widespread today.

After slaves were trapped, they were sent to forts on the West African coast to be collected and shipped to the New World. They were surrounded by people speaking a variety of different languages, and were taught the basics of Pidgin by the slave traders. This was the basis of their communication with plantation owners upon their arrival in America.

"Ebonics" generally refers to the evolved form of this Pidgin English spoken in the United States. It is different from the slave languages of the Caribbean. In the South, whites originally spoke a British style of English, while blacks originally spoke in Pidgin. However, white children were usually raised by a slave nanny, and often played with a slave playmate. These interactions during the formative stages of language acquisition meant that, Ebonics began to sound more like Queen's English, and the white southerners' speech began to sound, blacker. This was something they often tried to cover up in the circles of aristocracy.

The structure of speech in Ebonics can be analyzed and related to African language structures as well as to the black experience in America (for a detailed analysis, see Spears, 1984; Smitherman, 1991). Ebonics began its nationwide spread after the end of the Civil War, when many blacks in the South were suddenly free to move to major cities in the North. Soon, cities all over the country had black populations speaking Ebonics.

Coinage

'Ebonics' is a term which was introduced by Black linguists in the mid-1970s. The word Ebonics was coined by Robert L. William's from the words 'Ebony and Phonics' at the 1973 Conference on Cognitive and Language Development of the Black Child to describe Black English Vernacular (BEV) in the linguistic community. It refers not only to a particular grammar and syntax, but also to paralinguistic (i.e. noises such as laughing and crying) and to the gesture (movement) of African American communication. This term is the offshoot of a broader outlook called Afrocentrism, an ideology which holds that, identity is based solely on skin color and that blacks have a unique culture, history and even language.

Understanding Ebonics

"Ebonics" definitely qualifies in the definition of "language", which is a system of communication between humans through written and vocal symbols; a speech peculiar to an ethnic, national or cultural group. (*Noah Webster Lexicon Dictionary* 1980)

There are two schools of thought regarding the origin of Ebonics—the Anglican-based tradition and the African-based tradition. The Anglican tradition believes that Ebonics is traceable to British dialects of Old and Middle English, which the slave picked up from white immigrants who settled in the south during the colonial era. As a result, they assert that Ebonics is just archaic white speech that has been sustained by linguistic isolation (Krapp 1925, Kurath 1949).

The African-based tradition asserts that Ebonics is really Africanized English, which can be traced to the formation of English Pidgins and Creoles during the slave trade. This perspective views Ebonics developing as a result of a language combining various European languages (Joycelyn Landrum-Brown PHD 1995).

The following is an excerpt from a conversation between two fourth grade Ebonics speakers (Clark, Eschholz, Rosa 1994):

> Jimmy: Hey Ms. Smith, d'ya evvah watch Kung Fu on TV wif dat dude...wha's his name?
>
> David: He have my name, Jimmy. He David, too.
>
> Jimmy: Yeah, dat's right. Dat's duh dude's name.
>
> Ms. Smith: Yes, I've watched it a few times. It's really an exciting show.
>
> David: Did you evvah see how he throw all does dudes around', an' how he use his legs?
>
> Jimmy: Yeah, You know what? He can really fight. He don't fight to be mean dough (though). He fight to be good, and he he'p people. An' he always duh good guy.
>
> David: You know what? He one of does pries' or somefin'. Hey Ms. Smith, what is he? I can't remembah what dey call'.
>
> Ms. Smith: Have you ever heard of the word "monk"?
>
> Jimmy: No, what dat?
>
> David: It's one does pries', I think, ain't it? Yea, it one does pries' dat live wif ovvah pries', dose monks. He live in a convent like.
>
> Jimmy: In wha'? Wha's dat?

David: Ah man, ain't you know what dat is? It's where dey have people dat...people like pries' an' nuns live' dere.

Jimmy: No, but ain't he live in du desert? He always be walkin' on a desert on TV.

David: No, but he ain't live in duh desert. He don't walk dere all duh time. He don't live dere. He jus' be walkin' dere sometime'. He move aroun' a lot, you know. He travel all different places.

Jimmy: I'm wonderin' where he learn everyfin'.

David: He learn' in duh convent when he young, I think.

Dat's where dey say on TV one time.

Let's compare this excerpt to the properties of 1st language acquisition. The use of duh, dat, dose, dere, and dey is the same as the two year old usage of 'd' for 'th' during the 1st stages of acquisition. Another characteristic in the Ebonics' excerpt is the optional usage of the 's' ending for plurals. This is also a morphological characteristic during 2nd stages of 1st language acquisition. There is confusion in the use of the 's' by 1st language learner at about the age of three where plurality is concerned and they add 's' to every word such as 'foots' or 'feetes' or not using the 's' at all. Another shared characteristic between 1st language acquisition and Ebonics is the use of 'ed'. There is minor chaos with this addition to where it is added to everything as in 'walkeded' and 'wented'. (G. Yule, 1996).

As Blacks moved North during the Industrial Revolution displacing many immigrants in the slum areas of the big cities, their language became that of an isolated community. The restricted social environments fostered continuation of features of Black Speech development. The absence of sustained social and cultural contact with mainstream America created a linguistic situation in which Black Speech was relatively free from White American English influences.

Terms like "copping a plea" and "shucking" and "jiving" became terms used within the community of the Blacks when dealing with whites. When providing themselves minimal comforts and opportunities in cities that allowed "restricted access" to hotels and restaurants, Blacks were often forced to recognize that it was to their advantage economically and socially to play the "part". Images of Blacks and their speech were perpetuated through the entertainment world.

Radio also helped provide the stylized Black Speech and language to even a larger audience. The result was some degree of homogenization in at least the speech structures and styles used by those who had roles, which put them in association with whites. We must realize that Ebonics is a culturalized element of Black America and just as any other language; it carries the culture of its people. This is why so many Native American people are so concerned about losing their language because then they lose their history, their identity and ultimately their culture is wiped out.

There are, for sure, a lot of terms that are not always consistently used. Many of the terms come into use quickly and go out of use just as quickly. To some extent, this problem is hard or even impossible to avoid. When so much about human language remains only partially understood, it should come as no surprise that new attempts to understand will succeed only partially—if at all. Even basic terms such as language and dialect are subject to innumerable controversies. A problem with the language/dialect distinction is that history shows, that today's dialect can become tomorrow's language.

Many scholars in the social and behavioral sciences contend that the lexicons and grammars of different languages and sometimes of different dialects within the same language are associated with somewhat different cognitive patterns. Yet researchers report that groups who speak different languages often categorize their experiences in very different ways. This linguistic divergence presumably is not due to genetic variation among ethnic groups but instead to differences in their cultural conditioning and environmental exposures.

In 1976, Dr. Sheila Mayers, a Black linguist, wrote that African-American modes of communication and expression, or what she called Ebonics, are grounded in African World View, a view which she claimed emphasizes rhythm, analogy, metaphor, and intuition. Over the past twenty years, several other Black linguists have maintained that Ebonics is based on an African perspective which, they say, differs radically from Euro Western views of nature and reality.

If one actually researches the high concentration of specific tribes in geographically different places and then looks at how African language evolved in America, one notices that 'Ebonics' salvages cultural integrity from the European Wreck and honors the ancestors. It is an attempt by African-Americans to remember the African Holocaust and keep alive the tongues of their ancestors. Flagrant denigration of Ebonics is a demand by European-Americans that they deny their roots, their mother tongue, their ancestors and their curious ability to survive.

Many people are of the view that 'Ebonics' is actually a method for teaching Standard English to children who speak Black English. They consider that the goal of Ebonics is to make teachers aware that children who speak Black English are using a different grammatical structure, which causes misunderstanding, and allow teachers to use the children's knowledge of Black English as an aid in teaching Standard English. While, some people consider Ebonics as slang, this is a stereotypical term, and therefore cannot be used as an absolute to describe a multitude of people.

Standard African American English, or "Ebonics" as it is popularly known, is a legitimate, linguistically and sociologically accepted dialect of Standard American English. Its origin is a mixture of English and languages from the Niger-Congo linguistic group. The vocabulary is almost entirely English or modified English, but the grammar and pronunciation still reflect African language families in syntax and word order. It maintains other peculiarities like pronunciations that almost never end in a consonant or replacing "th" sounds with "S" or "F," which is something that new African immigrants still demonstrate in their efforts to speak English.

From a social perspective, Black Vernacular English or as it is often called, African American Vernacular English (AAVE), is fundamentally a spoken language, which encompasses the vernacular speech of blacks. Each of the black vernacular languages emerge within a particular racial and cultural context. Most significantly, the roots of Black Vernacular English lie in the experience of slavery and in the cultural collision between a multitude of African languages and an English-speaking dominant culture.

The initial evaluation of Black Vernacular English was that it was merely an imperfectly learned approximation of "real" English, differing from it because the speakers were careless and lazy and didn't "follow the rules". It was seen as dialect, in the deprecating use of the word, or slang. The hypothesis was that Black children were "linguistically deprived," and that they were either not exposed to the English language as much as other children or that the language they were exposed to was in some way vastly inferior and didn't allow them to develop linguistically as they should have.

Black English (or Black Vernacular English) has grammatical characteristics similar to other English based Creoles. There exists a continuum between Black Vernacular English and Standard English, as usually occurs with post-creoles and their "parent" languages. Individuals have large ranges of variance between their ethnic dialect and Standard English. Black Vernacular English is often unintelligible to speakers of Standard English. Cross-cultural misunderstanding, arising from wrong assumptions, often occurs when a speaker of Standard English encounters Black Vernacular English. The majority of English speakers tend to think Black Vernacular English, apart from the special slang; it is simply an impoverished version of English with a lot of grammatical mistakes.

There is a difference between making grammatical mistakes in Standard English and speaking correctly in a different variety of the language, one with a slightly different grammar, as is the case with Black Vernacular English which indeed has a regular, systematic grammar of its own. In African-American Vernacular English the copular verb 'be' can be omitted provided all of the following conditions are met:

- It must not be accented. You never leave 'is' out of something like 'There already is one!'

- It mustn't end the sentence. You never say, 'I don't know what it is' without the 'is'.
- It mustn't begin the sentence. You never leave out the 'is' in a question like 'Is dat right?'
- It mustn't be an infinitive. You never leave out 'be' in something like 'You got to be strong' or an imperative like 'Be careful', or in one of those habitual aspect cases like 'He be laughin'.
- It mustn't be in the past tense. You never leave out 'was' or 'were'.
- It mustn't be negated. You never leave out 'ain't' from something like 'He ain't no fool'.
- It mustn't be first person singular. You never leave out the 'am' of sentences like 'I'm yo' main man'.

From these and other readily observable examples, it isn't difficult to conclude that the only reasons for the early results that implied that Black Vernacular English was an "impoverished" version of Standard English were simply artifacts of invalid methods of data gathering and interpretation.

Actually, from a linguistics standpoint, it is still argued whether Ebonics is a form of slang or a dialect. It is a variant of English, but bears enough differences in vocabulary and grammar to exceed slang. Furthermore, it is spoken by a small, ethnically distinct group, which reinforces the categorization. It is assumed that speakers of Ebonics are lazy or uneducated smacks of racism.

Perhaps before we begin to decide whether "Ebonics" is a dialect or a slang, we should consider that African-American Vernacular English, also referred to as Ebonics, is a variety of English. It is a marker of ethnic identity and also a symbol of youth culture like rap. It is found among African-Americans but not all of them speak it and the features of Ebonics are more common in informal speech than in formal speech and it is more common among working-class than among middle-class speakers. The working-class speakers often see Ebonics as a marker of African-American identity and that the language can be used to gain a sense of community. They also feel that social networks may affect the influence of Ebonics.

Attitudes towards Ebonics bear the stamp of prejudice of what Ebonics is and what it says about the people who speak it. Many people think of Ebonics as broken English and the prejudices against Ebonics are closely related to racial and ethnic conflicts. There is a debate in the US among linguists about whether Ebonics is a dialect of English or whether it is a Creole language. One important issue that all linguists seem to agree on is that Ebonics is "structured and rule-governed". According to the Creole variety view Ebonics was developed on the plantations in the southern states of America when Africans were brought to America as slaves. The African slaves are supposed to have learnt English from only a few native speakers and this would then have led to the development of a Pidgin language which expanded to a Creole language. Other linguists do not believe in this theory. They argue that the conditions for the emergence of a Creole language were never met in the USA. They refer to a number of features of Ebonics which they claim come from older varieties of English that were once widely spoken. These linguists are the ones who argue that Ebonics is merely a dialect of Standard English.

Some of the differences between Ebonics and Standard English could prove the reason why Ebonics is perceived as broken English or lazy English. However, it is important to point out that Ebonics is not broken or lazy English. It is spoken by most of the black people in America.

Ebonics has the same vocabulary as other varieties of English. Of course, Ebonics speakers use some words that are present in other English dialects and have words that only exist in Ebonics. Sometimes it is hard to say where the words originally came from, some words can be traced to West African languages, other words to English and some can be traced to more than one language (multiple etymology). Pronunciation is one aspect that differentiates Ebonics from Standard English. One case where the pronunciation differs is when consonant clusters appear.

The consonant cluster reduction in Ebonics is when two or more consonants, which appear at the end of a word, are reduced. This happens not only in Ebonics but also in other varieties of English. The difference is that in Ebonics the reduction is variable and systematic. In words where a nasal is followed by a vowel Ebonics speaker nasalizes the vowel and deletes the nasal consonant. An example of this is the word man where the /n/ is deleted. Another feature of Ebonics is the merge of 'i' in 'pin' and in 'pen' before a nasal. 'Pin' and 'pen' are pronounced in the same way. Only a distinctive feature in the northern US. A distinctive feature of Ebonics is the conjugated verb "be". This verb is often not used in Ebonics speech.

Ebonics (ebony + phonetics), after having been called colored speech, Negro English, Black English, Black English Vernacular, and some abomination called Pan-African Communication Behaviors, it is identified as a slang, dialect, or language. But, whatever it is, Ebonics is as controversial today as it was in 1855 when the first major linguistic study was done. While the term "Ebonics" goes back to 1973, the system described by that term goes back much farther. Some linguists believe that all facets of Ebonics can be found in Southern white speech. However, linguists who study the sounds, words, and grammars of languages and dialects, though less rhapsodic about Ebonics than the novelists, were much more positive than the general public.

Every human language and dialect obeys distinct rules of grammar and pronunciation therefore, Ebonics is not slang. Slang refers just to a small set of new and usually short-lived words in the vocabulary of a dialect or language. Although Ebonics certainly has slang words such as chillin ("relaxing") or homey ("close friend"), to pick two that have found wide dissemination by the media—its linguistic identity is described by distinctive patterns of pronunciation and grammar. However, a look at Smitherman (1991) will reveal that Black English contains elements of Standard English, elements of West African languages, and elements unique to African-

Americans and researches on Ebonics suggests that it is not slang, but that it has a distinct structure all its own.

REFERENCES

Baron, Dennis, Department of English, University of Illinois—online discussion, e-mail:debaron@uiuc.edu, American Dialect Society.

Clark, Virginia P., Paul A. Eschholz, Alfred F. Rosa, *Languages—Introductory Readings*, St Martin's Press, New York, 1994, pp. 570-85.

Dorsett, Charles, *Black English—Looking to the Future—21st Century Racism*, 1/11/97, online—http://members.tripod.com /~cdorsett/ebonics.htm

Harris, J. (1996). *US Bilingual Education Funds Ruled Out for Ebonics Speakers*, Washington Post online—

http://jobs.washingtonpost.com/wp~stu/politics/gout/admin/stories/riley122596.htm

Landrum-Brown, Joycelyn, *Black English*, March 24, 1995, online—http://www.staff.uiuc.edu/~jlandrum/BlkEng.html

Labov, W. (1972). *Language in the Inner City: Studies in the Black English Vernacular*. Philadelphia, University of Pennsylvania Press.

Murphy, Cullen, *The Ebonic Plague*, Jan 8, 1997, online—http://slate.msn.com/GoodWord/97-01-08/GoodWoord.asp

Oubre, Alondra, *Black English Vernacular (Ebonics and Educabilitv): A Cross-cultural Perspective on Language, Cognition and Schooling*, 1997, online—http://www.phaelos.com/oubre.html

Rickford, John, *The Ebonics Controversy in My Backyard—A Socio-linguists Experience and Reflections*, online—http://www.stanford.edu/~rickford/papers/EbonicsinMyBackyard.html

Saldodo, Mufuene, University of Chicago, Chairman of the Department of Linguistic—online discussion, American Dialect Society.

Yule, George, *The Study of Language*, Second Edition, Cambridge University Press, 1996, pp. 171-89.

Smitherman, G. (1991). "Talking and Testifying: Black English and the Black Experience". In Reginald Jones (Ed.) *Black Psychology*, 3rd ed., Berkeley, CA: Cobb & Henry, pp. 249-68.

Spears, A.K. (1984). "Towards a New View of Black English." *The Journal*, 1, pp. 94-103.

17

Stylistics and the Teaching of Literature at the College Level

Prashant Mishra

Introduction

With the emergence of Linguistics as an autonomous discipline, its application in different fields of knowledge has been realized. One such domain of knowledge, where its application has been explored, is literary criticism which earlier was based on intuitive responses, subjective interpretations and biographical, historical and such other sorts of extra-textual details. Fed up with the subjective interpretations, criticism in the Twentieth century felt the need of objective methodology and consequently a host of the schools of criticism—Russian and French Formalism, Structuralism, Practical and New Criticism—came into existence. Linguistic Stylistics further extended the spirit of these ontological schools of criticism by treating a text as an autonomous entity and aimed at the objective description of the lexical, syntactical and phonological features in order to understand the meaning of a text. Stylistics has been based on the assumption that since literature consists of language, a linguistic analysis of literature can assist us in understanding it. Therefore, the aim of the present paper is to acquaint with the pedagogical potential and practical viability of stylistics in the teaching of literature at the college level.

I

Stylistics: A Conceptual Framework

Literature akin to language is also a means of communication. Its communication, however, is of a different sort and unlike mundane discourse, literary discourse is dressed in a different sort of fabric—a fabric which is not of a direct and plain nature but an embellished and foregrounded one. Literary language as well as literary content is a deviation from the day-to-day discourse which is denotative and of a plainer sort. Literary discourse is connotative as I.A. Richards regards it to be an emotive one because of its profound effect on the readers. This becomes possible due to specialized use of content and the language which encodes it. It is the specialized use of content and the language that comes under the purview of the study of style. Stylistics aims at the linguistic analysis of a literary text divorcing it from the biographical, historical and other such extra-textual details not given on a printed paper. It uncovers the linguistic repertoire that has been used by a writer to expand his theme. A linguistic analysis of a text, therefore, may help us in its decodification as it is language that encodes a text.

Stylistics is the linguistic analysis of a literary text. A writer exploits the principles of language creativity to express his content. Stylistics provides empirical and explicit methods of analyzing the phonological, syntactical and lexical elements of a text. It is an application of linguistics in the study of literature. It endeavours to comprehend a text by studying its linguistic features in the context in which they have been used. A brief account of the important concepts of stylistics has been given with examples from pieces of literary texts in the following discussions. In the last part of the paper practical applications of these concepts have been tested on a poem to see their pedagogical viability.

Style as Foregrounding

According to Jan Mukarovsky, the Prague school linguist, poetic discourse uses some highlighting devices to attract reader's attention towards some parts which are important for the theme and structure of the poem. This strategy of poets to bring some lexical and grammatical items into prominence to create special thematic and organizational effects is called foregrounding. Literary language differs from the day-to-day mundane conversational language which is direct, straight forward and unornamental. Mukarovsky in his essay "Standard Language and Poetic Language" writes, "The function of poetic language consists in the maximum foregrounding of the utterance...it is not used in the services of communication but in order to place in the foreground the act of expression, the act of speech itself" (J.A. Cuddon 1993:325-26). A poet foregrounds by using various linguistic devices like syntactical inversion (changing the normal word-order), repetition of words, phrases, clauses and sentences, parallelism (using parallel structures and patterns), unusual collocations (putting odd words side by side) and coupling (use of parallel phrasal, clausal and syntactical structures). According to Professor Leech, "As a general rule, anyone who wishes to investigate the significance and value of a work of art must concentrate on the element of interest and surprise, rather than on the automatic pattern. Such deviations from linguistic or other socially acceptable norms have been given the name of 'foregrounding'.... The unique creative innovations of poetry, not the routine deviations are what we must chiefly have in mind in this discussion of foregrounding" (Leech 1969:57).

Syntactical Inversion

Poets generally change the normal word order to bring to the front the lexical elements which are significant for the theme of a poem. For example in the following lines from Emily Dickinson's poem "I Taste a Liquor Never Brewed":

> Inebriate of air am I,
> And debauchee of dew,
> Reeling, through endless summer days,
> From inns of molten blue (I Taste a Liquor Never Brewed).

The usual word order "I am inebriate of air" is inverted to highlight the complement 'inebriate'. The complement 'inebriate' is brought into the front to highlight the poet's intoxication of the natural objects. The various words associated with addiction like 'inebriate', 'debauchee', and 'reeling' are put into the front to highlight poet's sensual indulgence in the various natural objects like dew, fresh air, etc.

Unusual Collocations

An unusual collocation refers to the juxtaposition of odd, uncommon and surprising words together to create foregrounding effect. Seturaman, Indra and Sriraman (1990) in their analysis of the poem "Flying Crooked Gift" by Robert Graves perceives the use of "unusual collocation" as the main foregrounding device used by the poet to develop the theme through the set of contrasting lexical items. According to them, the poem develops through the juxtaposition of paradoxical words like "honest idiocy", "a just sense of not to fly", "Hope and hopelessness", "guess and god" and "flying crooked gift". Even the title of the poem is built through the placement of odd words together. The poem contrasts the "straight flying" of birds which is regarded as merely an art and "flying crooked" of butterflies which is a gift. This contrast figuratively points towards the deviant activities of a poet which sets him apart from the ordinary mortals who always move straight like a common bird. It is the oblique activity (flying crooked) that differentiates him from the other members of his tribe and becomes a gift for him.

Coupling

Parallel phrasal, clausal and syntactical structures and patterns are also used by the poets to catch the attention of the readers towards some events or author's perspective about something. This device is known as coupling. In the poem "The Second Coming", W.B. Yeats highlights the arrival of the new civilization by means of parallel syntactic structures:

> Surely some revelation is at hand;
> Surely the second coming is at home.
>
> ("The Second Coming")

Repetition

Repetition of lexical items, phrases, clauses and sentences is also used as a foregrounding device to add force and clarity to a text. Generally, the parts which contribute to the theme and which are vital for the understanding of a text are repeated. In the "Wreck of the Deutschland" Hopkins repeated 'when' three times to foreground the idea of inevitable and unavoidable destiny:

> The frown of his face
> Before me, the hurtle of hell
> Behind, where, where was a, where was a place?
>
> ("Wreck of the Deutschland")

In Wordsworth's poem "Tintern Abbey" the numeral 'five' and the adverb of frequency 'again' are repeated to highlight the contrast between his present feelings and the past ones. The poet has a painful conviction that the past with its intense childish raptures can no more return to him:

Five years have past; five summers, with the length,
Of five long winters; and again I hear
These waters, rolling from their mountain-springs
With a sweet inland murmur, Once again
Do I behold these steep and lofty hills....

("Tintern Abbey")

In Frost's "Stopping by Woods on a Snowy Evening", in the last two lines, the speaker repeats the entire groups of words to emphasize his sense of duty:

And miles to go before I sleep
And miles to go before I sleep.

("Stopping by Woods on a Snowy Evening")

Poets employ syntactic repetition which involves repetition of types of phrases or clauses as a foregrounding device. In Wordsworth's "Solitary Reaper", in the first stanza, repetition of Imperative construction is used as a foregrounding device to invite the attention of the readers towards the solitary reaper and to highlight the same:

Behold her, single in the field,
You solitary Highland Lass;
Reaping and singing by herself;
Stop here, or gently pass!

("The Solitary Reaper")

Style as Deviance

An important exercise in stylistic analysis is to note down the deviances and novelties at the conceptual and linguistic levels. Through the use of deviant expressions, writers try to accomplish foregrounding effects. The deviations can be noticed at the level of subject matter and the use of language. Through the use of uncommon themes, analogies and figures poets create striking and fascinating works which when read automatically attract the attention of the readers and charms them by their novelties.

For example, the subject-matter of Emily Dickinson's poem "I Taste a Liquor Never Brewed" is unusual in the sense that the poetess creates an atmosphere of drunkenness and draws our attention to her as a strange tippler who is not intoxicated to the worldly drinks but to the beauties of Nature. Apart from the conceptual deviance, unusual spellings, punctuations and word formations are also sometimes used by the writers to add an element of surprise to their works. Deviance at the lexical level as has been seen in the use of 'unusual collocations' and 'syntactical inversions' have also been used by the poets to enhance the beauty of their content and rhythm. A beautiful example of syntactical inversion is noticed in Wordsworth's poem "The Daffodils" where the poet emphasises the large number of daffodils whose 'jocund company' overwhelmed him. Through the device of hyperbole (exaggerating the number of daffodils) and by bringing 'Ten thousands' from the position of object to the front, the poet highlights this treasure house of nature:

Ten Thousand saw I at a glance,
Tossing their heads in sprightly dance.

("Daffodils")

II

Stylistics: Its Pedagogical Potential and Viability

Our students at the college level are not competent enough to appreciate a text intuitively. Traditional literary criticism presumes that it is possible to evaluate a work of art through 'intuitive awareness'. It makes use of 'impressionistic terminology' in the process. But this way of looking at a literary text implies absence of explicitness. The interpretations of various teachers with no deep knowledge often contradict each other. As a result, students are baffled and unable to decide which interpretation is more helpful in the appreciation of the given literary piece. Stylistics, on the other hand, investigates the way language is used in a literary text with the aid of its linguistic description. It is concerned with patterning of language in a text. It helps us in arriving at a description which, to some extent, eliminates the need of impressionistic value-based judgements. Stylistics is objective and precise in its methods of inventions and descriptions. Therefore, our students are more at ease with it than those taught under the traditional impressionistic criticism which is subjective and differs from one individual to another individual.

Strength of stylistic approach is that it is practical. Stylistic analysis works on the assumption that the primary principles of linguistic analysis operate in the making of literature. It assumes that "the ordinary linguistic competence now being formalized in language theory offers powerful and unique perspective on the extraordinary imaginative interplay between writer, text and reader now dominating the concerns in literary theory" (Ching, Haley and Lunsford 1980:4). Its methods are objective. It deals with the study of lexical, syntactical and other relevant linguistic features of a literary text without reference to the author, the period, or other extra-textual data on which conventional literary appreciation depends completely. It confines itself to the literary text and does not put any extra burden on the students in knowing the writer and his background that has little to do with the aesthetic quality of a text. It helps the students in understanding the role of language in literature which comprises of words, structures and sentences. According to Ching, Haley and Lunsford, "Pure linguistics, based on 'ordinary' language competence can produce worthwhile insights into the formal properties of the 'extraordinary' discourse of literature" (Ching, Haley and Lunsford 1980:7).

One advantage of stylistic approach over the traditional approach is that it helps the learner more in improving his competence in language. Since language is the medium of expression in literature, any approach that ignores language component and pays more attention on the extra-textual information, is bound to put hurdles in the way of achieving language competence. The traditional approaches to literary criticism may be good for those who study a particular language as their mother tongue. The L2 learners who are studying literature as an aid to improve their language proficiency will, surely reap more benefits from the stylistic approach that is concerned with the study of linguistic aspects of a given piece of literature than from the traditional approaches.

Stylistics is the study of the use of language in literature. A literary work cannot be properly understood without a thorough knowledge of the language. The study of language of a literary piece will be a complement and an aid to the study of literature. In the case of a foreign language or the English language, this assumption becomes more significant for a literary work cannot be properly understood without a thorough knowledge of its language which is the medium of expression.

As a tool of literary criticism, we can rely to a great extent on stylistics because it provides us linguistic evidence to solve many puzzles of a literary text. It provides us the evidence of words and sentences which actually occur on the printed page in the literary text. That is why practical criticism relies more on linguistic evidence than on the extra-textual ones. Moreover, much of the fundamental terminology of literary criticism like 'metaphor', 'simile', 'irony', 'rhythm', 'metre', etc. cannot be explained without the help of Linguistics. Stylistics serves as a bridge between Linguistics and literary criticism and provides satisfactory answers to all the basic questions. It, thus, functions as a good pedagogical tool in the teaching of literature.

The traditional pedagogical methods do not ensure the participation of the students in the learning process. The teacher largely relies on the lecture mode with the motive to furnish background information related to the text and consequently students remain passive listeners whose main work is note taking rather than shedding any ideas on the text under study. The participation of the students in the learning process stirs enthusiasm in them. The teacher helps the students in identifying the deviant features of language which contribute significantly to the comprehension of a poem through foregrounding important thematic elements of a text. Stylistics which is the linguistic analysis of a text ensures the participation of the students in the learning process. In a stylistic analysis, a teacher spots out the linguistic elements which have been foregrounded and through them endeavours to arrive at the meaning of a text.

Too much background details given by a teacher distract the attention of the students from the text and kill their zeal to contribute something to the learning as nothing has been left for them. The main concern of a teacher in a traditional pedagogy becomes providing background details particularly biographical and historical ones with a little concern to help the students appreciate a text. Since stylistic analysis of a text involves the students in discovering the innovations and experimentations done by a writer at the phonological, syntactical and lexical level, it improves the linguistic competence of the students. H.G. Widdowson regards stylistics as a pedagogical tool and a pursuit that mediates between linguistics and literature. The work of a teacher in the classroom is to involve the students in tracing the various deviations that make the ordinary language prominent in a literary work. The students are involved in the process of exploration and make discoveries for themselves.

Stylistics helps the students in developing a consciousness of good style. At the school level, it is very difficult to achieve the aim of creating a sense of style in our students as they are not competent enough to analyze even the basic structures of language. But at the Post Graduate level, when our students become aware of the aesthetic qualities and the linguistic features of literature, a course in stylistics enables them to develop a sense of style. Students will be able to focus on the style markers of the passage which contribute to its effect. Once the sense of style is developed in our students, it will help them in improving their own writing style. A course in stylistics provides new insights into the phenomenon of style from the point of view of the reader and the message conveyed to him by the text. It teaches how a writer selects various components of language and exploits them to suit his subject-matter. In this way, through proper training in stylistics, our students are enabled to express what they imagine and dream.

Generally, in adopting a new approach acquaintance with its terminology is necessary and unfamiliarity with the jargon and register of the new approach distances teachers from adopting it. However, this is not the case in the introduction of stylistic approach at the college level. In the stylistic analysis of a literary piece, a teacher can exploit the rudimentary linguistic knowledge of his students and can explore its functional role in the genesis and comprehension of a literary piece. Certain common linguistic terms phonemes, syllable, sentence types—interrogatives, imperatives, exclamatory, etc. tenses—present, past, future; pronominals—first person, second person and third person; voice—active and passive voice, linkers and such other types of language items which have already been taught in the previous classes and with which our students are familiar and friendly may be used by a teacher in his analysis of a text. A teacher should ask the students to explore the significant linguistic items of a text and should help the students in interpreting and explaining a text with the help of them. Similarly various lexical items—nouns, pronouns, adjectives, verbs and adverbs which have a strong bearing on the theme and tone of the poem should be sorted out with the help of the students. Synonymous lexical items, related to the topic sentence, have to be spotted and explained with regard to the context. For example, in Wordsworth's poem "Solitary Reaper" various synonyms of 'solitary' have been used by the poet to highlight the loneliness of the maiden. Some of them have also been foregrounded. Through the analysis of various linguistic components, a teacher can explain a text which is a symmetrical synthesis of these component parts. Since a text is an organized whole, it is analyzed with an eye towards the understanding of the whole.

III

The Patriot: A Stylistic Analysis

"The Patriot" written by Nissim Ezekiel belongs to the group of poems titled "Very Indian Poems in Indian English". Even if the writer would not have termed it an Indian poem, the lexis and syntax of the poem provides us enough authenticity to its being an Indian poem in English. The text of the poem presents us sufficient clues to the marked deviations from the standard British English. The poem presents a socio-cultural ethos of India. It is Indian in both its form and content. The speaker who is a patriot expresses his concern for his motherland in an 'indianised' use of English. The use of Hindi words and the literal translation of phrases and idioms such as 'goonda', 'Indira Behn', 'Lassi', 'Hindi Wallaha', 'Ram Rajya' and "100% correct...200% correct" are common phrases adopted from Hindi vernacular and are common usages in Indian English. This use of the native idiomatic expressions makes Ezekiel's style colloquial, intimate and conversational as well as suitable to the Indian themes of his poetry.

'The Patriot' is a monologue. The addresser is a 'Patriot' who is speaking to an anonymous addressee as is evident from the use of second person pronoun in the last stanza of the poem when he says:

> You are going?
> But you will visit again

Any time, any day,
I am not believing in ceremony
Always I am enjoying your company. ("The Patriot")

The use of present progressive in place of the simple present is also a typical feature of Indian English usage that makes it deviant from the standard British English. This feature has been used throughout the poem in verbs like fighting, following, understanding, neglecting, reading, thinking, etc. Since the speaker is a 'Patriot' who believes in the past glory of his country, he expresses his discontent with the current scenario in a deviant medium. In the first stanza, he says:

I am standing for peace and non-violence.
Why world is fighting fighting
Why all people of world
Are not following Mahatma Gandhi,
I am simply not understanding
Ancient Indian Wisdom is 100% correct.
I should say even 200% correct. ("The Patriot")

Non-inversion of the Aux in the lines "Why all people of world/ Are not following Mahatma Gandhi" is a common grammatical mistake committed in Indian English. This trait has been exploited by the poet in the above-mentioned line to provide it an Indian flavour and to maintain his identity of being an Indian Patriot. Through the repetition of 'fighting' in the interrogative sentence, the speaker expresses his aversion towards the violence going on in the world. In spite of the violence going on in the world and the modern generation's neglect of Gandhian thoughts and the Ancient Indian Wisdom, the speaker is hopeful of the coming of "Regeneration, Remuneration and Contraception", however slow their pace may be:

Lend me the ears.
Everything is coming
Regeneration, Remuneration, Contraception.
Be patiently, brothers and sisters. ("The Patriot")

Further, in the second stanza, the speaker authenticates the cultural content in his characteristic manner by the use of non-inversion of the Aux and the omission of the Aux and Prep in the interrogative sentence making it a deviant expression from the

British English grammar. For example, in the expression "you want one glass lassi", the substitute Aux 'Do' and the Prep 'of' before the Noun 'lassi' are deliberately omitted by the poet. In the third stanza through the repetition of 'total' the speaker's distaste for drinking has been foregrounded. He expresses his preference for 'a glass of lassi', an Indian summer drink in a simplified use of English by omitting the Aux 'Do'. The following line 'Very good for digestion' continues the same simplification of grammar. For example:

> You want one glass lassi?
> Very good for digestion
> With little salt lovely drink,
> Better than wine;
> Not that I am ever tasting the wine
> I am the total teetotaller, completely total
> But I say. ("The Patriot")

In the fourth stanza, the speaker expresses his displeasure over the irresponsible behaviour of his neighbours—Pakistan and China:

> Pakistan Behaving like this,
> China behaving like that,
> It is making me sad, I am telling you,
> Really most harassing me. ("The Patriot")

'Pakistan Behaving like this, China behaving like that'; 'You tolerate me/ I tolerate you'; 'I am thinking/ I am saying' are the parallel syntactic patterns employed by the poet to provide rhythm to his blank verse.

In the next stanza, the speaker expresses his confidence that one day 'Ram Rajya' will surely come to his country as in spite of diversity in the country and idiosyncratic habits and tastes, people are tolerant of each other's ways of life.

> In India also
> Gujaraties, Maharashtrians, Hindiwallahs
> All brothers
> Though some are having funny habits.
> Still you tolerate me,

I tolerate you,
One day Ram Rajya is surely coming. ("The Patriot")

The simplicity of language, use of colloquial words and phrases, use of repetition and coupling are some of the stylistic devices used by the poet to provide an additional merit to the poem. The deviant expressions like the use of present continuous tense in place of simple present, non-inversion of the subject and the Aux, omission of function words are some of the deviations from the standard British usage. These features not only generate humour but are suited to the cultural content of the poem. Since the addresser is a 'Patriot', he therefore expresses his concern for his motherland in an 'indianized' use of a foreign tongue. Thus, the deliberate use of 'Swadeshi Angrezi' is an integral aspect of the theme and technique of the poem.

Conclusion

The above analysis of the poem "The Patriot" by Nissim Ezekiel shows that at the college level Stylistics can be used in the classroom as a means to investigate and appreciate literature. Since students at the college level acquire necessary competence in the use of language and are already familiar with the main ingredients of language, their linguistic knowledge can be brushed up with the aid of a teacher in the classroom to analyze and understand literature. What is required from a teacher is to train his students in the learning and application of the rudimentary principles of stylistics. In the first few classes, a teacher should acquaint his students with the basics of stylistics like foregrounding devices—repetition, coupling, inversion, unusual collocations and various deviant expressions like morphological, lexical, syntactical, thematic deviations which may assist us in the comprehension of the theme of a literary piece. Once students are taught the fundamental principles of stylistic analysis and a few applications of the same are shown by the teacher, they can apply these principles independently. In this way stylistics can be an interesting exercise in the classroom to comprehend and enjoy a literary discourse.

REFERENCES

Ching, M.K.L., M.C. Haley, R.F. Lunsford (Ed.) (1980). *Linguistic Perspectives on Literature*. London, Boston and Haley: Routledge and Kegan Paul.

Cuddon, J.A. (Ed.) (1998). *A Dictionary of Literary Terms and Literary Theory*. Delhi: Maya Blackwell Doaba House.

Krishnaswamy, N., K.N. Sivaraman, C.T. Indra (Eds.) (1995). *Teaching Poetry at the Advanced Level*. Madras: T.R. Publications Pvt. Ltd.

Leech, G.N. (1969). *A Linguistic Guide to English Poetry*. London and Harlow: Longsman, Green and Co. Ltd.

Parasher, S.V. (1991). *Indian English: Functions and Forms*. New Delhi: Bahri Publications.

Prakasam, V. (1996). *Stylistics of Poetry: A Functional Perspective*. Hyderabad: Omkar Publications.

Seturaman, V.S., C.T. Indra and T. Sriraman (Eds.) (1990). *Practical Criticism*. Madras: Macmillan India Ltd.

18

Globalizing English Studies in India

Harish Narang

This presentation is in three parts. In the first part, I submit, briefly, my association with and advocacy for the introduction of African Writings in English as a part of English Studies programmes at various levels—B.A. (Hons), M.A., M.Phil and Ph.D., solely because it has a direct bearing on my main presentation later. In the second, I narrate a few academic anecdotes. In the third and the final part, making a few deductions from the personal bit of history and the anecdotes presented above, I present my case for a radical relook at the canon of English Studies in India.

It was a little over two decades ago—in the early eighties—that I started teaching a course on Introduction to African Writings in English to my M.A. students at the J.N.U. It was unprecedented in the history of English literary Studies in India in the sense that no English department in a university in India had made African literature a part of its curriculum, giving it the space of a full paper. Hitherto, African writers had been taught and studied as a part of the Paper on Commonwealth Literature which as we know was a kind of 'Khichdi' wherein students were exposed to texts from writers representing various former colonies of Great Britain ranging from Australia to Africa and Asia to the Caribbeans and also included at times—strangely enough—authors from Great Britain. Even this was more true of the scheme of courses in universities down south rather than up north. Strange as it may seem, departments of English in north have always been more slow in introducing changes in their syllabi than their counterparts in the south. There has been a definite north-south divide as far as updating of courses in English Studies is concerned. I distinctly remember being asked by a very senior Professor from the North—'Chinua who?'—when I tried to explain to him the authors I taught as a part of my paper on African Literature. It was more than just ignorance. His tone made it very clear that he was poking fun at the exotic-sounding names of literary nobodies whom I had canonized by making their writings a part of the sacred territory of English Literary Studies trod by Sovereign Shakespeares and mighty Miltons. Mind you, by then Achebe's history-making novel, *Things Fall Apart,* had been published for over 25 years, had gone into several editions, had been translated into two dozen languages or so and had been hailed as a modern classic. Achebe had already visited India, having been to University of Mysore.

Next ten years or so of my career were spent persuading friends in English departments in universities in the north—HP, Jammu, Panjab, GNDU, Panjabi, Kurukshetra, Lucknow, Jamia, IGNOU—wherever I went on academic assignments—to introduce writers from the African continent in their courses of study, register students for M.Phil/Ph.D. programmes of study on topics relating to African writings in English. I made it a point to formulate all my lecturers in various departments, presentations in seminars and refresher courses around African literature in English, persuading, cajoling, bribing (promises of books and research material, what else) students and teachers to give those authors a chance. When invited to contribute articles to journals and books I wrote only on African literature. All my translations during that period were from African writers. Wherever I went, I initiated a debate about the need for creating academic space for not only Achebe, Ngugi, Soyinka, Gordimer, Ousmane and Emecheta who were big names from the continental writing but also lesser known writers like Ekwensi, Nwapa, Mwangi, Ogot, Armah, Bessie Head, La Guma, p'Bitek and Aidoo.

Why was I doing all this? Why this obsession—if this could be called so—with African writings? The reasons for this follow in another section of the presentation. It may suffice to observe here that today, most of the departments in the universities named above and many more have included full papers on African Writings in English and many scores of students have written their M.Phil and Ph.D. dissertations on topics relating to this very vibrant body of literature and authors whose names are no more a matter of fun. Even a conservative department like the department of English at the University of Delhi that took more than twenty-five years to revise its B.A. (Hons) syllabus has now included African writers in their undergraduate programme of study. In my presentations, I also made a point to mention that my arguments for introducing African literature were equally valid for the introduction of other similar literatures, namely, Indian, Australian, Canadian and the Caribbean. Of course, there were some departments which overdid it in a hurry to score brownie points over others. I still remember one student from a university in what is now Uttrakhand landing up in my office one day, armed with a letter from her Professor and Head, who had requested me to help her find material on her M.Phil research topic. When I asked her the title of her dissertation, she replied that she was working on 'The Theme of alienation in the writings of Bessie Head'. When I asked her about her primary readings, she informed me that she had not read anything from Bessie Head; nor from any other South African writer, for that matter. She had no answer when I asked her as to how she had arrived at her dissertation topic without having read anything from the author. The only observation she made was the both her supervisor and she wanted to be the first in the department to work on an African author. Then there was this colleague of mine from a university in Jammu and Kashmir who referred to Buchi Emecheta as 'my Buchi' only because she had taught a text of the novelist for a couple of semesters. Jokes apart, students' exposure to African writings in English was what could be called in popular, colloquial parlance 'a hit'.

Let me now move on from this personal bit of history to the reasons for such a sustained campaign for African writings in English to be included in the scheme of courses of departments of English. But before I do so, I'd like to narrate to you a few anecdotes—in fact, as you can see I have done nothing else so far. But then to me, wisdom lies only in anecdotes and what we make of them.

Here is the first one—and the latest one. A student of mine—she is brilliant—went for an interview for a teaching job in a college in a neighbouring university in Delhi. She is already teaching in another college on an ad-hoc basis. During the interview, a member of the selection committee and a very senior Professor from the department of English in the university, asked her to quote something from Dryden's poetry. As she told me, she tried to wriggle out of an awkward situation but the Professor persisted and finally she confessed that she could not. She knew she had lost her chance to get the job although she had done well in her answers to other questions. Not to be able to quote from a British poet whose writings were a part of the syllabus and course content in most Indian universities was a big sin in the eyes of this Professor.

By a sheer coincidence, another student of mine had faced a similar situation a few weeks earlier where the same Professor had asked her to tell him the publication dates of all the plays of Shakespeare. She too could not be selected.

And now the second anecdote. This one is quite recent too.

Last month, I was invited to preside over a seminar on Shakespeare in a college in University of Delhi. I tried to get out of it by pleading that I was not a scholar of Shakespeare—it is true and I can hardly quote anything from his writings, to the utter shock and consternation of so many—but the organizers shall have none of it. The three speakers included two scholars from the United States of America and the third one was a colleague from the department in the university. One of the Professors spoke, among others, on Kalidas's *Abhigyan Shakuntalam.* During the discussion on his paper, a teacher who was in the audience and who has been known for teaching Shakespeare for a long time and whose obsession with him is proverbial—he can't stand a word of criticism against Shakespeare and has picked up serious quarrels with scholars for running down Shakespeare as an imperialist, racist or anti-feminist, traces of all of which can found in his writings—made the observation that Kalidas was the Shakespeare of India. His observation reminded me of another one, made many years ago, when in an international seminar an Indian scholar had put forth a proposition that Shakespeare was in fact an Indian whose real name was Sheikh Piir.

And now the last one. One of my students who teaches in one of the colleges in Delhi came to see me recently. Over a cup of coffee, I asked her about her teaching—the books and authors she was teaching currently. She said that among others she was teaching Restoration Comedy in general and a play by William Congreve in particular. Before I could say anything, she added—'It's so boring and such a pain in the neck for both me and my students who are simply not interested in that kind of writing. Sir, I really wonder as to who put *The Way of the World* there and why. I did not answer her then. In fact, I was sure she knew part of the answer and her question was only tautological—at least partly. But it did set me thinking—once again—about the what and the why of the English Studies in India. That, in fact, is what I intend talking about now in the last part of my presentation.

The anecdotes narrated above seem too disjointed and unrelated to one another except that all of them relate to teaching/learning of English literature in India. To me, however, these are all pointers to the basic mystery—who done what to our English literary studies in India when and why? The mystery does not lie so much in the who done it part since we all know that it was the British who first introduced the teaching and learning of English language and literature in India as a part of the British education system. The why part is also well-known by now, thanks to the wide publicity that Macaulay's Minute of 1835 received both during the colonial rule and after the Indian independence. What is also known but less cared for is that the teaching/learning of both the language and literature has remained essentially the same for the last 200 years or so. Let me show you how—first the language part. Not more than two weeks ago, may be even less, a student who has just finished his Ph.D. in Linguistics from our university and who has been teaching at University of Delhi met me recently, and once again over a cup of coffee—sometimes I wonder as to where would Indian scholarship be without tea or coffee—told me that he has been given an interesting project to work on. The Bodos of North-East have asked him to render for their school going kids Nesfield's English grammar in their language. On being asked 'why Nesfield', he replied to me that they—the people in the North-East—swear by that grammar and do not want 'even a comma or full stop' to be changed. Now, many of us are familiar with that book of grammar and are also full of liking for Nesfield's scholarship and manner of presenting the pedagogical part of grammatical facts but the English language has undergone so much change—even grammatically, more so in India—since he first wrote his book. How do you account for this in the teaching/learning process of the young kids in school if you insist on Nesfield's grammar is anybody's guess. No wonder then what I was once told by an observer of our English: you speak a written variety of Empire English. I could not agree with him more. Let alone others, teachers of English—both in schools and in universities and colleges—speak like that, write like that and teach like that. You don't believe me. Let me give you one solitary example. In most schools they still teach kids the strict, rigid, empire-given manner of starting and ending a letter. And the students are taught that while writing an application to a superior—an officer, for instance—you must begin it with the following words—'I beg to state that...' Or end it with the words—'Yours faithfully'. And if any student deviates from that beginning or ending, he/she is penalized by losing marks even if the content of the letter is in acceptable English. Has any one—any teacher—ever wondered as to why did the British teachers in colonial times insist on that particular format? We were in a master-servant relationship with them and any request—even the most legitimate one, for instance, a half-day casual leave in an emergency like attending to a seriously ill wife or child—had to be 'begged' for before it was granted. Also, you had not only to show but state your 'faithfulness' to your master every time you addressed him. Even though 'sincerely' may be a very decent word, it cannot be used in a master-servant relationship. It has to be 'faithful' which is English version of the MCP 'aapke charano ki daasi' which is what women were taught to write to their husbands at the end of their letters—that is if they ever dared to write to them or have it written by someone who could write. I understand that the scribe added it on his own at the end even if the woman forgot to mention it specifically. In short, the language content of our English is still replete with colonial intent and we continue to insist on teaching the language the same way.

And now let us turn to the field of literature and its teaching/learning in India. In fact, here I would like to refer to the Kalidas anecdote. How many of us agree with that evaluation? Well, I can tell you this that when that observation was made in the seminar, there was not even one—except yours truly who was in the chair and therefore could not say anything, at least not immediately although it drew a long comment from me eventually—who raised any objection to Kalidas being referred to as the Shakespeare of India. No, not even an eyebrow was raised. Well, here are two great playwrights representing two different linguistic and literary traditions and the greatness of one was being compared with that of the other, being measured in terms of the other. What was there to object to? Nothing except that it is an absurd statement to make—as absurd as to state that Narasimha Rao, the former Prime Minister of India influenced the thinking of Chanakya. Or, Nalanda was modelled after the Jawaharlal Nehru University. Incidentally, the last comparison—made appropriately, of course—was made by the President of India two weeks ago when he visited the JNU campus and said that Jawaharlal Nehru University could become the modern Nalanda. To return to our original point, Kalidas wrote ions before the English learnt to write their language. They hadn't even invented their alphabet perhaps. If Kalidas had, while writing his plays, achieved a level of excellence in dramaturgy that was later—much later—to be reached by Shakespeare, writing in English, would it not be more appropriate—chronologically, at least—to state that Shakespeare is the Kalidas of England. This is certainly not absurd and it does not take away from Shakespeare his greatness as a playwright.

However, does it mean that the critics—and it was English critics who first formulated this comparative evaluation—were ignorant about or unaware of the absurdity involved in the statement. Or is there more to it than meets the eye when one reads it? Of course, those elucidating the comparison were not innocent, nor ignorant. Of course, there is more to it than meets the eye. What is being proposed here is to set up Shakespeare's dramatic writings as a universal benchmark against which all others pursuing the profession of writing plays must be evaluated and graded. It really did not matter whether the playwright being compared wrote before him or after. In fact, there is more to the statement than just setting up Shakespeare as a benchmark, making him as a kind of universal of dramaturgy. The statement is an illustration of what has been called Euro centricity which as we know is a phenomenon of setting up Europe as the centre of universe and Europeans as the source of all-encompassing superiority in every field of knowledge—chronology or no chronology. It is no surprise that most Indians fail to see the real intention behind such a formulation. In fact, many a scholar—from Sanskrit or culture Studies—considers this evaluation to be a compliment, a recognition of the greatness of Kalidas and parrots it at academic gatherings or in his/her writings thereby reinforcing the myth of Euro centricity. At the same time, it is also a sign of our colonized mindsets which are still obsessed with Anglophobia. The continued domination of English literary texts and authors in our scheme of courses and syllabi is the most significant example of such a mindset and this is what I propose to discuss now.

Let me go back to the point where I stated that the British introduced teaching/learning of English language and literature in India as a part of the British education system and also mentioned that the Minute of Macaulay gave out the political objectives and goals of such action. The philosophical foundations for this proposition could be found in the now infamous *raison d'etre* of colonization—to civilize the non-Europeans. It did not matter that this flew in the face of history which told everyone, including the British, that there were developed civilizations in India, China, parts of Africa, the Middle-East and North America much before Europe evolved to that stage. It really did not matter to the British that before their first writers—Chaucer and others—began to learn their craft of putting words together to create poems or prose narratives, India had developed literature, including in the written form, in almost a dozen languages. In fact, "Sangam" poetry in Tamil is perhaps among the oldest existing written forms of literature in the world if not the oldest. And what about Sanskrit, and Pali and Prakrit? Even many modern Indian languages—Kannada, Malayalam, Marathi, Gujarati, Hindi and Bengali had significant writings to boast of at the time of their encounter with English.

Against this body of literature, the British put together a motley crowd of all and sundry authors and books—more sundry than all—and touted this as a tradition of an outstanding literary achievement that must be studied by others in order to emulate. True that among them were some really significant writers—Shakespeare, Milton, Swift, perhaps Chaucer, may be Dickens or George Eliot, or Virginia Woolf, and a few more. But what about the others—Dryden, Pope and Congreve, for instance? And one could multiply the list without much effort—Webster, Johnson, Jane Austen. What is so great about their poetry or plays or novels? Well, I am not denying that these writers could be significant for the British—significant for being important links in the chain of evolution of English Literature as a sign of the cultural development of the English; significant for distilling socio-political milieu of their times; or significant because of the ideological positions that some of these writers took in the writings. Incidentally, do you know that English Literature Studies as it was introduced in India and as it obtains in India in more or less unchanged form even today, was introduced in India before it was introduced in England itself. Strange, you may say, but it is true. Incongruous, you may observe, but it is true. May be, it appears funny to some of you, but it is true. However, to me it is neither strange nor incongruous, nor even funny. Why? Let me elaborate a little.

The British needed to introduce such a programme of study here in India but they did not need to introduce such a programme of study in England—at least not at that point of time. The British introduced English Literature and Language Studies in India for the very same reasons for which they introduced English law and governance, English administrative norms and procedures, English dress and related codes, English food and English manner of eating, English speech and English manner of speaking and a hundred other similar things. The strategy was to first run down all existing Indian—I refuse to use the word indigenous, which in the context could be derogatory since most British anthropologists, historians and sociologists have used the term loading it with a value judgment *vis-à-vis* European unversalism—traditions and practices in these walks of life as inferior if not savage and uncivilized, thereby creating a cultural vacuum and then planting everything English in the name of superiority—philosophical, political and cultural.

Thus we were forced to study these British authors as representatives of a superior literature, superior culture. Since the British had no such point to prove back home in England, there was no need to introduce such a programme of study—at least at that point of time. Later, of course, it would be made a part of the curriculum for familiarizing their students of their cultural evolution and heritage which would be as valid a reason as the introduction of Hindi literature for Hindi speakers in India or Tamil literature for students from the Tamil community. I need not overemphasize the point that this point of enforcing cultural superiority was not an end in itself but only a means for colonizing a space the British considered more significant in their scheme of things than the physical space most of which they now controlled—the Indian minds. Colonization of minds, all colonizers believed—and rightly so—would be a more effective weapon in the continued colonization of physical space than the weapons of gun and technology that had helped them in the first instance. And let us not lose sight of the primary objective of British colonization—all colonization: greed, economic greed. Friends, I am asking you to remember that behind the introduction of English Literary Studies in India was the basic objective of continued colonization of India—no more, no less. That's simple truth—stated as simply as I can. And while being subjected to such learning, we were being exposed to some truly significant writers—gold coins—like Shakespeare who could compare well with our own Kalidas, there were also some counterfiet coins—*jaali sikke*—like William Congreve of the Restoration Drama who had no value for us—for any one else except perhaps the British—as part of the world literary heritage. And yet, as I showed in that observation from my students she is doomed to teach it and her students have to suffer it by not studying it but also answer questions on it and a part of their evaluation and possibly career depends on it. How stupid, how utterly stupid for a nation of one billion independent people to go on studying year after year writers and authors who have no relevance to our lives, our culture, our history, our vision, our anything! Just because when we were servants, our masters—our colonial masters—forced us to do so. It is not a question of Congreve alone. There are scores of them—I named some like Dryden, Pope, Austen—who have no relevance at all in our scheme of things—national as well as individual—and we go on putting them on the pedestal of literary learning and worshipping them as if they were stars on the world firmament of literary excellence. There is hardly any university English department that does not teach them. As I tried to show through the narration of some of the anecdotes above, careers of brilliant students are made or marred on the mere ability or lack of it to quote from Drydens and Popes, ability to remember as to when the first folio edition of Hamlet was published or who edited the Arden edition. Criminal, callously criminal to perpetuate mental slavery through such frivolous inanity. Well, until political independence, we had no choice in reviewing the English literature courses and their contents in the same way that we had no choice in reviewing certain other things—perhaps more important—because of the master-servant relationship we had with the British. However, there is no such compulsion on us any more and I see no reason as to why it cannot be done now. In fact, it should have been done here before—long before.

Some of us might turn around and say that it has been done. Did I myself not begin this presentation by stating the efforts in the introduction of African Literature as a part of the curriculum and the way I succeeded? Also, do English Literature Courses not include Indian Writings in English, Canadian Writing, Australian Literature, Caribbean Writings, Literature of the Indian Diaspora and many more? True, but despite these changes which have been piecemeal, the core of the content still remain very English or at best British. Most of the literatures listed above are offered either as choices—optional papers as we call them—as against a much bigger, substantial part that is sometimes called core courses, sometimes compulsory courses. The new literatures content is offered as an appendage and is more often than not either lumped together in a single or at best a couple of courses or these are offered as 'either or' choices in the same manner in which certain caterers offer you choices between dishes while deciding a menu at a predetermined tariff: a tomato coriander soup or a clear chicken soup, gobhi masala or alu-methi, moong dal halwa or rabdi-jalebi. But should this not be like this, some friends—both students and teachers—may argue? After all, it is a programme of study in English literature. What else should it contain if not English literature? True, very true. But what is English literature—now? What is the definition and status of English literature at the beginning of the 21st century? And how should that impact not only the teaching and learning of English literature but also the content of courses, including their quantum? Answers to these questions are very crucial and necessary inputs for having a 'relook' at the English Studies Programmes that I spoke about in the beginning of my presentation. Let me try and provide some answers.

David Crystal is a leading British Linguist who has been investigating the evolution of English language around the globe for the last four decades or so and has written extensively about it. Crystal was in India some time ago and gave a series of lectures on the State of Englishes, globally. In a seminar presentation at the British Council at New Delhi, he doled out statistic after statistic to show how English speaking English persons were now a small minority—a very small minority—in total gamut of English speaking persons globally. Even if statistics were to be examined of English speakers of European descent—and that would include those in the United States of America, Canada, Australia and New Zealand, among others—the numbers would still fall short of English speakers of non-European origin, thanks to the contribution of India, about 30 per cent of whose over a billion strong population has some control over English language. This, according to David Crystal, is impacting—and why shouldn't it, he said—not only the evolving character of English language but also its teaching/learning processes, including the course content. That is why when one speaks of the plurality of the English language, no one is surprised anymore. In fact, not only other parts of the world but in England itself, they are speaking of—besides the usual Irish English, Welsh English and Scottish English—Gujarati English, Punjabi English, Bengali English, Nigerian English, Jamaican English and a score more. This also meant—and David Crystal said in as many words—that in the changing global perspective of English language—its character, its teaching and its learning—India had a very significant role to play. He reinforced the point by adding that India's global domination of the software industry was a result of this number game being in its favour and that this in turn would lead to India impacting the English teaching/learning more significantly in future.

My contention is that what is true of English language and its teaching/learning today is equally true—if not more—of English literature. Indians producing literature in English are many more than the English—even the British. Also, besides the Americans, the Australians, the Canadians and the New

Zealanders—most of whom are of European origin—the Kenyans, the Ugandans, the Tanzanians, the Zambians, the Zimbabweans, the South Africans, the Nigerians, the Ghananians, the Liberians, the Srilankans, the Pakistanis, the Bangladeshis, the Nepalese, the Afghanistanis, the Singaporeans and the Malayasians, the Trinidadians, the Jamaicans, the Guyanese, the Fijians—most of whom are of non-European descent—are also creating literature in English. Together, the total output of this body of literature is many times more than the literary output of English and even British writers. If this is how things stand today in the field of literature production, why should English or British literature get a major share of syllabi and course content in English literary studies? Why shouldn't we show it its place—its proper place—in the scheme of things in the world of English Literary Studies. David Crystal said that India is in a position to and should impact the teaching/learning of English language because it is contributing a very large number of learners of the language—and competent ones at that. In the same way—and this is my contention—that India should take the lead in impacting the teaching/learning of English literature in a significant way. And one of the first priorities should be a more democratic and more equitable distribution of various English literatures listed above, including the English English literature and British English literature.

Let me now conclude by saying that while a large number of scholars and critics have spoken of the role of history in critical evaluation of works of literature, hardly any have emphasized the need for invoking history for having a 'relook' at the course content of English Literary Studies programmes. There are hardly any who speak of the need for a historical justice even in determining the quantum of courses while framing the details of syllabi. I am invoking history for reevaluating the quantum and content of our English Literature Courses in Indian universities. A course in African or Indian or Australian or Canadian literature written in English included here and there as an after thought is hardly the kind of justice that I am sticking my neck out for. I am asking for a radical revision of the Anglican quantum of our English Literature programmes of Study. There was time, twenty years ago, when some of us demanded independent places in the sun for various constituents of the so-called Commonwealth Literature—Indian, African, Australian, Canadian, Caribbean, etc. Now is the time to demand a proper deanglicization—and for us this means decolonization—of the canon. If we do not do so now, we would continue to speak of Kalidases as the Shakespeares of India. What could be more absurd than that!

19

Decolonising Teaching Materials and Strategies: Towards an Alternative Pedagogics

C. Kannan

Indian education system in general and English Language teaching in particular still endorse the colonial paradigm. The colonial paradigm always concentrated on projecting and imposing the attitude of the British. The aims and objectives of teaching English at various levels, though changed occasionally, a considerably respectable efficiency in ELT has not been achieved. An important lapse is the identification of teaching of literature as teaching of language—the literature aspect or component as content, with emphasis on the literariness ignoring language aspects. Language is both a vehicle of communication and an instrument of thought. Paradoxically enough our learners are not able to appreciate the literary aspects of the texts as they haven't acquired the required language abilities to enjoy the learning materials. The language of literature has peculiar linguistic aspects and these nuances appear as strange and complex modes of communication to the learners. As a result, appreciation and enjoyment of literature tend to be an exercise in futility. So it is desirable to acquire the required basic language skills before venturing into the task of appreciating literature as such. Pre-independent India had a philosophically sound and psychologically reasonable pedagogics widely practised with a culture specificity though the cultural forms and nativistic elements of the Indian colony were ignored. But in the modern times we haven't succeeded in establishing an Indian Education system based on our ethos.

The main task of this paper is to look for an alternative pedagogics, considering the contemporary Indian scenario. The contemporary Indian scenario alludes to the socio-cultural milieu and the 'needs' of the nation. Is it possible to develop a tenable and viable mode of teaching strategy to modernise India? Modernisation is not westernisation. It is an attitudinal change of the individual in his attempt to keep the world changing. It does not mean a thorough deviation from the established norms, of course with the Anglo-Saxon tradition as a springboard. It is not surprising that ELT in India still depends much on the colonial systems—especially the teaching materials. Indian pedagogics has heavy dosages of the old imperialistic dictates in the form of colonial discourses even in the postcolonial context.

Most of the books prescribed for the degree and postgraduate courses in English in our universities are acclaimed masterpieces. But how many learners are familiar with the cultural context and environment envisaged in those works. Even if they are not familiar with the culture matrix, it is possible to grasp the literariness of the prescribed materials with the already acquired linguistic competence. Another dichotomy pointed out by literary critics is the total neglect or ignorance of the 'Basha' literatures. The learner's mother tongue and its literary tradition along with the present writings must serve as a prerequisite for the task of encountering an alien culture and literature.

Learner's real life experiences and familiar contextualisation must be the main chunk of the teaching repertoire. How can we tackle this with a judicious selection of learning materials from familiar contexts? Formulation of well-developed modules emphasizing the aspects of ELT is the preliminary step. Very often the learners from the rural background who were not exposed to new methods and language situations experience a sort of 'culture shock'. The learning materials with unfamiliar culture components baffle our young learners. To develop communicative skills, multidimensional projects can concentrate on familiarising unfamiliar cultures. This will save the learners from culture shock and will increase the effectiveness of the instructional materials. Culture shock will ultimately lead to 'stigmatization' and to avoid this discomfort of the learners, new learning tools and learning tasks based on the real life situations are designed.

> ...the inability to relate to a given educational environment productively has social stigma attached to it. The learner who does not fit in will be socially stigmatized by other people and, probably more damaging, will internalize the norms of the culture; failing to fit in with these norms, the learner will stigmatize himself or herself. (Joyce 1997:391)

British educationists of the period tried to impose the cultural forms of the west through the learning materials. Imperial ideologies became the objects of studies totally ignoring the native Indians still endorse this as a positive virtue and boast ourself as specialists in accepting and assimilating all alien ways of living and thinking. Perhaps the western education system must have resulted in a 'liberating influence' upon the Indians. And this liberating influence was achieved at the cost of rejecting our own identity and way of thinking.

Breaking away from the conventional mould, ELT should focus on the expressive skills of the learners. Though teacher has become learning facilitator, effective changes in approaches, methods and techniques in ELT have not been adapted. The teaching of English as a Second Language (ESL) in the Indian context has been the major concern for educational planners, curriculum framers materials producers and language teachers. Striving for improving the existing teaching strategies points out the need for reconsidering the quality of the teacher, teaching materials, learner and the environment. The changes in the language classroom can be achieved through learner interaction and teacher learner interaction. Learning environment with learner centeredness concentrating on learner activity is an aspect of the new pedagogics. But here a difficult task is the proper arrangement of the materials for varied purposes and also how to organize them. For this teachers must be highly resourceful and creative to innovate new classroom techniques. Teaching is an art and a teacher has to play the role of a creative artist to incorporate and design strategies. The challenges in English Language Teaching have made teaching a tedious task. But it must be treated as a joyful responsibility of the teacher. It is neither a task nor a jobbery. The professional competency and content enrichment will make the ELT experience a joyful avocation. Unless the teacher is delighted he cannot delight the learners. Effective teaching will lead to effortless learning.

There are certain preliminary steps in the context and process of teaching English as a second language. We know that the concept of second Language Teaching has psychological principles. The various methods hitherto followed were replaced by new techniques incorporating notions like Error analysis, Contrastive analysis and Pedagogic analysis. Error analysis and Contrastive analysis are familiar terms in education contributed by linguistics. Error analysis will be followed by remedial teaching to test the common errors of the learners. Exposure to the target language is inevitable for the effective and quick learning of a foreign language. And as such many may object the idea of contrastive analysis in the teaching of a second language. But at the higher level it is desirable to have an idea regarding the basic similarities and contrasts in the mother tongue and the target language.

Pedagogic analysis is an attempt to analyse the subject matter through the eyes of the learner. It is an endeavour to help the learner in the process of making the learning material into a receivable form. The learning materials/lessons are the major preliminary data available. Pedagogic analysis with special reference to a teaching module in English language teaching consists of the following major components.

Identification of the major and minor concepts is the first component in the module. In a prose passage the important content (lexical) words are identified. Content analysis is carried out with special reference to the Key concepts. In a poem, the concentration is on the imagery pattern, figures of speech, linguistic nuances and stylistic devices. All these elements which render 'poetic' qualities are to be assimilated by the teacher and the identification of the teaching items is the basic step.

The language aspects like vocabulary and structure are important to acquire competency in a language.

Vocabulary consists of synonyms and antonyms. The apt phonetic realizations of the newly introduced words, stress and other features must be identified. To achieve intelligibility at least in India, the learners need some basic training in phonetics. In the pedagogic analysis of language items, the suprasegmental features of the English Language with its unphonetic nature must be stressed. The newly introduced words are phonemically transcribed (Broad transcription) and the phonetic scripts with their distribution system (whether the particular phoneme can appear word initially, word finally and word medially) are also introduced. Another step is the identification of the functional aspects reflected in the lesson as structures.

Identification of the pre-requisites is the next stage. It is an attempt to realize the essential learning items that are required for the acquisition and transfer of the new learning experience. This identification regarding the pre-requisites includes the language aspects as well as the cultural context.

In the next stage, preparation of pre-diagnostic test items are made to identify the lapses. It is an attempt to identify the language skills which are to be inculcated. If the material is based on any socio-cultural milieu, the required 'preparedness' of the learner is assessed.

After preparing a detailed analysis and relative significance of the instructional objectives, appropriate learning experiences at different stages are chalked out. These stages are followed by comparing and identifying new topics and items aiming at an interdisciplinary approach. Further, items are divided into lesson grids considering the following.

The units are divided into hierarchical stages. The anticipated errors and difficulties of the learners are listed. In the achievement and diagnostic tests the errors are identified. It is followed by a long list of home assignments. The process of pedagogic analysis is completed with a comprehensive list of language projects and suggestions for further reading.

ELT has to realise that language is both power and discourse. As a powerful tool of negotiation, language has a need factor. Language activities with relevance to real life and near life situations are conducive to effective learning. The following observations support the rationale for proposing a shift in the methodology.

In spite of all the experiments and innovations in the field of ELT, the learner performance is disheartening. When a learner easily picks up the rudiments of the first language, why does he feel difficult to learn a second language? It is pointed out that communication in a second language (English at present is taught in India not as a foreign language, but as a second language) becomes a near improbability in a teacher-dominated classroom. In a learner-centered environment, he becomes an active participant in the communication strategy. The role of the teacher is a marginal one, but has to provide activities for linguistic communication. Ultimate aim of this strategy is learner autonomy—learners should be independent learners with necessary support and guidance from the learning facilitator. Here the prescribed materials have greater importance. Recent research has proved that learners show greater interest in reading and writing non-prescribed materials. Let things from the outside world come to the class-room either in original or in duplication. The teacher must be active to make students 'function' English. Drag the outside reality into the classroom and in the speech act try to overcome the communication gap between the interlocutors. Along with these classroom activities the teacher has to reflect on the experiences. Theorizing can start from the analysis of experience. Techniques are evolved to form new language teaching methods suitable to the present Indian context and needs.

This tendency can be exploited to improve the language ability. The redistribution of priorities is the beginning of a renewed curriculum.

To a second language learner, the teacher has to communicate the different facets of the target language. Familiarisation of the linguistic nuances through carefully designed frames ensures easy learning. Failure to relate the study of English to the actual needs of the learner insists for a need-based syllabus, which ensures maximum exposure to the target language. A clear perspective of the entrant behaviour of the learner and a vision regarding the terminal behaviour will help to formulate an 'internal syllabus' for the individual learners.

In the second language learning situation, the learning materials help to achieve a reasonable degree of communicative competence. This can be achieved through the development of language skills (Listening, Speaking, Writing, Reading), the mastery of Language elements, (speech sounds, words, phrases, sentences and discourse), the development of communication skill (involving accuracy, fluency and appropriateness) and the inclusion of literary skills such as the ability to understand, interpret and aesthetic enjoyment. The materials developed based on principles of second language learning will also take care of the development of study skills and reference skills.

A critical evaluation of ELT will reveal different approaches during certain specific stages. Thus Oral Approach or Situational Language Teaching associated with the British Linguists was popular during the 1980's. The Audio-lingual Method flourished during the 1950's was derived from the structural linguistics. It emphasised learning as habit formation. Communicative Language Teaching emerged as a method during the late 1960's considered language as a tool for interaction and communication.

Learner-centeredness and activity-oriented teaching are the signs of the new pedagogics. In the present situation, it is inevitable to identify the concerned needs and levels of language proficiency. Jack C. Richard and Theodre S. Rogers emphasise the importance of 'Needs Analysis' in ELT situation:

> Needs analysis is concerned with identifying general and specific language needs that can be addressed in developing goals, objectives, and content in language program.... Needs analysis focuses on what the learner's present level of proficiency is and on what the learner will be required to use the language for on completion of the program. Its aim is to identify the type of language skills and level of language proficiency the program should aim to deliver. Needs analysis acknowledges that the goals of learners vary and must be determined before decisions about content and method can be made. (1995:156)

A harmonious development of all the language skills transforms the learners as effective communicators. The improvement in the language competency is achieved through constant interaction. And during this process the learner is not viewed as an empty receptacle. The learner, in the changed context is considered as an immense potential ready to pick up language elements quickly. This readiness for linguistic communication from the learner automatically invites the continuous involvement of the teacher in interacting with the learner. Finally, a good teacher of English who requires a lot of teaching skills, will formulate a design to improve the same. While presenting a lesson, the most important stages are Presentation, Practice, Production and Review. The following teaching skills will improve the professional competency of the teacher:

1. The skill to speak comprehensible English to the learners, simple in structure and coming down to the level of the learners.
2. Developing interest and appropriate language activites to motivate them.
3. Providing opportunities to the learners to interact with the teacher and the learners.
4. Try to develop good rapport.
5. Develop interaction and conversation between the learners.
6. Provide regular opportunities to ask questions.

7. Integrate the mastery of grammar with other language skills. These are some of the learning activities and new and interesting items can be included further.

Balancing between traditional culture and global exposure can be attained through both Frontline curriculum and Fast track curriculum. The former permits anything that appears new to be included in the syllabus while the latter provides more freedom of selection to the leaners.

New learning activities and teaching strategies are to be formulated with well-defined objectives. As the reality keeps on changing there is no validity in insisting any fixity of strategy. Sermonising any particular approach or technique in ELT without any consideration for the context and environment specificity is not feasible. A deconstructive thinking in ELT from the Indian perspective has to be initiated. English Language Teaching in the colonial period had the main objective of westernization. Language was a mere tool to the imperialists with a specific aim. There is an inevitable need for demolishing the conventional methods manipulated by the dominant culture. The traditional approaches and objectives of ELT must be redefined to balance them with the present 'needs'. The concept of need-based language teaching may force us to remould pedagogics against the canons of acceptability—thus resulting a sort of deconstruction of ELT, a march towards an alternative pedagogics, decolonising the colonial materials and strategies.

Let us consider the priorities in the decolonised pedagogics. We have to check whether the curriculum is framed to form a solid base in life skills. Considering the present world scenario, our curriculum has to promote cardinal human virtues and a willingness to live together. It should consider ecological balance and harmony with nature to promote environment sensitivity. Curriculum should also ensure gender equality. It should satisfy the lovers of traditional cultures and inculcate work culture.

Adequate instructional materials based on the above priorities with well-defined specifications will focus on all the aspects of language—communicative, interpretative and expressive.

Enrich our pedagogical strategies according to the current trends and needs of the society. We have to consider the integration of the sensibility of the present society with a clear perspective of the developing world. For the successful orientation for conceptualization of any method, the learner-teacher relationship as interlocutors is an essential factor. Train the learners in productive language skills (Writing and Speaking) is the main task of the teacher. In the teacher-learner interaction, adequate selection and identification of the variety of spoken English is essential. The unphonetic nature of the English Language with its suprasegmental features make the task of teaching spoken English an enormously challenging one. Teaching spoken English with the main objective of achieving intelligibility within India is, however, not a complex process. Received Pronunciation has become a myth. "The time has come to abandon the archaic name 'Received Pronunciation'. The model used for British English is what is referred to as BBC English: this is the pronunciation of professional speakers employed by the BBC as newsreaders..." (Roach 2003:V). The concept of General Indian English has become out of context, and in the context of globalisation, international intelligibility is a desirable factor. Training in this skilled activity must begin with loud reading practice followed by other procedures like ear training and listening comprehension. How to make our learners as good communicators? One way is to deviate from the conventional grammar teaching by laying stress on 'functions'. As an approach it endorses communicative aspect of the language. 'Form' alone is irrelevant to the learner and this shift would help the learner to respond to different functions in a meaningful way. Responses to a number of life like situations will help the learner to identify easily the functions of language items and can use them in similar situations. This change from 'form' to 'function' in ELT has to tackle the following:

Who are we teaching?
Why are we teaching?

What are we teaching?
How are we teaching?
How do we know that teaching has taken place?

The perfect instruments of learning—the materials must be supplemented by 'theoretical understanding' of the transaction of learning experiences. Ronald Wardhaugh's views on the subject is a good reminder:

> Good teaching practice is based on good theoretical understanding. There is indeed nothing so practical as a good theory. Teachers should focus from time to time not on techniques, not on methods, but on approach, that is on theory, and should try in those moments to capture some of the excitement of the many challenges that confront us in teaching English to speakers of other languages. (1972:19)

An unhealthy trend in the English teaching scenario is the case against literature, trying to argue for language teaching. This competition between the advocates of language teaching and supporters of teaching literature component urges the need for the integration of language and literature. A synthesis of language teaching and literature—inclusion of literature with language perspective can act as a rationale. Literary texts and learning materials based on real life situations with abundant linguistic and language components will create an awareness regarding the strategy of teaching language through literature.

ELT during the colonial period concentrated on two kinds of motivations. English was taught as a foreign language and it was studied for operational and integrative purposes. Geoffrey Broughton and others in *Teaching English as a Foreign Language* discuss how a foreign language learnt for operational purposes (examples cited are the sales man, and the tourist) is instrumental. The thesis also refers to the integrative motivation—a sort of effective comprehension of the culture and social milieu of the English (1978:5). During the colonial period the politics and culture of the dominant group were endorsed. The urge to decolonise directly alludes to the need to include alternative discourses instead of the old stereotyped. By alternative discourse I mean the popular culture and literature of the marginalized. With different perspectives of teaching, we have to establish culture space to subaltern life, avoiding 'fossilation'—a state or stage in which we continue to remain in what we are. Evaluation of the materials prepared on the basis of alternative discourse is an important procedure in the teaching strategy. The relevance and appropriateness have already been stated earlier. Teaching strategies formed to exploit the materials will improve the classroom performance. The procedural process with specific motivational objectives is another stage. We have to teach English to our learners with some obvious reasons. In the Indian context there is an allegation against English for no obvious reasons. The English Language Teaching situation in India can be improved by analyzing the entry-level competence and the needs envisaged.

ELT should not be a continuation of the out-dated age-old tradition—should not be a residue of the colonial attitude. A postcolonial attitude must be evolved in terms of English Language Teaching. In preparing teaching materials, we have to select and talk about our own literatures, languages and values through English. The movement from the third world literature towards the fourth world—the indigenous literatures must find place in the English classrooms. Existing courses in English do not entertain alternative discourses. We still endorse the dominant politics and culture of the mainstream which is leading towards 'interior colonialism'. Decolonising teaching strategies, however, does not nourish a negative attitude against the teaching of English. ELT has to accommodate the ceaseless implementation of changes taking place in the present global scenario, but without surrendering completely to the process of globalisation.

REFERENCES

Broughton, Geoffrey et al. (1978). *Teaching English as a Foreign Language*. London: Routledge & Kegan Paul.

Brumfit, C.G., and K. Johnson (eds). (1979). *The Communicative Approach to Language Teaching*. Oxford: Oxford University Press.

Cook, Vivian. (1991). *Second Language Learning and Language Teaching*. London: Edward Arnold.

Doff, Adrian. (1988). *Teach English: A Training Course for Teachers—Trainer's Handbook*. Cambridge: Cambridge University Press.

Gardner, R.C. (1985). *Social Psychology and Second Language Learning*. London: Edward Arnold.

Joyce, Bruce and Marsha Weil. (1997). *Models of Teaching*. New Delhi: Prentice Hall of India.

Richards, J.C. and T.S. Rodgers, (1995). *Approaches and Methods in Language Teaching*. Cambridge: Cambridge University Press.

Rivers, W.M. (1981). *Teaching Foreign Language Skills*. Chicago: University of Chicago Press.

Roach, Peter (ed). (2003). *English Pronouncing Dictionary*. Cambridge: Cambridge University Press.

Wardaugh, Ronald. (1972). "TESOL: Current Problems and Classroom Practices" in *Teaching English as a Second Language*. Ed. Harold B. Allen & Russell N. Campbell. Bombay: Tata McGraw-Hill.

20

Foreign Influence on English Language

Mallikarjun Patil

Many times we do not know the language we speak. Still we must care for it as it plays an important role in projecting our existence in society. Knowledge is power. Simeon Potter argues, "The power of rightly chosen words is very great, whether those words are intended to inform, to entertain, or to move."[1] English is one such language which we must take care of.

English is an Indo-European/Germanic/Aryan language which was spoken in Ukraine and Southern Russia five thousand years ago, between 6000 and 4000 BC. It was a proto language in the Neolithic Age. Lithuania bears many forms of that still.

Indo-European family had eight branches Greek, Latin (French, Spanish, Italian and Portuguese), Germanic (East, West and North Germanic languages), Indo-Iranian (Indian languages relating to Sanskrit family plus Iranian languages like Persian and Arabic), Armenian, Albanian, Celtic (Briton, Cornish, Welsh, Irish and Scottish) and Balto-Slavanic (includes Lithuania and Latvia). The unique features of these languages are that western languages, maybe, due to proximity, have a similar structure (example: Parts of Speech) and vocabulary (common root forms). Such primitive words like *father, mother, brother, sister* denoting blood relations exist in many Indo-European languages as evidenced below. For example the helping verb is:

Sanskrit	Greek	Latin	German	Russian	Italian
Asti	*esti*	*est*	*ist*	*est*	*e'*
Pitru		*pater*	*vater*		

It is believed that Sanskrit must be the oldest Indo-European language.

Another thing is that western languages use *c* or *k* dominantly and they are called *Centum* languages, while eastern languages use *sh* for *k* and they are called *Satam* languages. This is to say those languages that do not have a common structure such as parts of speech or common roots of lexis are not included in the tag Indo-European. Chinese, Dravidian and some European languages like Uralian, Finnish and Hungarian do not have one or the other features of the above family. Some of these are agglutinative.

The sub-family Germanic, also called Teutonic or Gothonic, developed three geographic divisions: East Germanic (Burgundian, Vandal and Gothic), North Germanic (Norwegian, Icelandic, Swedish and Danish) and West Germanic (German, Dutch, Flemish, Frisian and English). The proto-Germanic language existed before the Christian era. The unique features of these languages are that they have common stress and intonation patterns, two-tense verb system (present and past) and strong and weak verbs (as Grimm's Ablaut series explains. Example: drive, drove, driven). Tacitus (1st century) speaks of this in his *Germania*. Scandinavian runic inscriptions evidence this. Wulfila (311-83 AD), a bishop of Vasigoths translated the Bible into Gothic and this work is the earliest extant proto-Germanic work. Now the question arises why this proto-Germanic language vanished? Maybe because of disintegration. If that be what per cent of words of that language have come into the present day English?

Certain events like the arrival of Germanic tribes Jutes (from Jutland, the Jute brothers Hengist and Horsa arriving in England in 449 soon after Romans left England in 410), Angles (from Schleswig) and Saxons (from Holstein) to Romanized Britain, England's conversion to Christianity (in 597), Scandinavian invasion, Norman conquest, revival of learning, the English migration to America and colonization have played an important role in the development of English.

Anglo-Saxons created a sort of history. They helped British kings but they refused to go back. Jutes settled in the present day Kent, Saxons in South-West and Angles in mid-north. First literature grew in the north which being divided into Northumbria and Marcia. Hilda, Abbess of Whitby, Caedmon, Benedict Bicop (founder of Jarrow monastery) and his pupil Bede (the Venerable), worked there. When Saxon kings became dominant the literature-area was shifted to Wincanster (Winchester), the capital of West Saxons. The Scandinavian or Viking invasions in the 7th, 8th and 9th centuries disrupted all this. But King Alfred (871-99) himself a man of letters stopped them and encouraged the growth of literature in his region. Wulfstan and Alfric created a literary renaissance.

English as a Germanic language has certain position and grandeur. The English spoken by these tribes was nothing but a low Germanic language like Dutch, Flemish and Frisian. In fact, this was common to all low Germanic people. English people called it Saxon or Anglo-Saxon. But 'King Alfred called his language and nation as *Englisc.* The phrase Old English was used in the 13th century. Not to speak of Old English was a pure language with little Latin and Norse.

The unique features of Old English are:

1. Inflections,
2. Free word order,
3. No silent syllables, and
4. Dialectability.

Then came Norman Conquest in the 11th century leading to the eventual influence of the French. Already Christianity had brought in Latin. The French also brought in Greek indirectly while Renaissance increased real Greek influence. Likewise, due to trade, there was felt the influence of other Romance languages like Italian, Spanish and Italian. During the Middle English (1100-1500) period, English changed greatly and its unique features were:

1. Loss of Inflections,

2. Leading to Fixed Word Order,
3. The use of Preposition, and
4. Creating Spelling Confusion (because of French scribes).

These features continued in modern English as well. The use of French and Latin was heavy. As we know, gradually Chaucer and other writers' effort for strengthening English succeeded. London emerged as the center of learning and of standard English language. The reasons were not far to seek. It was a Norman capital; near it lying Anglia, a wool trade center and Oxford and Cambridge universities. Besides, London had Caxton's printing press. Renaissance and Shakespeare enhanced the prestige of English and during the time of Dryden it reached its highest growth. British colonialism in the next centuries was to expand English further. Modern times are in favour of it. So it is a global language today.

The arrival of Germanic tribes plus Scandinavian and Norman invasions and Latinization led to the death of many native Celtic languages such as Breton, Cornish and Gaelic, while others Welsh, Irish and Scottish exist weakly.

First, Anglo-Saxons used Germanic runes as a script. Later they used Roman script from Phoenicians via Greece and Rome. English is not England's native language. It is a Germanic language with Scandinavian, Greek, Latin, French and other influences. Because of heavy influence, its structure, spelling and pronunciation systems changed considerably. As a result, the language fluctuated in its look, and great men did not like heavy changes. Some said it is a wild and chaotic language. Though it attained maturity in Dryden's time, Dryden himself said it had no prosody, no tolerable dictionary and grammar.

As we know English is a West Germanic language. The Scandinavian languages are North Germanic. Racially these people were once living in proximity. Once Germanic tribes settled down in England some Scandinavian tribes wished to follow the suit. After sporadic raids (beginning in 787 at Dorset), Alfred and Guthrum had the Treaty of Wedmore in

886 and Scandinavians were permitted to settle down in Danelaw (between London and Chester. That is to the north of Thames). So they had their own rule there. Danes plundered again and defeated Athelred in 991. He ran away to France. Again in 1009, they plunderd Oxford and took Winchester. Athelred came back and sacked them. This provoked Sveinn's son Canute and he arrived in 1015 with forces and defeated the king. In fact, he ruled England from 1016 to 1036. At the same time he was also the ruler of Denmark and Norway. After him his son ruled for another six years. The Danes settled down in Anglia, Midlands and the North from 850 and lived there for three centuries. Though they came as plunderers (Vikings), after their common originality asserted, they blended with the English. The Icelandic poet Gunnlang would recite his poem to king Athelred effortlessly. A Scandinavian chronicler says, "The language in Norway and England was one and the same when William won England."

As a result of Scandinavian influence, the words of Scandinavian languages like Norsė, Danish, Norwegian and Swedish left their marks on manorial organization, local government and law liberally. Yet this was through spoken media. Words like *law, statue, outlaw, husband, fellow, wrong, walk, want, weak, wing, sky, ski* and, *skull* came into English. Scandinavian influence is still strong in Cumberland, Riding and Anglia. Some people use that language's numerals there. Since Middle Ages Scandinavian influence is occasional. Such new words like *skii, saga* and *tungsten* are rather of Common European stock.

Since Danelaw, a colony between London and York where Scandinavians lived, had not yet developed much writing, Scandinavian influence was not felt in writing immediately. It was to be seen only in Early Middle English. Names of certain parts of human body *(leg, skin, skull)*, animals *(calf bull)*, prepositions *(fro, thwart, till* (meaning *to*), *until)*, pronouns, *(they, their, them)*, pronominal adjectives *(both, same)*, verbs *(are)*, phrasal verbs *(take, take off)*, verbal operator *get*, and-*s* (in goes) affix of the third person singular (for English *th)* are Scandinavian.

Scandinavian endings are seen explicitly in place names as:

—*by* means 'village' as in Normanby (Norse men, and, 'by' means village from *byr* = village of the (Norsemen, Norwegians). Likewise, Derby and Denby.

— *beck* 'brook' in Birkbeck

— *brick* 'slope' in Norbreck

— *fell* 'hill' in Whinfell

— *garth* 'yard' in Applegarth

— *mel* 'sand-dune' in Cartmell

— *Figg* 'ridge' in Lambrigg

— *thwaite* 'clearing' in Braithwaite, etc.

Some Scandinavian words remain with their English counterparts as doublets. Of course, they have slight difference in meaning.

English	**Scandinavian**
no	nay
from	fro
rear	raise
shirt	skirt
ditch	dike

There was a competition between English and Scandinavian words for survival and the latter shot to fame: *sister* against English *swester, egg* against *ey.*

John of Trevisa (in 1387) said Scandinavian influence defiled and corrupted English. But 45% of English language is of Germanic in its origin.

Next to Scandinavian Greek influence is felt heavily. The ancient Athens from the 6th century onwards led the world in knowledge. Pericles (95-429 BC), Socrates, Plato, Aristotle and a host of others, particularly writers, created an everlasting corpus of writings.

The seven ancient arts Grammar, Logic, Rhetoric, Arithmetic, Geometry, Astronomy and Music are Greek in origin.

Greek, as an Indo-European language, was mature enough to sustain growth. So it helped European languages like Latin, French and English grow with its word-power.

Therefore, Greek was taught in all European universities.

Chaucer, Petrarch and Boccaccio regretted to have not learnt Greek.

Greek words either in toto, or in adaptation and assimilation, or in translation came into English abundantly enriching English. But it is difficult to distinguish Greek words as they came through Latin and French. The common words like *phone, atom* and *graph* are Greek. When it comes to Literature basic words like *drama, tragedy, comedy, catastrophe* and *climax* are Greek; and many science words like *psychology* and *neurology* are Greek.

The classical renaissance led to the importance of Greek learning. The rediscovery of ancient classical Greek knowledge brought a new way of looking at life. There was a wealth of thought. Greek brought a new set of ideas and terms for political science, art and literature.

Greek has given us affixes like, *un–, –ness, –ly, post–, anti–, a–, –ology*, etc.

Latin is another important Indo-European language that influenced English heavily. Contacts with Roman Empire during several centuries introduced Latin words to the people of England. Roman Britons had a good number of Latin words like *Chester* appearing in place names like Dorchester. But Latin influence was through written language.

Once Christianity came to England with St Augustine in 597, the English began picking up Latin. Latin words like *street, mill,* and *cheese* became quite common. Words like *minster, monk, mass, church* and *priest* spread immediately. Secondly church fathers created new words and assigned new meanings to English words. For example: the English festival *Easter* and the rite *Baptism* acquired new meanings.

Latin words came through religion, science and literature. The 9th century Benedictine revival with Dunsten and Alfric, and other trends brought as many as 400 words. One thing is that English then had its own power to create new words and it created words like *Gospel* from Latin *God spellboc.* Alfric wrote a Latin grammar using technical terms like *part taker* for *participle* and *nama* for *noun.*

The Greek borrowing continued in Middle and Modern English too, in areas like technology, law, science and religion. So words like *index, pauper, legitimate, scribe, simile, collect* and *tolerance* came into existence.

Some Latin words like *exit, genius, specimen, album, inertia, alibi* and, *extra* were taken into English as they were, while most others were anglicized, acclimatized (example: *telephone),* adapted and translated. Latin affixes like *-ment, -ation, -able, -ate, -ic* and *-al,* came into English for word creation. Likewise, Latin *-or* was used as *-our* (as in labour) and Latin *-er* as *-re* (example: *center* as *centre).* Latin words came in legion, sometimes creating synonyms/doublets as *blame-blaspheme, frial-fragile, poor-pauper, reason-ration, respite-respect, sure-secure, equal-egal, adventure-aventure, confer-collate* and *construct-resurrect.* The latter words came through French. *Sin* basically wrongdoing means *crime* now. This is called semantic borrowing.

Latin affected the structure of English. For example: we say *It is me* for *It is I.* We use *whom* in place of *who* sometimes. This is because of Latin influence. Secondly some English metrical system is Latinate. Though English is a stressed language, Latin syllabic length decides English stress.

Latin became the first language and useful. It was taught in schools and colleges. It was a religious language upto the 16th century, haunting many intellectuals. Many writers and scientists used it. Roger Ascham, Bacon, More, Harvey and Newton wrote in it. The English intellectuals thought that Latin was a more durable language.

Similarly French is a fundamental (second big) influence on English for dignity and eloquence. This was there even before Norman Conquest as English kings had relations with Normans. Such pre-Norman words include *castle* for the English *burg,* suggesting a new way of life.

Scandinavians as that of Huns were heroic and nomads. Their king Cnut ousted the English king Athelred the Unready (978-1016) in 1016 and ruled England for 26 years. So the English king who had married a Norman princess took refuge with Norman king William and later his son Edward regained his father's throne. Edward as a mark of gratitude, because of his issuelessness, assured William that he would, on getting back his kingdom and on his death, pass it over to him. Once Cnut's successor son died in 1042, Edward regained his kingdom and ruled for 26 years. But when he died in 1066 his adviser Harold (former minister Godwine's son) who became the king of England refused to pass it over to William. This angered William and the latter defeated the English in 1066 at the battle of Hastings.

Norman conquest was a landmark in the history of Britain. Normans changed the face of earth in England. William with him brought French nobility and culture. The French held all high posts. It is said the king banned English in office. The English kings neither learnt English nor married English women for the next three centuries. French became the first language and its use became common in administration, court, education and social life. Anglo-Norman was the French used in England. It was a written technical language as well as a dialect. In fact, Normans placed all the four Old English dialects on a level. Likewise they shifted the capital from Winchester to London. Bokenham says the French barbarized English. A chronicler Robert wrote 'unless a man knows French one counts of him little.' A lady at Charles II's court was despised if she could not speak fashionable French.

As a result, French words like *arrest, market, rent, justice, prince, duke, duchess* and *baron* came into English. But *king* and *queen* remained English. Those of more elegant occupations are French: *carpenter, draper, mason, painter* and *tailor,* while simple occupations remain of English. Another thing is that French words like *table* and *chair* got assimilated in English but words like *garage* and *amateur* did not. They retained their original spelling, stress and pronunciation. Some English and French words are synonymous. So are *shire, town, home, house, cows, sheep* and *pig* English, *county, city, palace, mansion, beef, mutton* and *pork* French. Yet English words are stronger, more physical and more human. Some English words competed with the French: *writ* with *scripture* and *board* with *table* and the latter succeeded.

When Henry II extended his rule in Norman provinces and England's royal contacts with France grew, Paris French influenced English. This introduced Paris French soft sounds *(ch* and *w)* for Norman hard sounds [c (from Latin *k)* and *g*], creating doublets. For example:

Norman French	Paris French
catch	chase
canal	channel
warden	guardian
reward	regard
real	royal
count	compute
colur	colour
dainty	dignity
wile	guile
prisun	prison
warrantee	guarantee
wage	gage
gaol	jail

The Norman French monks altered the look of English profoundly. Some letters like *k*, *q*, *x* and *z* were seldom used. So Old Englis 'cyning' became king, *cw* became quath, *cw* becoming, *qu*, and (1) c, (2)-er, (3)-te, (4) sc and (5) g, becoming (1) ch, (2)-re, (3)-ty, (4) sh/sch and (5) gg/dg respectively. There are many French affixes like *-able,* metres and stanza forms, literary genres and syntax being used in English.

The English kings lost their Norman possessions in the 13th century and they merged with the nation. In 1362 the English parliament passed a law that English must be used for all purposes. Still the events of Hundred Years War,

Restoration and its repercussions in literature, French revolution, colonization, world wars and multiculturalism brought enormous contact between the two nations influencing each other.

But too much of French influence was criticized. Mulcaster in his spirited plea asked "Why not all in English?" He said:

1. a) English is needless (but look at the time wasted in the learning of foreign languages!), b) It is coarse and uncultivated (uncouth) (but look at the state of Latin before Cicero made an effort to polish it!). Dryden made fun of French in his play *Marriage à la Mode*. Dr Johnson said "English would become a dialect of French if this influence continued."

The other European languages have their own share in the formation of English as a world language. Celtic languages like Welsh, Irish and Scottish have a small share. Most of the river *(Thames, Avon, Ouse)* and some place names are Celtic. *Druid, trousers, brat* and *galore* are Irish; *clan, bog, glen, slogan* and *whiskey* are Scottish; and *bard, crag, flanne* and *cradle* are Welsh. Cornish left some marks and now it is no more.

Germanic languages like German, Austrian, Dutch, Flemish and Frisian affected English. For example: the beginning of a sentence with predicate as in 'said he,' 'came a pause' and 'Down went king royal George' is a German feature. This was predominant in Anglo-Saxon, and half of Alfred's writing is like that. The English 'better' is German 'besser,' the *t* and *s* being interchangeable. Words like *zinc, bismuth, cobalt, quartz* and *nickel* are German. Dutch influenced English with words like *plunder, bear, skipper, deck, excise, guilder, dollar, yacht, tea* and *brandy*. *Island* from *tea and* is Frisian.

Of the Slavonic languages Russian contacts produced words like *rouble, sable, Czar, steppe* and *mammoth*. *Intelligentsia* is Polish and *robot* is Czech.

Other European languages like Italian have their share. Italian's main contribution is through French. Italian words in painting *(studio)*, music *(opera, solo, temp* and *gusto)* and architecture *(portico, villa, balcony* and *arcade)* came into English retaining their original spelling and pronunciation. Italians were surprised at Englishmen's visiting Italy and behaving like the natives. They said: "An Italianate Englishman is a devil incarnate."

The English contact with Spanish for trade and war brought in some Spanish words like *renegade, vanilla, cork, banana, sherry, cigar, matador, armada, tornado* and *potato.* The English contact with the Portuguese brought *marmalade, buffalo, caste, coco, mango, copr a, teak* and *apricot.*

C.L. Wren says, "In view of the world-wide contacts of the English speakers—through competition with the empires of Spain, Portugal, the Netherlands and France, in Africa and the East, the Red-Indian languages by way of America, British dominion in India, Africa, and the Far East and the British settlement of the newly discovered continent of Australia in the 18th and 19th centuries—English language absorbed a variety of words from almost every where."

Turkish means Arabic and Persian. First Arabic deserves a special mention, for it was Arabs or Moors of Spain and of Arabic centers that introduced many technical terms into English. Arabic science, renaissance learning and Islamic studies influenced Europe and English language. Words like *algebra, alcohol, zenith, cotton, amber, magazine, fakir, ima* and *harem* are Arabic. Persian words like *azure, jasmine, shawl and paradise* came into English through Arabic.

Hebrew words include *cherub, messiah, sabboth, seraph, torah, bethel* and *log. Zebra* and *mumbo jumbo* are African.

From India came Sanskrit, Hindi and other vernaculars' words. Religious technical terms like *guru, pundit, nirvana, yoga, karma, maharaj; jute, jungle, sahib, pariah, sahib, cot, rupee, pukka, coolie, nabob, khaki* (Hindi), *mongoose* (Marathi), *bungalow* (Bengali), *juggernaut* (Oriya), *chatni* (Kannada), *curry* (Tamil) came from Indian languages.

Tea is Chinese, *rickshaw* is Japanese, *boomerang* is Australian, *bamboo, paddy* and *cckatoo* are Malay, *igloo* is Eskimos and *canoe* is Haiti.

Thus English is a world language as the world has made it over the centuries.

21

Gesture in the Fine Arts

R. Chanana

Knowledge is like 'Sinking Star'. Every language abounds in style and expression of a particular culture. Language is "intuitive science of experience" (Sapir). Every language has its own psyche. The art of intuition and innate art of expression are synthesized in a way to evolve aesthetic factors which constitutes the psyche of language. Language, we all know, is made of words and it is equally well known that gesture is made of motion. The motion may be of hands, of the lips, of the eyes, of the facial muscles, or even of the body as a whole. Gestures, made of such motions are highly expressive and often convey much more than mere words can. They stress what words convey, charge them with emotions of the speaker and in semi-articulate rustics, they are an important means of communication. Thus the language of gesture is as important, perhaps, much more, than the language of words. When the language of words fails, we use the language of gestures. The language of words is most successful and most expressive when it turns into gesture. Language of words becomes gesture when it conveys emotions and passions which are usually not conveyed by the words used. Such emotional and passionate gestures are more expressive, more meaningful and more powerful than the ordinary language in which words have not acquired the emotional force and vigour of gestures. We all are aware of the sign language which is practised for the physically challenged persons. Gesture is almost inherent in language.

Blackmur writes, "Gesture, in language, is the outward and dramatic play of inward and imagined meaning."

Not only is gesture inherent in language and necessary to impart to it emotional force and vigour, it is also inherent in architecture, in sculpture, in painting and in dancing and music. It is of as great an importance structurally in these fine arts, as it is in poetry. The present paper aims to explain the point in detail with reference to the fine arts.

This universe is painted by the Greatest Artist Almighty—the creator of the universe. This Universe is imitated by different mediums—literature and fine arts. In imaginative *painting* the gesture is imparted to portraits or figure-painting by the skilful use of texture and light. No knowledge is so great or so skilled, as our knowledge of what we see in people but when we try to express this visual knowledge in words, we fumble and remain unsuccessful in communicating it exactly. This visual knowledge of human nature is best expressed in imaginative painting, and such expression is the gesture in portrait-painting. An imaginative painter catches such gestures, such meaningful moments, while they are lacking in portraits not so imaginative. Many an excellent portrait, perfect in its fidelity to truth, are caught or imagined by the inspired artist, and it is such gestures that startle the portrait into the maximum of life. Such meaningful gestures impart not only life and vitality to the portrait, but also universality. That is why in great portraits we see ourselves. They have a gesture which conveys one or the other of the universally felt emotions. Paintings of suffering humanity, horror images, smiling flowers, running streams, lively forests, burning trees and the stump of the tree, the painting of Monalisa throb with life and spirit lurks in them.

In *sculpture* the artist carves out human or animal shapes out of stone or wood or some other physical mass, and in this way arrests human or animal movements. But in a good piece of sculpture, the essential human or animal shapes, though arrested, move within themselves, whether the movement is from outward to inward, or from inward to outward, and in this way they make a timeless gesture. There is an essential difference between gesture and act. In a bad sculpture, there is always a sense of action. We feel that the horse is about to leap or the athlete wants to leap. There is always a sense that some movement or the other has been arrested, and that it wants to go on and complete itself in action. A good sculpture does not create any such sense of some movement arrested, in the moving stillness, there is a gesture completed at the moment of its greatest significance. In this way it creates the effect of fulfillment and perfection. For example, caves of Ajanta and Elora, marble rocks of Jabalpur, temples of Khajuraho. The tourist is spurred mentally and wishes to reach Khajuraho. While observing the stone statue they are spell bound and feel some spiritual satisfaction. Erotic sculpture invites him but he returns gaining something spiritual that enlivens his soul. The gesture illuminates and enlivens the medium of the artist, be it heavy or light. It is gesture which makes a stone figure a sphinx, and it is gesture again which makes the great sphinx a smile. It is gesture which gives the impression of meaningful movement in repose, of great momentum in great repose. Man has always brooded upon himself and upon the world round him, and good sculpture is the result of such brooding. It is this brooding which imparts meaningful gestures to stone figures. The gesture results from the momentum and the repose of man's brooding upon himself.

The finest example of gesture in architecture is a church-spire. A good church-spire gives a sense of life and movement. So is the architecture of the temple and mosque. It is like an arrow aimed at the Almighty. In it the form has become identical with the subject, and so is expressive of the religious aspirations of which the church or temple or mosque is a symbol. It creates a sense of movement as a tree or a shrub gives the sense of a process of growth, or as a beautiful room gives the effect of extending space rather than enclosing it. This very gesture is there when we feel, that pillars are mighty, that a bridge spans or leaps, and that a dome covers us. "This sense of movement is 'actually' inert mass and empty space is what we all gesture in architecture. 'Lotus temple of Delhi. Iskcon of Bangalore, Bombay, Delhi and European countries, White

House in America, many bridges multi-storied buildings five and seven star hotels in all the great capitals of India, India Gate, Rashtrapati Bhawan, Rock Gardens of Chandigarh and many memorable buildings speak for themselves.

In *dancing* gesture is of supreme importance, for when the gesture breaks down or does not communicate, the dance does not speak at all. Gesture must be built and infused into the movements of the dancer, otherwise they remain merely meaningless movements. Gesture makes dancing buoyant, and makes it possible for it to come to a middle or end to a dance. Gesture is the means through which the movements of the dance complete themselves. The movements of the dance become gestures with the help of either ritual, as in the Mass (a Christian ceremony) or music, as in the ballet. In ritual gesture is important. It is gesture which transforms mere movements into ritual. Gesture is the stable and moving element in ritual; it is born out of native feelings, and it controls and stresses the meaning of the ritual. To quote Blackmur, "Dancing delivers gestures otherwise conceived. It is the natural, wayward play of the body, controlled." Mirabai will go dancing in love of Lord Krishna and she is accepted as a symbol of *bhakti* for all Indians thus religion and philosophy cannot be separated from life in the Indian context. It is a cultural cohesion and identity. In Bharat Natyam, the performer expresses the whole story, through his 'bhav-bhangima' the 'Tandav Nritya' of Natraj represents the whole scheme of destruction of this universe. In Kathak-Nritya, the dancer represents Radha and Krishna through the movements at the same time on the stage and the audience feel and enjoy the spirit of Prakati and Purush. Here lies the significance of gesture in dancing.

Acting is the purposive control of the body's movements which produces meaningful gestures. Such control is necessary for transforming the movements of dancer into gesture, and such control is equally important in acting. It is the reduction, condensation, and telescoping of free movements that transform them into gesture both in dancing and acting. Historically considered play—acting grew out of dumb-show which is essentially mimicry or mummery. Mummery is an extraordinarily resourceful and complex art, using the full personality of the actor, and it receives life and vitality through his gestures. It is by his gesture that a good actor enlivens even a badly written play. It is because of the power of gestures of a good actor that even a play, written in a language we do not know, moves us and hold us spellbound. I myself once enjoyed such a play, and was enthralled by the supreme control of the actor over his movements. His gestures rose from beauty to more lucid beauty, and the gestures impressed and moved the author, though he could not at all understand the spoken word. It was a delightful experience, even though he was not familiar with the language. The experience clearly brings out the importance of gesture in acting. "Great acting bodies forth the gestures of great words; no more." Vasu's very first appearance in R.K. Narayan's *Man Eater of Malgudi*, marks him out from the rest. "His movements—quick, energetic, violent as they are—appear to be in tune with his gigantic appearance—a tanned face, large powerful eyes under thick eyebrows, a large forehead and a shock of unkempt hair, like a black halo." It would be worth quoting the acting performed by Shakuntla suffering from high-love-fever on the flower bed fanned by her friends Priyamvada and Ansuya.

Music is a much purer art than acting. It is purer because it works entirely through the medium of sound; and is entirely independent of all other mediums. All its movement is the movement of sound. It proceeds exclusively according to its own purpose, without any other considerations as is the case with the other arts. That is why Roger Sessions wrote in his work *The Intent of the Artist* that music, "creates gestures of the human spirit". Successful music is the result of most severe discipline. Through this severe discipline the musician secures the freedom of repetition, of development, of variation within, upon or around a theme to an extent which in any other major art would be not only ineffectual but boring; the freedom, in short, to play with the elements of musical meaning until they become gesture. In music the soul of the artist is expressed through gestures of sound, controlled and manipulated by the severe discipline to which the musician has subjected himself.

That is why Pater said that all the arts tend to the condition of music, and this condition is gesture. Music is the means for the expression of the gesture of the soul. Music also has a technique, a form and a theme or substance, but for a good musician the technique is everything, and he takes joy in it irrespective of the theme. The technique the whole object of his attention, for it is the means through which the gesture of the soul finds a befitting expression. In moments of highest success and achievement, the form and the substance become one, both in the process of expression and at the end. Both form and substance are united as gesture in moments of inspiration. That is why we are happy when we sing, and sing when we are sad. Music is the expression of the total personality and not of a part of it as is the case with the other arts. It is gesture expressive of the heart and mind of the musician. Music changes the atmosphere, even the instruments play a great role in changing the moods. Nowadays music is practised as a remedy for the patients. Doctor should have some knowledge of music so that they may treat the patients in a better way.

Such is the significance of gesture in the six fine arts, of which *poetry* is the natural child. Poetry shows the influence of the other arts, but it also creates a fiery gesture all its own. Poetry is the gesture of poetic judgment, the judgment of all the gestures, which make up our full being. Poetry is the meaning of all meaning, or at least the prophecy of it. There is a fury in poetic words which we understand, though we may not understand the words themselves. This fury is always there in a poem worth the name of poetry and it arises from a poetic gesture which carries the prophetic meaning of poetry, and poetic gesture which carries the prophetic meaning of poetry, and poetic judgment. Through rhythm, cadence and interval, all the gesture of the spoken word, the look and feel of man while speaking, can be well expressed: "physical gesture with face and hands and vocal gesture in shifting inflections". The whole technique of imaginative writing is concerned with the making of words play upon each other, both in small and large groups. Words acquire gesture and become more expressive only when they are delivered within a form and these forms or patterns are as many as there are gestures. *Repetition* of words or groups of words is one of the simplest devices by which words acquire the force and effectiveness of gestures. Take for example Macbeth's, "Tomorrow, and tomorrow and tomorrow", or Lear's, "Never never never never never". The words become an obsessive gesture, made out of a single repeated word intensified into a half throttled cry on the heart of the speaker. The words thus acquire a fury which they do not possess in themselves. The titles of great works of art, and also of immortal figures of literature, are transformed into symbols. Thus Hamlet has become symbolic of a man trying to resolve his doubts in great spiritual agony. Macbeth, Don Quixote, Dante, Plato, Michelangelo, etc. all equally symbolic. In the opinion of Blackmur, "A *symbol*, I take it, is what we use to express meaningfullness in a permanent way which cannot be expressed in direct words or formulas of words with any completeness; a symbol is a cumulus of meaning which once established, attracts further meaning to it until, overloaded, it collapses." Gestures are the first step towards the making of symbols, and those symbols which endure are the residuary legates of the meanings earned through gesture. In *punning* there is an effect to make one word act like another, or several. Rhyme, which is the terminal form of punning, and alliteration, which is the initial form of punning, are the commonest uses of this form of word-play. Every successful pun is a gesture, the only direct means for the expression of the undifferentiated sense of the poet. It is through pun that the poet joins together the perception of the different senses, heightening them into a single sensation. It produces an undifferentiated gesture of meaning. In other words, "the play upon words is both the most immediate and most final congries of signs; it is the very gesture which identified the elements of sound with the elements of meaning." Words transformed into gestures convey what ordinary words fail to convey. Transformed into gestures they carry a load of meaning, a fury which is felt even through the meaning be not understood. *Obliteration* plays a great role in literature and life. It is the stress and urgency of plot which determine what gestures are wanted and when they are to be put into operation. *Plot* does this on a larger scale, *meter* and *refrain* also do it, but on a smaller scale. *Coleridge* defined meter as, "the motion of meaning", but it would be also true to say that, "motion is the meter of meaning". Meter as motion brings meaning to gesture, and motion as meter ties gesture to meaning. Refrain also serves to impose order on the perceptions of the poet. It is a means of emphatic ordering. But it also does much more than that. It modifies meaning by giving to gesture a conventional form. Refrain gives a particular form to gesture that might otherwise be formless. All these devices stir up us deeply and we feel it as if it were a gesture, the gesture of our uncreated selves.

Thus gesture plays a great role in convincing the unsaid story. Gesture issues forth from human psyche that never requires any language of its own. It requires only a genuine understanding. When lips are broken, sweet tunes are remembered not. In the end of this paper I would like to state that all kinds of animals, birds and creatures of this universe express themselves through gesture which is a universal phenomenon.

WORKS CITED

Blackmur, R.P., "Language As Gesture", *Accent.* Summer, 1943.

Coleridge, S.T., *Biographia Literaria.*

Hoijer, Harry, "Linguistic and Cultural Change", *Language in Culture and Society.* Ed. Dell Hymes, New Delhi: Allied Pub., 1964.

Sapir, Edward, *Language*, NY Harcourt Brace: 1921.

Sessions, Roger, *The Intent of the Artist.*

22

Role of Regulatory Bodies and Quality of Technical Education

K. Sudha Rao

This article and the data provided has an imposing aim—to provide a guide to the role of regulatory bodies in education in general and Technical Education in specific, and a useful analysis of this field of study in the Indian context. Because the field has grown so dramatically after the independence, it is only possible to confine to limited area. This is a good time in the sense Technical Education has become a prime concern in India and the role of regulatory bodies is the major issue in settling issues concerning quality, equity, excellence and relevance. The views expressed in this article are those of the author and are in no way a part of the policy and programmes of the Council. The article, provides for definition of the regulatory body, its placement in the Indian context, existing scenario of Technical Education in India and finally the role of regulatory bodies in improving the quality of Technical Education in India.

Before proceeding on the topic as such an understanding as to what exactly the regulatory body means would be of great help. As per the Encyclopedia of Education, Regulatory agency is an "Independent governmental commission established by legislative act to set standards in a specific activity or operations in the private sector of the economy and to enforce the standards". In general, regulatory agencies function outside executive supervision, because the regulations that they adopt have the force of law, part of their function is essentially legislative, but because they may conduct hearings and pass judgements concerning adherence to their regulations, they also have a judicial function—often carried out before a quasi-judicial official called an administrative law judge, who is not part of the court system. Regulatory agencies have become popular means of promoting fair trade and consumer protection as problems of commerce and trade have become more complex particularly in the 20th centurty.

The idea of the regulatory agency was first advanced in the United States, and it has been largely an American institution. The first agency was the Interstate Commerce Commission (ICC), established by Congress in 1887 to regulate the railroads. It remains the prototype of such an agency. It was organized in the belief that a commission of specialists would know more about the railroads and their unique problems than Congress would, that a permanent commission could provide a more unbroken line of policy than could an elected body, and that it could combine the two functions of legislative and judicial that are necessary for effective regulation. Originally, the ICC was to serve only as an advisory body to Congress and the courts, but it was soon granted powers to itself. Also, an independent commission could be impartial and nonpartisan, a necessity for equitable regulation.

The assertion of governmental control in other organisations led to the creation of many other regulatory agencies modelled upon the ICC.

Regulatory agencies use a commission system of administration, and their terms of office are fixed and often very long. In almost all other countries outside the United States, the role of regulatory agencies is taken by the regular administrative departments of government and India is no exception.

With this understanding, I proceed to visualize the role of regulatory body in a given context. It is obvious from the above definition that the performance of a regulatory body depends mainly on the powers vested in it. Further the exercise of power of a regulatory body is dependant upon many more factors such as:

- powers vested in the bodies that are being regulated by the regulatory bodies.
- powers vested with the other central and state govt. bodies that are also simultaneously regulating those bodies that are being regulated by the regulatory body.
- powers vested with the bodies that are supposed to be providing inputs (financial and others) to the regulatory body.

All these vary depending upon the place, time and environment in which it operates. The regulatory power of a given regulatory body may experience ups and downs depending upon the magnitude of the contextual variables operating on it. For example performance appraisal of teachers or Autonomy to the institutions. Though UGC is the regulatory body with all powers to implement still in actuality it remains unimplemented.

Let us look at the Technical Education in India and how it reached the stage where we are today. I would not be filling it up with too much of data as they are available in AICTE documents for those who are interested in except the three tables in the Annexure.

(i) List I entry 66 of the Constitution makes the center responsible for the maintenance and coordination of standards. UGC and AICTE are the outcomes of this provision.

(ii) Degree level institutions are affiliated to universities and it is the universities that grant affiliation, conduct examinations and awards degrees. Universities are autonomous institutions.

(iii) In statutory terms education was originally in the state list. List III entry 25 of the Constitution 42nd Amendment brings education in the concurrent list in 1976. Both center and state thus have shared responsibilities.

(iv) Technical Education is a subcomponent of the higher education component which inturn is a part of the main education system which in turn is a part of the main society. Changes at one level has its impact on the other levels. For example the liberalization policy, industrial policy, technology policy, and foreign policy though they are the decisions taken outside the Technical Education system, all these have direct bearing on the Technical Education system.

(v) The institutions themselves: Number, nature, location, and courses.

(vi) The accreditation system as it is today in the country.

(vii) The practice of strong affiliating system existing in higher education.

(viii) The employment structure in educational institutions.

(ix) The mass psyche for resistance to change.

These are only a few examples of contextual variables that can operate simultaneously between the regulatory body and the bodies that are being regulated in influencing the quality that is there.

Fig. 1 depicts the placement of regulatory body/bodies in Technical Education in India.

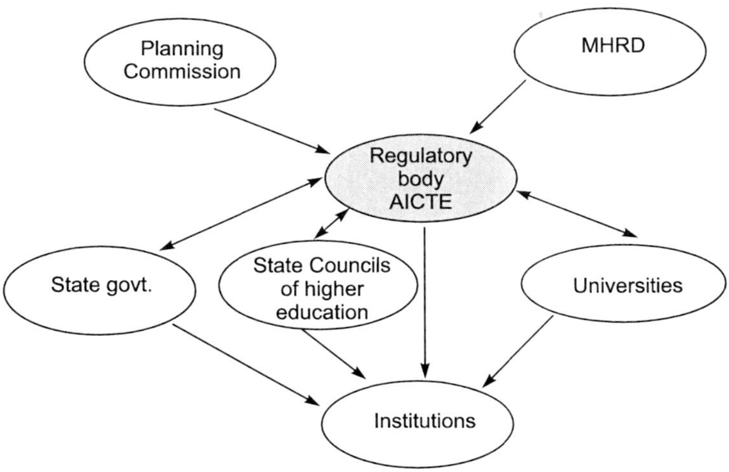

Fig. 1: Placement of Regulatory Body/Bodies

Keeping in view the above factors it might be necessary to redefine the roles of different agencies which have been providing facilities for education in the country viz. central govt., state govt., UGC, universities, the local authorities, etc. Their present roles have arisen, not out of conscious planning, but from historical circumstances, many of which, might have now ceased to have any relevance. It is also possible that at times they have created confusions with regard to powers and hence the need for frequent intervention of supreme court.

With this background, let me now proceed to visualize how regulatory bodies can influence the quality of Technical Education. No doubt, it has a major role and probably all the power required in a given scenerio for ensuring quality of Technical Education. AICTE is a regulatory body for Technical Education, like UGC for higher education, established by parliament Act 52 of 1987 as a statutory body.

The Act of 1987 reads "To provide for the establishment of an All India Council for Technical Education with a view to the proper planning and co-ordinated development of the Technical Education system throughout the country, the promotion of qualitative improvement of such education in relation to planned quantitative growth and the regulation and proper maintenance of norms and standards in the Technical Education system and for matters connected therewith."

From this arises the three major responsibilities—

(i) Planning and coordinated development of Technical Education system.

(ii) Promotion of qualitative improvements.

(iii) Regulation and maintenance of norms and standards.

—for engineering and technology, computer science and engineering, management, architect, town planning, pharmacy, hotel management and catering technology, applied arts and crafts. The chapter on "powers and function" in the act further clarifies the areas of operation.

The existing scenario of Technical Education has significance to both "the Role" and "the Quality". As on today Technical Education is supported by many:

(i) Technical Education is supported by several organizations. Out of the total 34 schemes in operation only 15 schemes are with AICTE and the rest are with others such as UGC scheme of assistance to Technical Education Institutions, RECs, IIMs, NERIST, ICST, ICET, IITs and Engineering College at Jammu.

(ii) Out of the total outlay of Technical Education for the plan period of 94-95 only 25 or so is with AICTE,

(iii) Funding of the govt., engineering institutions are done by state govt.

(iv) Private institutions have their own arrangements.

In other words, other agencies that are mentioned earlier do have regulating roles by laying down conditions for grants, affiliations, etc.

The statewise distribution of institution provided in the tables 1-4 indicates the govt., and pvt. enterprises in Technical Education. This varies from state to state and also from region to region.

It can be seen from the tables below that:

- Maximum number of institutions are located in four major states viz. Maharashtra, Karnataka, Andhra Pradesh and Tamil Nadu.
- Maximum number of pvt. institutions are located in those four states and still there is high demand for starting many more institutions.
- There are states like where there is no private Technical Education institutions at all.
- States like Kerala and West Bengal have started govt. Eng. colleges in private lines.

Of course, one can justify the existence of these institutions on the basis of intake and demand for new courses. Yet one can also argue on the other side on the basis of output, and outcome or unemployment and underemployment.

With such large variations in the present scenario, it is obvious that no single policy can be suitable for all parts of the country. Even in the same state policy might have to vary from one type of institution to the other.

Keeping all these in view, it appears, that role of regulatory agency remains limited. Limited to the extent of a "Facilitator". In other words it is to facilitate quality, equity, relevance and excellence of Technical Education in the country through its activities. In doing so, it might have to play different roles at different points of time, or with different states or with different institutions. In other words it might have to play the roles like active, passive, supportive, proactive and reactive roles. But all these are within the powers and functions provided to the regulatory body by the Act.

The detail pertaining to powers and functions are listed in the Act itself. Yet while implementing all these, decision as to choosing the right role and adopting the managerial style required to suit the situation determines the kind of quality that we experience in Technical Education. More so, in a country like ours where at the one end we have institutions like IITs and at the other, the remote private engineering colleges, teachers highly qualified and also minimum qualified. Students entering the system with high merit facing tough competition and at the other by paying high fees, institutions having facilities at par with any developed country and others with minimum possible. All together contributes to the quality. Obvious it is that regulatory body has taken into consideration all these and still evolve policy, promote programmes, set norms and standards, other to the stated norms while approving the institutions, intake and courses and ensure monitoring and evaluation. In addition initiate activities for removal of imbalances and provide for equality.

Table 1: Statewise Distribution of Engineering and Technology Institutions with Percentages of Different Types

S.No	State	Total No. of Insti-tutions	Percentage of Diploma Institutions				Percentage of Degree Institutions			
			Govt.	Univ. Dept.	Private	Private Aided	Govt.	Univ. Dept.	Private	Private Aided
1.	M.P.	56	72	–	–	2	16	–	5	5
2.	Orissa	25	48	–	28	–	16	4	4	–
3.	Andaman & Nicobar Islands	2	100	–	–	–	–	–	–	–
4.	Arunachal Pradesh	2	50	–	–	–	50	–	–	–
5.	Assam	12	75	–	–	–	25	–	–	–
6.	Meghalaya	1	100	–	–	–	–	–	–	–
7.	Mizoram*	1	100	–	–	–	–	–	–	–
8.	Nagaland	1	100	–	–	–	–	–	–	–
9.	Tripura	2	50	–	–	–	50	–	–	–
10.	West Bengal	48	71	–	2	2	19	6	–	–
11.	Uttar Pradesh	130	60	4	2	16	6	9	2	1
12.	Bihar	44	59	2	14	–	21	–	2	2
13.	Chandigarh	5	40	–	–	–	60	–	–	–
14.	Delhi	27	37	4	33	–	15	7	4	–
15.	Haryana	29	55	–	10	14	14	–	7	–
16.	Himachal Pradesh	7	57	–	29	–	14	–	–	–
17.	Jammu & Kashmir	15	33	–	40	–	27	–	–	–
18.	Punjab	46	50	–	21	2	9	9	9	–
19.	Rajasthan	36	58	3	14	–	14	8	–	3
20.	Andhra Pradesh	107	53	–	15	3	1	7	21	–
21.	Pondicherry	4	75	–	–	–	25	–	–	–

Table 2: Statewise Distribution of Pharmacy Institutions with Percentages of Different Types*

S. No	State	Total No. of Insti-tutions	Percentage of Diploma Institutions				Percentage of Degree Institutions			
			Govt.	Univ. Dept.	Private	Private Aided	Govt.	Univ. Dept.	Private	Private Aided
1.	M.P.	4	100	–	–	–	–	–	–	–
2.	Orissa	23	13	–	65	–	–	–	22	–
3.	Assam	3	67	–	–	–	–	33	–	–
4.	Tripura	1	100	–	–	–	–	–	–	–
5.	Sikkim	1	–	–	100	–	–	–	–	–
6.	West Bengal	6	83	–	–	–	–	17	–	–
7.	Uttar Pradesh	29*	83	–	4	–	–	3	3	–
8.	Bihar	8	–	–	63	–	25	–	–	12
9.	Chandigarh	3	34	–	33	–	33	–	–	–
10.	Delhi	7	14	14	43	–	15	14	–	–
11.	Haryana	10	40	–	50	10	–	–	–	–
12.	Himachal Pradesh	3	67	–	33	–	–	–	–	–
13.	Jammu & Kashmir	2	50	–	50	–	–	–	–	–
14.	Punjab	22	27	–	64	–	5	–	4	–
15.	Rajasthan	14	–	7	72	–	–	7	14	–
16.	Andhra Pradesh	22	55	–	9	9	–	9	18	–
17.	Pondicherry	1	–	–	100	–	–	–	–	–
18.	Tamil Nadu	24**	–	–	21	–	–	4	75	–
19.	Karnataka	98***	–	53	–	–			47	
20.	Kerala	13		93					7	
21.	Gujarat	14	29	7	–	36	7	7	–	14
22.	Goa	2	50	–	–	–	50	–	–	–
23.	Maharashtra	98	3	1	45	19	1	3	23	5

* Some of these are departments in polytechnics and medical colleges.

** Eleven Diploma programmes are also run in degree colleges.

*** Diploma programmes are also conducted in degree coileges.

Table 3: Statewise Distribution of Management Institutions with Percentages of Different Types

S. No	State	Total No. of Institutions	As Percentage of Total No. of Institution				
			Govt.	Univ. Dept.	Univ. affiliation Deemed Univ./Autonomous	Private No Grant	Govt. Aided
1.	Madhya Pradesh	15	–	60	40	–	–
2.	Orissa	15	–	27	27	46	–
3.	Assam	5	20	60	–	20	–
4.	Manipur	1	–	100	–	–	–
5.	West Bengal	11	9	37	–	45	9
6.	Bihar	14	7	7	50	36	–
7.	Uttar Pradesh	34	12	29	–	59	–
8.	Chandigarh	1	–	100	–	–	–
9.	Delhi	22	5	5	5	85	–
10.	Haryana	8	13	25	25	37	–
11.	Himachal Pradesh	1	–	100	–	–	–
12.	Jammu & Kashmir	2	–	100	–	–	–
13.	Punjab	3	–	100	–	–	–
14.	Rajasthan	7	–	42	29	29	–
15.	Andhra Pradesh	58	–	9	79	12	–
16.	Tamil Nadu	69	1	9	80	10	–
17.	Pondicherry	1	–	–	100	–	–
18.	Karnataka	21	10	24	33	33	–
19.	Kerala	8	–	50	38	12	–
20.	Goa	2	–	50	–	50	–
21.	Gujarat	11	–	65	–	36	–
22.	Maharashtra	106	4	5	85	6	–

Table 4: Statewise Distribution of Architectural Institutions with Percentages of Different Types

S.No	State	Total No. of Institutions	Govt.	Private	Govt. Aided/Funded
1.	Madhya Pradesh	5	40	40	20
2.	Orissa	2	50	50	–
3.	West Bengal	3	100	–	–
4.	Bihar	2	50	–	50
5.	Uttar Pradesh	3	100	–	–
6.	Chandigarh	1	100	–	–
7.	Delhi	3	33	33	34
8.	Haryana	2	50	50	–
9.	Punjab	2	100	–	–
10.	Rajasthan	1	100	–	–
11.	Andhra Pradesh	2	100	–	–
12.	Tamil Nadu	12	17	83	–
13.	Karnataka	13	8	69	23
14.	Kerala	2	50	–	50
I5.	Goa	1	100	–	–
16.	Gujarat	4	25	50	25
17.	Maharashtra	32	6	88	6

Contributors

Balachandran, K., Professor of English, Annamalai University, Annamalai Nagar-608 002, Tamil Nadu.

Chanana, R., Head of the Department of English, Govt. Maharaja Auto P.G. College, Chhattarpur, Madhya Pradesh; [Resi.] C/o S.S. Motors, Nupur Bhawan, Bus Stand, Chhattarpur, Madhya Pradesh-471 001.

Dhaka, Mahendra Singh, A-208, Defence Colony, Meerut, Uttar Pradesh.

Evelyn, Anita, St. Peter's Engineering College, Chennai, Tamil Nadu.

Gupta, Pratibha, Department of English, L.N. Mithila University, Darbhanga, Bihar.

Kannan, C., Head of the PG Department of English, Government College, Kasaragod, Post Office: Vidyanagar, District: Kasaragod, Kerala-671 123.

Kirubahar, J. Samuel, Department of English, VHNSN College, Virudhunnagar-626 001.

Lata, Pushp, Assistant Professor, Languages Group, BITS, Pilani; [Resi.] 458/2, Mandir Marg, Pilani, Rajasthan.

Lyon, Michael H., Research Consultant, Hive Design & Consultancy, 69 Jute St, Aberdeen, AB24, 3HA, Scotland, UK, email: mb.lyon@btinternet.com

Mishra, Krushna Chandra, Lecturer in English (S.G.), Govt. College, Bomdilla-790 001, Arunachal Pradesh.

Mishra, Prashant, Professor and Head of the Department, Government P.G. College, Neemuch, Madhya Pradesh; [Resi.] 92, Rajaswa Colony, Neemuch, Madhya Pradesh-458 441.

Mahapatra, N.P., Lecturer, M.D. College, Narayanpur, Assam.

Narang, Harish, Department of English, JNU, New Delhi.

Patil, Mallikarjun, Reader, Department of English, Karnataka University, Dharwad-580 003.

Ponni, K., Lecturer in English (S.G.), Government Arts College, (Thrivalluvar University), C. Mutlur, Post Office: Chidambaram–608102, Tamil Nadu.

Raman, Meenakshi, Assistant Professor of English and Group Leader, Language Group, BITS, Pilani-333 031, Rajasthan.

Raviya, Hitesh D., Reader in English, Department of English, KSKV Kachchh University, Mundra Road, Bhuj, District: Kachchh, Gujarat; [Resi.] 202, Hem Shikha Complex, Vidyanagar Road, Karamsad, Gujarat-388 325, email: hdraviya@rediffmail.com

Rao, K. Sudha, Advisor (CD), All India Council for Technical Education, Indira Gandhi Sports Complex, I.P. Estate, New Delhi-110 002.

West, Bernice J.M., Acadèmic Director (Research Students and Supervisors), Postgraduate Studies, Room C 513, Clarke Building, The Robert Gordon University, University Schoolhill Campus, Aberdeen, Scotland, UK, email: b.west@rgu.ac.uk

Yadav, Karan Singh, Lecturer in English, Govt. College, Ateli M. Garh, Haryana.